GOD
SAVE THE
Queens

GOD
SAVE THE
Queens

The Essential History
of Women in Hip-Hop

KATHY IANDOLI

DEY ST.
An Imprint of WILLIAM MORROW

Grateful acknowledgment is made for permission to reprint the following: Victoria Ford/Sneakshot Photography (pages x, 184, 226, 258, 284, and 290); Raymond Boyd via Getty Images (page 70); Evan Agostini/Hulton Archive via Getty Images (page 126); Jeff Kravitz/FilmMagic, Inc. via Getty Images (pages 162 and 200); and Johnny Nunez/WireImage via Getty Images (page 270).

HarperCollins books may be purchased for educational, business, or sales promotional use. For information, please e-mail the Special Markets Department at SPsales@harpercollins.com.

A hardcover edition of this book was published in 2019 by Dey Street, an imprint of William Morrow.

FIRST DEY STREET PAPERBACK EDITION PUBLISHED 2020.

Designed by Suet Chong

Library of Congress Control Number: 2019948733

ISBN 978-0-06-287851-9

20 21 22 23 24   BRR   10 9 8 7 6 5 4 3 2 1

In loving memory of my mother, Anna Acquaviva Iandoli,
my Queen who saved me. Love always, Your Snooky

Contents

I

Girls to the Front

II

Class Acts

III

Only Female in My Crew

IV

So Much for the Afterglow

GOD
SAVE THE
Queens

Decades later, Lil' Kim still steals the show.

LADIES FIRST

IF DJ KOOL HERC IS THE FOUNDING FATHER OF HIP-HOP, THEN HIS sister, Cindy Campbell, is the founding mother. We've all seen the flyer countless times. The date was August 11, 1973. The location: 1520 Sedgwick Avenue, in the mighty South Bronx. At the bottom of the flyer is a list of special guests (in this order): Coco (better known as Coke La Rock), Cindy C, Klark K (aka the early pioneer Clark Kent—not to be confused with Jay-Z/Biggie's DJ Clark Kent), and Timmy T. "A DJ KOOL HERC PARTY" is scribbled in shadowed graffiti-style block letters across the top of the flyer—yet it was Cindy C(ampbell)'s idea to throw the party in the first place.

Clive "Kool Herc" Campbell was already dabbling with music, as his and Cindy's father had his own sound system, which was stored in Herc's room. Herc and Cindy would sneak in and play with their father's equipment when he wasn't around, though Herc wanted his own. So he built it from scratch, using makeshift pieces and spare parts to customize his powerful system. He originally christened it The Herculord, later using the same name for his crew.

That next-level sound system would soon become Kool Herc's trademark, though that August 11th party would kick off his legacy of throwing the best jams and performing with the highest caliber of sound. But again, it was all his sister Cindy's idea.

The story goes that Cindy wanted to throw a back-to-school party and charge guests at the door (a quarter for ladies, fifty cents for the fellas, per the flyer). The proceeds would go toward the $25 rental fee for the rec room in Herc and Cindy's Sedgwick Avenue apartment building, along with Cindy's high school wardrobe for that fall. See, Cindy didn't want to wear the same old gear from local Bronx department stores, so this jam would fund her shopping spree on Manhattan's Lower East Side. But Cindy took it a step further. The building super would only grant her access to the rec room with a parent's permission, so once her dad gave the OK, Cindy thought of a master plan. First came the refreshments (hot dogs, sodas, etc.), most of which were purchased at a wholesale distributor so that she could turn a profit. Some of the parents in the building worked security at the event. Cindy's mom manned the kitchen and Dad helped with the food, as Cindy collected tickets at the door. Of course, Herc was on the wheels of steel.

That first party—the now infamous one that hip-hop celebrates every year—brought in about three hundred guests between nine P.M. and four A.M. Photos of the rec room show just how small it is, making its packed attendance even more impactful in hindsight, as partygoers rotated in and out for a solid seven hours. Sixteen-year-old Kool Herc spun an unorthodox mix of hits based on his diverse musical palate. By the next morning, he was a legend. Herc and Cindy continued to throw more jams, with Herc's credibility steadily growing. Eventually, MCs picked up the microphone to expound upon Herc's skills and the records he was spinning. The jams were recorded, with the audio played back as if it were an album. A similar occurrence would happen when the late Mr. Magic unveiled the first hip-hop radio show, *Rap Attack*. But that very first party marked the birth of what we now consider hip-hop music, and it all began with Cindy wanting to throw her own personal wardrobe fund-raiser.

Truth be told, though, that party wasn't the first appearance of what we've come to know as the broader hip-hop culture, nor was it the first time a woman did something awesome in hip-hop's earliest days. In 1972, a year before Kool Herc's party, a Sugar Hill B-boy by the name of Kurtis Blow hit the scene. At thirteen, Kurtis was added to a crew of older kids up on Amsterdam Avenue who had a score to settle. "A lot of people don't know this, but we used to dance against the girls. That's how it started," Kurtis tells me. A year before he joined his crew, they were at a club called The Factory and got their hats handed to them by the B-girls, the fiercest breakdancing competitors for the guys. "They would mush your face, take your hat, throw it across the room," he recalls of the female dancers. His crew went home, practiced, came up with some new routines, and returned for revenge, but losing against a team of girls came with a price. "The whole thing about that was if you danced against a female and you lost, your reputation was over," he says. It was a wrongful assumption of thinking (or rather, *hoping*) that a group of girls were the weaker species of dancers, yet still worthy breakdancing opponents.

Kurtis built his reputation as a B-boy at a venue called the Chuck Center on 115th Street and Second Avenue, but once again, he was dancing against girls. The leader was named Kellogg, known for her intricate style and unapologetic attitude when she had the floor. A crewmember of Kurtis's named Maurice battled Kellogg one night. "She went down and did her moves, came back and mushed him in the face," as Kurtis tells it, "and when she did, he fell back and tried to hold himself and do a backstand on his one hand. When he landed, he broke his wrist. That's how Kellogg got her reputation." Maurice even tried to return the next week to battle Kellogg with a cast on his arm, but the damage was already done.

Kellogg's best friend was a sixteen-year-old B-girl named Stephanie. "I was in love with her," Kurtis says, who was then fourteen years old. "One night I burned her dancing against her, and the next week she stopped talking to me. So, for me? It was like, okay, we've gotta find another way to get this competition going. That's one of the reasons why we stopped dancing against girls, because, one, if you lost, your reputation was ruined, and two, if you won, you couldn't take the girl out on a date. As I was getting older, that became more important to me than B-boying in a competition."

The girls won Kurtis Blow over, so he moved over to deejaying and emceeing. That worked out pretty well for him, to say the least. As for Kellogg, her reputation remained intact.

Prologue

A MORNING IN PARIS

IT WAS BARELY NINE O'CLOCK ON A MONDAY MORNING WHEN I was called a "cunt" on live radio. The year was 2009, and I was working as the urban program director of a French Internet radio station, built on the back of a major American broadcasting company. The two French owners were named Armand and Matteo (not really, I'm just being dramatic), and they were polar opposites. Armand would always wear a tight suit with his hair perfectly slicked back. He would fidget with the buckle on his designer belt as if to draw attention to its price tag. He hardly made eye contact, yet when he did, it always looked as though he were calculating your worth in the event of a layoff. Matteo dressed in linen like he was headed to a yacht party in Saint-Tropez, accessorized with a permanently annoying smile. He would force conversations upon everyone within reach. Whenever I saw him, a line from OutKast's "Elevators" played in my head: "But he kept smilin' like a clown, facial expression lookin' silly." They both claimed my position was the most important in the company, since they *loooooooved* hip-hop, yet they would mysteriously vanish to their offices whenever rappers entered the building for interviews. *Loooooove?* Yeah, right.

One of the shows was helmed by a hip-hop legend—one whom I had grown pretty close to in a Tony Soprano–meets–Dr. Melfi kind of way (I'm clearly Lorraine Bracco's character in that equation). We'd have talks about rap's glory days, and he helped me through some pretty absurd moments when guests would come to the station and act up. Then there was the one time I nonchalantly mentioned the size of MC Hammer's package in the "Pumps and a Bump" video to him (you can YouTube that to validate my claim), and the next day he called me into the studio with Hammer on the line. "Kathy has something she'd like to tell you," he said live on-air. Mortified, I mumbled something about a Speedo and ran out of the studio. Cool way to assert my #boss status.

As I walked through the employee entrance that Monday morning, I was flagged down by the morning show's associate producer, Nix. His eyes were like saucers. We had dealt with guests smearing shit on the bathroom walls (I'll save that story for another book) and others threatening to shoot up the place, so in that moment I was prepared for anything. Everything but "cunt."

Nix pulled me into his studio and said, "You need to hear this." He rewound the show to the segment before, when the host (my Tony Soprano) asked an intern to run an errand on air. A week prior, an intern had attempted a similar task for "Tony" and was almost plastered to the front of a light rail train in Jersey City for not looking both ways before crossing the tracks. So, I made it mandatory that no intern could leave the premises during the day for work-related duties. They could save that train-dodging business for after work. These interns were far from children, too; grown adults attempting to break into radio through the back door of tagging music to be played on air. We all have to start somewhere, right? Best to avoid getting smeared on the road in the process.

The grown-ass intern nervously said no to Tony on-air. "No?" Tony bassed. "No? Get your manager in here." The intern manager, Alex, walked in and laid it down: "Kathy said no more interns leaving the building . . . for insurance purposes." To this, Tony barked, "Why do I have to listen to her? Fuck that cunt!"

CUNT. CUNT. CUNT. The word kept echoing in my ears. To this day when I hear Tony's voice speaking over one of his most notoriously classic tracks (and admittedly still one of my favorite rap songs of all time), I *still* hear the word *CUNT* instead.

Nix stopped the tape and stared at me, trying to read my face for a reaction. I saw red, but maintained my composure, since I'm prone to anger-crying. *Not today, Satan. Not today, Tony.* I smiled at Nix and walked out of the studio. In the main area, everyone was staring at me, especially Alex—who had just finished his own fight with Tony and his cohost. Apparently while I was having the word *cunt* pummeled into my ear in Nix's studio, Alex was bravely battling Tony and his team of three, who were mocking him for abiding by my rules. Alex soon had to be dragged from the studio by another radio jock so the cops wouldn't have to be called. He left the office that day and never came back.

(When I called Alex recently, ten years later, to recount this story, he said to me, "I remember that same day you told me, 'This story won't end here,' and that it would show up in a book one day." Well, here it is!)

I opened the door to the studio where the show was recording. By then, Tony and his cronies were on the phone with some random employee at a nearby mall, entreating them for lunch from the food court (one of the many other errands he liked demanding of the interns). With a middle finger roll and the push of a button, I took the show off the air and left white noise for all his listeners to enjoy. I pulled the heavy door back open and walked out. It was all eyes on me in the open area. I entered Armand's office, where he was reclined and staring off into the New York City skyline. He did his best Don Draper impersonation, back turned, as I huffed and puffed through the play-by-play. After I paused my rant for a reaction, he spun his IKEA office chair to face me, leaned forward—his skin paler than mine—looked me dead in the eyes, and said:

"You're a white wooooooooman."

His accent layered the word *woman* like a dollop of mayonnaise on a French baguette.

"You work in Black music."

With his accent, "Black" sounded like "block," but he certainly wasn't referencing Sedgwick Avenue. Then came the coup de grâce:

"Who will ever respect you?"

With that, he walked right past me, out of his office, and put the show back on the air. I resigned a week later.

A few months prior to taking that job, two days before my thirtieth birthday, I had been laid off from an editor position at AllHipHop during what I now like to call the Hip-Hop Internet Crash of 2009. For nearly a decade, rap websites were grabbing their proverbial dicks and rocking back and forth on their heels, so proud of themselves that they had proved print media wrong and survived while print magazines were all scrambling to stay afloat. After all, the "hip-hop Internet" needed to be filled with something other than music, since Napster put the RIAA on high alert in '99 and random postings of songs didn't qualify as #content (at least back then). So, websites were erected in hip-hop's honor, full of interviews and album reviews in a place called "There is no limit to this bandwidth—every artist is a part of rap's new real estate!" It all came to a head in 2009 when web content basically switched to song clips with blurbs (and stayed that way for like five years), once ad dollars for the written word didn't materialize as readily as everyone had hoped. Making real money was an anomaly, so we all took what we could get.

Women in hip-hop were slowly becoming more empowered, thanks to voices like my dear friend Kim Osorio, who made history by becoming the first female editor in chief of *The Source* in 2005. By 2006, she was suing the hip-hop Bible in a four-way suit for sexual harassment, retaliation, defamation, and gender discrimination after *Source* co-owner-slash-figurehead Raymond "Benzino" Scott harassed her then threatened to ruin her name. Ironically, Kim won only for retaliation and defamation ("It was a federal case and only two women were on the jury," she tells me), but the suit sparked a fire under women not only to push harder to succeed in the hip-hop business but to speak up when something foul is a afoot.

In 1999, I began my journey in this weird fantasy world that we call the hip-hop music industry. In high school and college, I worked at a local Sam Goody as a "sales associate" (okay, *cashier*), with the added important job of organizing the rap and electronic music aisles. They both lived on the same endcap, since 95 percent of the store was pop music and in 1996, hip-hop was far from pop. Little did we know that a year or two later, Puffy would be the first to really nudge hip-hop music into the mainstream. I started that job in November 1996, two months after Tupac was murdered. The rap section was all jumbled together, with the exception of one extra tab: gangster rap. That's where the bulk of the *air quotes* explicit music lived. Sometimes, that little Parental Advisory tag was enough for a CD to land in that section (thank Tipper Gore for that one). Or the obligatory gun-wielding-artist photo on the cover made it qualifiable as gangster rap. Think N.W.A and every rapper they ever inspired in Locs sunglasses. Looking back and remembering that era, that category was such a slap in the face to the state of hip-hop. Like, "Oh, here are the dangerous selections carefully separated and labeled as such." So I placed Death Row legend The Lady of Rage (you know her from "Afro Puffs") in the gangster rap section. Bo$$, a rapper from the D, was added there, too. Both artists talked the talk and walked the walk (keep on reading and you'll learn why). "No, they go in the main section," my manager told me. "Why?" I asked. "They're more *gangster* than any of those guys." His response was, "Yeah, but they're women." Eek. I immediately wanted to create a separate tab titled WOMEN and place all the female hip-hop artists in there (including The Fugees, because let's face it, Lauryn carried that whole group). My manager walked away and I slid Rage and Bo$$ back into their rightful home. Eventually I just alphabetized the whole section with letter tabs and threw that stupid "Gangster Rap" tab away. Even the Crips and Bloods compilation CDs earned their rightful place under "Various Artists." The best part about working in a record store during the '90s and early '00s was watching hip-hop transform right before my eyes, including the ascent of women in the hip-hop industry. When I started working there in November 1996, I watched as Lil' Kim's *Hard Core* and Foxy Brown's *Ill Na Na* were released back to back, igniting what would become a whole new era for female rappers. Then I was able to witness the astronomical success of *The Miseducation of Lauryn Hill* on a brick-and-mortar level in August 1998, which is something I will forever cherish. I saw customers buy entire crew collections—from No Limit Records to Three 6 Mafia—as I casually reminded them not to forget the ladies in the mix: Mia X's and Gangsta Boo's CDs, respectively.

From there I handed out flyers for The Roots and helped work on their all-women concert series called Black Lily back in '99, after responding to a call for street team members on their Okayplayer message boards. I was hired as an in-house writer in the publicity department of a major label (as a favor from one of the executives, since I needed internship credits for my master's at NYU) in '05, worked at an artist management company in '08, and wrote for every publication that would let me in—some more respected than others.

So as I stood in Armand's office, my entire CV flashed before my eyes as he smugly asked who would ever respect me. I had taken that radio job out of sheer desperation. But unbeknownst to Armand and Matteo, an old friend from AllHipHop named Jake Paine had recently brought me on board at HipHopDX, so I was already preparing to leave my position at the station. Cunt-Gate only sped up the process.

And it wasn't the "cunt" that led to my expedited exit. I've since seen my Tony Soprano, and he's welcomed me warmly and "cunt"-free. He was angry in that moment, but that word should never have been used. That much I get, and even revealing his name now would serve no purpose since A) I've been called a lot worse since then by everyone from music executives to Internet trolls, B) as much as we try to think otherwise, no one really cares about your stories of disrespect, and oh, let's not forget good ol' C) it could kill my career way faster than it would ever kill his. Let's be honest about that. Really though, what got me was Armand asking, "Who will ever respect you?" That stung the most. It's a question that's lingered in my mind for far too long; a question that every woman in any industry asks herself. But in hip-hop, I've now come to realize that if *I* keep that question omnipresent, imagine how other women (especially Women of Color, the most underappreciated) must feel to varying degrees and in varying circumstances, when this industry has continuously othered us in everything from the artistry to the business side. This is why I wrote *God Save the Queens*.

Angela Davis has this quote: "Radical simply means 'grasping things at the root.'" That applies to really any facet of society—from politics to religion, film, music, art, gender, whatever. It's the notion that pearls will be clutched if you dig into the deepest underbelly of whatever it is you aim to transform and fuck it up from the inside out. Sometimes it's for the good; other times, not so much. That was essentially what women have done from the start with hip-hop. The problem—and for all intents and purposes, let's call it a *problem*—was that hip-hop in its purest form was radical in and of itself. In the late '70s and early '80s, no one had a clue what to make of hip-hop as a genre, let alone a culture. Throwing women into the mix so early was seen more as a liability than an asset. So now you're posing a threat by being a radical within a radical.

In 1982, journalist and *Beat Street* story writer Steven Hager used the term *hip-hop* in an article about Afrika Bambaataa for the *Village Voice* (RIP), validating the idea in print and calling it by name. Two years later, we would meet Roxanne Shanté. There were heavy sprinkles of women in the space prior to that, but Shanté was a radical rapper. She had no qualms about challenging anyone (male or female), while still in braces, no less. But to jump on in as the whole hip-hop culture was still grappling with being seen as a rebellious (read: *radical*) art form while still gaining the respect of the masses was a bold move that was met with significant push-back from any man who felt they deserved the clout Shanté was acquiring—especially when she was gaining radio airplay when most male hip-hop artists weren't. More on that later.

So now we're three and a half decades removed from the start of that narrative, and sometimes it feels like nothing has changed. I'm typing this as I scan photos of Cardi B with a knot over her eye from being elbowed by Nicki Minaj's security guard during New York's fall 2018 Fashion Week. Cardi threw her very expensive shoe in protest, a signature move of hers since her *Love & Hip-Hop: New York* days. Their marketing-driven battle would later continue, one questioning the other on everything from having rhymes ghost-written to accusations of payola, questionable chart positions, and tour dollars diminishing, plus the peanut gallery's question of whether there can ever be more than one woman at the top. Still. Only with women, it's considered the Regina George complex. The villainous *Mean Girl* can't accept another woman on the scene, so every move is strategic and calculated, with the sole intent of sabotage and successful solitude. This is far from new, and you'll learn within these pages just how similar Queens native Nicki Minaj is to her predecessor, fellow Queens native Roxanne Shanté. The top is only lonely when you want more people beside you.

When Cardi B addressed the whole situation over Instagram (which will probably go down in infamy, despite the post being now deleted from social media), she had this to say to Nicki Minaj: "You're out here fucking up your legacy, looking like a fucking hater." Fucking up her legacy. There's some merit to that statement, though not necessarily due to the extent of the damage Nicki caused, but because there was an attempt at all to make waves when as women, our space is designed to be soundproof. We whine, we complain, we are too emotional, perpetually in a state of PMS. Never mind the countless grown men who retaliate with words, fists, and at times far worse to get both their pain and point across. And when any of this is brought up, we're playing the "gender card." With all that going on, how can any women get along? Some do, and that's great, but many don't, and what I've learned from writing this book is that some, sadly, never have, while others viewed it all as a sisterhood of commonality with one singular cause in mind: to just keep going.

It would have been really great to write this prologue about how cool it is that women in hip-hop have emerged from the ashes and reinvented the wheel hand in hand, or at the very least side by side. We know better than that, though. The scenery has certainly changed; gone are those basement jams where women lyrically slap-boxed the shit out of each other and their male peers. Now there are shoe-flinging fights at one of the biggest fashion events of the year with security present. There are also Dolce & Gabbana gowns in attendance, which used to be the fantastical fodder of Lil' Kim and Foxy Brown lyrics circa '96–'98. These days, designers are a dime a dozen and come frequently to the doorsteps of the top-tier women in rap, Lil' Kim still being among them. We could call that progress, but we'd be lying to an extent. What does it mean if the baddest women on the planet can't get along? Maybe a peace treaty between Cardi B and Nicki Minaj will be announced by the time you're reading this, but since we're still waiting for Foxy Brown and Lil' Kim to release that *Thelma & Louise* project, I wouldn't hold my breath.

This book has taken on so many forms since I started writing it, because as hip-hop continues to grow in strength, in numbers, and in power, its evolution has been rapid. Regardless of who hates whom, there are many women's success stories. It's a change from the historically slim collection of girls who would decorate the regions of hip-hop music, typically appearing one per crew. These shifts make it nearly impossible to create one linear history on the forty-plus years that women have touched all corners of the world with their raps. We could list them one by one like *VIBE* did in 2001 with their *Hip-Hop Divas* book, but someone would be excluded who deserved to be there, and that would be unfair to even the female rappers who contributed on the smallest of scales. Progress is progress.

What I learned from the stories contained within this book was that the people may change, but the circumstances remain the same. How they handle those circumstances is the real plot twist. I learned things I never imagined I would when I started this journey; I thought I could write this book with my eyes closed—after all, I, too, was a woman in hip-hop and had my own set of stories. I couldn't have been more wrong.

My stories are completely different from those of the women presented in this work, beyond just my not being a rapper. The most primary distinction is that I'm white—but as Bahamadia once told me, that didn't matter. "You're still a woman," she said. "That alone puts you at a disadvantage." And she's right, though I will never be one to step to Black and Brown women and say, "Amirite, ladies?" because my struggles pale in comparison to theirs (pun intended), and I will never claim otherwise. But yes, I'm still at a disadvantage, and as a writer for nearly two decades, I wanted to contribute to the history of my gender in hip-hop. This book has been a long time coming.

Years back, another writer and I attempted to write a book that discussed women's contributions to rap, but it never fully solidified. The world simply wasn't ready. I was, though, and I vividly remember the moment when I knew definitively that I was going to write a book on the subject one day: it was at that radio station, as I packed up my office.

The greatest question is, how do you backtrack over forty-five years to tell the full story of how women not only musically contributed to what has now become a widespread phenomenon but also how they pioneered it from day one? The answer is: you try your hardest, especially when history has it all wrong and those blurbs to which women have been relegated in hip college textbooks and coffee-table books barely skim the surface. This is a collection of stories; a compilation of moments, bound together not to form a linear history, but rather a greater understanding of just how impactful women were and still are to the evolution of hip-hop. I found as many women as I could who were willing to talk (and some men who helped along the way), and I simply pressed record. Since covering women in hip-hop has been my primary beat for nearly twenty years, I also dug back into my archives from interviews, conversations, concerts, and even friendships.

It took the thirty-five years since Roxanne Shanté dropped her prolific "Roxanne's Revenge" for the book to actually happen. I'm honored to be the one who wrote it. *God Save the Queens* isn't a female rap encyclopedia or a listicle book of facts. It's a narrative homage to all the women in hip-hop—from all facets of the game—who have pioneered movements and opened doors that were previously shut and locked. They've weathered storms through all different climates and eras, often without any credit or proper recognition. This book is for them; it's for us. For the women who grasped hip-hop by the roots in order to make that radical shift, from day one and all the days thereafter. Because contrary to popular belief, the ladies have always been first.

And the story goes a little somethin' like this . . .

I

Girls to the Front

Chapter One

THE BRONX
IS BURNING

I'M SEATED IN A BOOTH AT A STEAKHOUSE IN NEW JERSEY WITH
Harlem-born, South Bronx–bred, hip-hop pioneer Debora
Hooper, known as "Debbie D." Now a preacher and ministry coach,
Debbie is referred to as a hip-hop matriarch, one of the treasured
few female pioneers to arrive during hip-hop's genesis. She lays before me one of the only real hip-hop informational artifacts of the
late 1970s and early 1980s. It's a binder-bound collection of flyers. They're amateur in design, when compared to the loud, glossy
ones that would become a hip-hop nightlife staple. The flyers are
all packed with names scribbled across multicolored photocopy
paper, separated in lists at times by groups and solo performers.
Debbie's name is listed quite often as a soloist, the only woman
on the scene for a solid three years, at least judging from the flyers
she has. Sometimes local high schools were listed, letting the kids
know which of their friends had been invited to attend. It's a subtle

testament to just how young this art form and its participants truly were at its inception.

"If your group name was on the flyer, then you weren't a soloist yet," Debbie explains. "A soloist performs alone onstage with her DJ. The proof is in the flyers." Debbie D was one of the first to break from her group DJ Patty Duke & the Jazzy 5 MCs. She added DJ Wanda Dee to her setup and started performing solo in late 1981.

If you scan the webpages and social media sites of women from that era, many refer to themselves as "the first" female MC soloist. It's a footnote that at face value feels like a moot point, but for so many women, it's a necessary detail to secure their supremacy in hip-hop's tangled history. The qualification for some is having a physical recording; for others, it's the number of times they were billed on flyers by themselves (with no crew attached), yet many lay claim to that spot as the first female soloist.

"Actually, none of them were first," DJ Cutmaster Cool V tells me. Cool V was Biz Markie's DJ and producer for over three decades. "What we're getting caught up in now is first and last. All of these girls are relevant because they came out at a time when it was hard for girls to come out." Perhaps they all arrived at once and never knew each other. He references Virginia's Golden Gate Quartet, a group founded in the 1930s whose cadence was nearly identical to that of the Sugarhill Gang. They're all men, though Cool V's point was that maybe the music was being made, but not everyone was hearing it. It's kind of like the "tree falls in the forest" question. Maybe someone was "first" cultivating this same sound somewhere in Mississippi or Hawaii. Maybe it was a woman. Who really knows, and back then there wasn't significant documentation to prove anything. This leads to a lot of history being rewritten in later years, since the only cards that can be pulled are word of mouth and those flyers. "You have to remember, everybody was young, they never went to different places," Cool V adds. The young hip-hop pioneers rarely ventured beyond the confines of their respective boroughs. It's not like they were frequently traveling and experiencing the sounds of neighboring cities, states, or countries. *First* is subjective. "We're older now, we can't say 'first' or 'last,'" he continues. "We can say 'pioneer female MCs,' from the importance of being at the top of the pioneering list, which is something essential for women from the Bronx." Still, at that time, considering how hard it was for women to even have the opportunity to pick up the microphone, there's an added layer of wanting to be cited as one of the scarce few who were actually offered an opportunity to flex their skills. The waiting game to get onstage was frustrating for women in hip-hop's early days, though it wouldn't last forever.

In 1977, the block was hot in the South Bronx. Literally. A series of fires swept across New York City during the '70s, decimating the Bronx especially. The blame has always been a mixed bag— from rumored arson to cashing in on insurance policies to the poor quality of the building structures and the negligence of the fire departments who came to the rescue once a blaze hit. Tensions were high, so when the infamous New York City blackout arrived in July '77, widespread looting across the boroughs became the delayed response to everything else that was going on. For the Bronx in particular, that looting was serendipitous for the expansion of hip-hop. DJ Kool Herc was one of the very few leaders of the burgeoning hip-hop movement to own a sound system. He'd had a solid four-year run as king since that infamous rec room party at 1520 Sedgwick Avenue, based largely upon his access to that boomin' equipment. If your sound system was weak, you shouldn't even bother showing up. Herc always showed up. During the blackout, young hip-hop kids looted, too, targeting electronics stores and boosting their own sound systems. While not everyone shoplifted their gear, that moment sparked a desire to DJ beyond the Bronx and into the neighboring boroughs. So now everyone got in on the action and threw their own parties. With countless jams happening that summer, there was plenty of room on the mic for women.

One pioneer in particular was Debbie D. Hailing from the Bronx's Webster Houses, Debbie was one of the first female MCs to emerge during that historic summer of '77. "I'll never forget it, Kathy," Debbie recalls to me, over four decades later. "I can see it plain as day. I was living in the projects, on the nineteenth floor, and I'm sitting on the bed. It's warm outside, the windows are up, and I'm like, 'What is that noise? What is that?' I asked my mom if I could go outside, and I followed the music. I come to find out it was in this area called the Middle Building. There were like a million kids outside, thirteen, fourteen years old. There were no adults." Parks were flooded with kids all congregating around one loud stereo system powered by a hookup to a street lamp. The DJ was spinning, the MC was rhyming. It was an open opportunity to strut your stuff, and right away Debbie D was all in.

After a few visits to the jams, Debbie posed a life-changing question to the DJ: *Can I get on your mic?*

"One of the major differences between old school and new school is that new-school hip-hop artists go straight into the studio," Debbie remarks. "Old-school hip-hop artists went straight to the streets when it was time to rhyme. So what happened was, you had to prepare your rhyme and you had to say the same rhyme over and over in your house, because by the time you went to the street, you had to know it. You couldn't mess it up." It was trial and error leading to an art form that she would soon master, first joining the group DJ Patty Duke & the Jazzy 5 MCs and eventually bringing her skills to the silver screen in Harry Belafonte's hip-hop flick *Beat Street* and aligning with the legendary Juice Crew, a crossborough (though primarily Queensbridge-native) hip-hop collective founded by radio DJ Mr. Magic and producer Marley Marl.

There was a certain level of cachet to women joining all-male groups. First, it gave their presence a sense of purpose. For years, women were waiting for that fateful moment to jump on the mic in the midst of an already-forming male-dominated platform. Standing out from a mix of guys meant greater novelty, since back then, as an MC, male or female, you were merely an accessory to the DJ to begin with. "Now it's all about the MC, but back then the DJ was at the forefront," Debbie D says. As such, the best way to pop as an MC was to be different alongside your groupmates. Being an entirely different gender certainly helped, though skills were also crucial. Second, you had to join a crew no matter what. "Nobody was running around like a lone ranger," Debbie adds. "Everybody was looking for a crew." If your crew had a DJ with a strong sound system (back to the Herc business model), then you were guaranteed heightened visibility. If their system was weak, you had to work that much harder for recognition.

Crews were blooming left and right during that period, too, and women were becoming more popular as members, though only one woman per male crew could exist. Everything was moving fast. One of the first groups to incorporate a woman was the Funky 4, when it took on Sharon "Sha-Rock" Green, who is regarded as the first female MC. Eventually, MC Sha-Rock and fellow member Rahiem left the group, with Rahiem joining Grandmaster Flash and the Furious Five. The Funky 4 then recruited Li'l Rodney C! and Jazzy Jeff, but became the Funky 4 + 1 when Sha-Rock rejoined. "I was the original part of the four," Sha-Rock confirmed in an interview with VICE in 2014. "There were three other guys and myself." When she returned, she received the moniker "Miss Plus One," and the group changed its name to the Funky 4 + 1. "MC Sha-Rock was the most incredible MC," Kurtis Blow says of Miss Plus One. "I would put her against any guy during that time. She was just devastating, and she was pretty too. She, to me, was the epitome of a female MC." Funky 4 + 1 was the first hip-hop group to get a recording contract through Enjoy! Records with their 1979 single "Rappin' & Rocking the House." They later joined Sugar Hill Records under the leadership of CEO Sylvia Robinson. That same year, Lady B—a radio DJ hailing from Philly—released her song "To the Beat Y'all," along with Lady D, who released her namesake track "Lady D" on the same 7-inch vinyl single as MC Tee's "Nu Sounds."

In 1981, after Blondie's Debbie Harry made history when "Rapture" became the first rap music video to air on MTV, she introduced Funky 4 + 1 on *Saturday Night Live,* making them the first hip-hop group to appear on national television.

More female artists and their groups flourished throughout the early '80s, many under the umbrella of the Zulu Nation, led by pioneer Afrika Bambaataa. Lisa Lee, who was the first (and only) female in the Soulsonic Force (of "Planet Rock" fame), later joined the Cosmic Force. Sweet and Sour was part of Kool Herc's crew The Herculords, along with Pebblee-Poo, who was with her brother's Master Don & the Death Committee. Pebblee-Poo was also one of the first women to fly solo.

The "firsts" debate carries over into all-female groups as well. South Carolina's The Sequence was the first all-female hip-hop group to cut a record (with Sugar Hill Records), though group member Angie Stone would later switch over to R&B. "They had the first hook I had ever heard on 'Funk You Up,'" Kurtis Blow says of The Sequence's 1979 single. Kurtis released "The Breaks" a year later. "A lot of people give me the credit for having the first hook— 'These . . . are . . . the breaks'—but no, 'Funk You Up' actually came before that. I have to give them their props."

Then there are the Winley sisters, Tanya and Paulette. Their father Paul Winley turned his doo-wop label Winley Records into a hip-hop label, the first label to actually cut a record with Afrika Bambaataa. Tanya Winley was known on the solo front as the original Sweet Tee, predating Toi "Sweet Tee" Jackson, the prominent female MC who in 1986 scored a hit called "It's My Beat," featuring the legendary DJ Jazzy Joyce. As a group, the Winley sisters recorded the single "Rhymin' and Rappin'" in 1979, and Sweet Tee dropped her solo track "Vicious Rap" in 1980. There's a debate over whether Sweet Tee was the first female soloist to cut a record, since she recorded her song in 1979, the same year as Lady B's "To the Beat Y'all," but it wasn't released immediately.

However, the Mercedes Ladies are universally regarded as the first all-female hip-hop group. Formed around 1976–1977 and composed of both MCs and DJs, it took the teenaged group a few years to gain significant traction, especially when male egos trickled into the equation. "When I first started deejaying, it was because I had seen [Grandmaster] Flash when I was fourteen," remembers Baby D, a Mercedes Ladies MC/DJ from 1978 to 1983. Baby D was self-taught on the turntables, rocking house parties with the guys at the James Monroe projects in the Bronx. Baby D came into her own, however, when she met her mentor, Grand Wizzard Theodore, through an artist named MC Smiley (not to be confused with her groupmate RD Smiley). Theodore taught her the art of scratch, and it was on ever since. Baby D's rep preceded her. "I was on par with Grandmaster Flash and Theodore, which kind of pisses me off because men back then . . . they would not acknowledge the females," she says with a pitch in her tone.

"At one point, Grandmaster Flash . . . when we were talking, he told me, 'You know what group really made us afraid?' I said, 'What?' He said, 'Mercedes Ladies.' I said, 'Why?' He said, 'Because you? You are me. But you're a female. Your MCs, they can rap. They're like Melle Mel, Kid Creole, all of them. And what's even worse is that you spin like me.'" Baby D credits Theodore for the skills, but Flash for the knowledge as it pertains to her navigation through hip-hop.

"Baby D was an incredible DJ," Kurtis Blow says. He later made history when he took Baby D on tour, making her one of the first female DJs to tour with a male MC. "I actually stole her from the Mercedes Ladies and took her on the road for about two years," he explains. "She was very fast and accurate on the turntables. Her style of cuts reminded me of Flash or Theodore. I think she was the best female DJ I ever saw."

As much as Baby D was regarded as a skilled DJ, her rhymes were equally potent. She called herself "double jeopardy," and Grandmaster Flash agreed. "But then when you sit back and listen to these cats talk, I'm like, 'So when are y'all gonna talk about Mercedes Ladies?'" she says. "Sometimes I have to sit down and question myself if we were even there."

Considering Mercedes Ladies still have to fight for a name check at all, Baby D isn't particularly concerned with being first, but is adamant about being known as the foundation for all others that followed. "Mercedes Ladies is without a doubt the foundation of females within hip-hop," she says. "We are the ones that busted our ass so that [Roxanne] Shanté and Sequence and Salt-N-Pepa and everyone else could go and do what they did. We did that. We fought that. We fought Starski."

Starski?

It was a night in downtown Manhattan, maybe at the Palladium, but Baby D's memory of the venue is cloudy. The era of the outdoor sound system wars had come to a close at the end of the summer of '77, and performances had moved into the clubs during the colder weather. Lovebug Starski and Busy Bee Starski had just performed a clean set. Mercedes Ladies were onstage, but Baby D was in the back fighting with Grandmaster Flash. Various acts would often share equipment, and she had forgotten her needles and her records. All she needed were those records and needles, but Flash wasn't giving them up without a lecture. She was annoyed, and Flash was angry. He raised his voice and D lost her mind. "You will not talk to me that way because I'm a female," she yelled back. It was part gender war, part lovers' quarrel. "Of course at the time, me and Flash were going out," she says now, with a laugh. Meanwhile, their bickering was drowned out by loud booing from the crowd. D ran out onstage behind RD Smiley's turntables, the same set successfully used by Starski moments prior. Except now, they're not working. "We were sabotaged," Baby D says, believing Lovebug Starski to have been the culprit. "They would do crap like that to females that were good." Whether refusing to lift heavy equipment or climb fences they had already climbed to plug in their own sound systems during outdoor sets, the men had a frequent response for women who asked for help: "Do it yourself."

This time the saboteurs weren't going to ruin Mercedes Ladies' shine. Baby D and RD Smiley figured out the glitch (it came down to a simple dial turned all the way down). Flash handed her his records and needles and said, "Go save the show." D walked back onstage, tapped her groupmate Sheri Sher on the shoulder, and said, "Let's do this." Victory was achieved.

"We lit the stage up that night."

Chapter Two

US GIRLS

IT DIDN'T TAKE HIP-HOP VERY LONG TO MAKE THE PIVOT TO FILM. The early '80s were spent surfing a consecutive wave of movies that depicted the various angles of hip-hop's elements. From *Wild Style* (1983) to *Style Wars* (1984) to *Breakin'* and *Breakin' 2: Electric Boogaloo* (1984), the narratives of breakdancing and graffiti writing were well documented onscreen. It took *Beat Street* in 1984 and *Krush Groove* in 1985 to truly marry the two aforementioned elements of hip-hop with the remaining two, emceeing and deejaying. *Beat Street* was something special, though, because without it, we wouldn't have *Krush Groove,* which tells the story of the most successful hip-hop label, Def Jam.

In the March 12, 1984 issue of *New York Magazine, Beat Street* producer Harry Belafonte was interviewed in the "On Location" section for an article titled "Harry's Kids," highlighting how Belafonte was doing right by the hip-hop community, especially by hiring non-actors for the film and using real locations like abandoned buildings and actual NYC nightclubs to shoot the film's scenes. The article's author, Amy Virshup, writes, "Belafonte hopes that *Beat Street* will prove that blacks can make 'bankable' films, and that hip-hop will communicate to a mass audience the strength of black culture in America." In many ways, his vision for the film was realized.

Beat Street provided a panoramic view of hip-hop in New York City at that time, and more specifically of its birthplace, the South Bronx. The lead character Kenny "Double K" Kirkland is both an MC and a DJ, with a brother named Lee who is a B-boy. His best friend Ramon writes graffiti, and Chollie is Kenny's manager/promoter. Chollie's character was a foreshadowing of what many both hoped and feared hip-hop was becoming: a business. The film grossed $16,595,791 domestically, $5,218,040 in its first week alone.

And right smack in the middle of its success were Us Girls.

By the fall of 1983, many all-female rap groups had faded, leaving a handful of soloists still actively on the scene. Debbie D got a call from Sha-Rock one day, asking her to join a group with her and Lisa Lee. Debbie met with Lisa at her apartment on the other side of the Bronx. "This happened in October of 1983," Debbie verifies to me, handing over a small piece of paper marked with a date. On it is the word *Empress,* and the names Debbie D, Lisa Lee, and Sha-Rock. "I think Lisa came up with the name," she says, though they wouldn't be Empress for very long.

Word got out to the hip-hop community that Harry Belafonte was producing *Beat Street.* Lisa Lee had already made history as the sole female MC in *Wild Style,* but with her girls beside her, a *Beat Street* cameo was a no-brainer. "You've got the three baddest girls in hip-hop together," Debbie says. "We had to be in that movie." So, the three of them pulled up to the Roxy nightclub, where a *Beat Street* scene was being filmed, and asked to speak with Mr. Harry

Belafonte. The sight of three girls ready to rap was shocking in and of itself. "They weren't in their element," she adds, "they" being the Hollywood hands maneuvering the hip-hop film, "but we were in ours, so it wasn't threatening. All of our hip-hop people were in there." They approached Belafonte. "'You should have us in the movie. We're the first girls. We're bad,'" Debbie remembers saying. She now giggles at her youthful gall. "I don't ever think we auditioned or anything. We just had a conversation." The girls later met Belafonte in his office to discuss their part in the film. In her 2010 book *Luminary Icon,* Sha-Rock talks about almost missing the opportunity. As a Sugar Hill Records signee, her part in the film had to be okayed by CEO Sylvia Robinson. Being the shrewd businesswoman that she was, Robinson managed to parlay Sha-Rock's role in the film into an opportunity for her other group, Grandmaster Melle Mel & the Furious Five, to record the "Beat Street Breakdown" theme, along with a cameo in the film.

There were no MCs in *Beat Street* before Empress joined the fold, though after their place was locked, *Beat Street* shifted gears, adding more artists to the cast.

When the trio enter the abandoned building party scene in the movie, it's like a whole new world. The film's star, aspiring DJ Double K, is spinning records at the party, interjecting DJ cuts with his own rhymes. The girls are spotted dancing in the mix, so Double K beckons them to the front. "Well, here's three ladies from my neighborhood, guaranteed to rock the beat and rock the beat good," he rhymes. The three ladies walk up to the front where Double K is spinning. "Us girls can boogie, too," they sing in unison. "We can dance, we can shake it." Then they break into a unified rap: "Us girls are the best of friends. If one ain't got no money, the other one lends." It was a utopic moment for the introduction of girl power into rap, especially on the silver screen. Each girl had her turn to rhyme, all with a specific mission and style in tow: Debbie

D opens with the no-nonsense bars. She's a fly girl and she knows it, and if you respect her and "wine her mind," then you're good to go. If not, there's the door. Sha-Rock will leave a guy with his back soaking wet. It's pretty obvious what she's referring to. And then comes Lisa Lee, wooing the fellas with how good she'll treat them and how she's looking for love. (Three years later, LL Cool J would release "I Need Love" with coincidentally a similar message directed toward the ladies and a vaguely similar rhyming pattern.) At the time, the girls were still known as Empress, but their song became their signature during the filming of the movie. "Everyone on set kept saying, 'Where the Us Girls at? Where the Us Girls at?'" Debbie says. "So that's how we became Us Girls."

"That did it for me," legendary female MC turned radio personality Monie Love tells me about that pivotal movie scene. "It had a really big impression on me." At the time, Monie was still living in London, slowly catching up to the hip-hop explosion happening in the States. *Beat Street* made it across the pond, though, and by proxy so did Debbie D, Lisa Lee, and Sha-Rock. The power of their reach superseded all the male-driven marketing of the film—Us Girls was never featured on any promotional posters or photos, despite being a part of the first musical scene in the movie. It was a buried gesture of sexism on the part of Hollywood, along with an attempted slight to the pockets of every hip-hop artist in the film, considering they almost weren't paid to participate.

Debbie was working as a legal secretary in Rockefeller Center during the filming of *Beat Street*. When she asked her boss for time off, explaining that she was a rapper appearing in an upcoming film, her boss requested to speak with Harry Belafonte to verify the request. "I'm thinking, 'For what?'" Debbie says. She told the switchboard operator to prepare for a call from *the* Harry Belafonte, who actually called himself and spoke with Debbie's boss. When the call ended, Debbie's boss told her that when she appeared on set the next day, there would be something waiting for her. "When I got to the set, they say, 'Who is Debora Hooper?' I'm like, 'Oh God!' Because they didn't say, 'Who is Debbie D?' They're using my government name. So, they said, 'Fill this out.' It was a paper to sign up for the Screen Actors Guild, and it was the paper to sign up for [publishing through] EMI. Because of that, we still get paid to this day. For the rest of my life—even when I'm gone—everywhere that movie plays around the world, we get paid." Us Girls even get a bonus. "We're paid twice because we sang in the movie, and we're in the movie," Debbie adds.

There's a sore spot in hip-hop history when it comes to the pioneers. They ultimately invented a culture that has translated into billions of dollars, yet they lived in a pre-radio, primarily pre-recorded world, where their only source of currency was their credibility. Thanks to Debbie D, everyone who starred in *Beat Street* has the luxury of receiving a residuals check, unlike those who did the graffiti-inspired film *Wild Style,* which gave its performers a few hundred bucks and sent them all on their merry way. *Beat Street* led to many opportunities, especially for the newly christened Us Girls, who toured overseas with their film notoriety and even won awards, like the one Debbie D mentions to me: an award for Best Female Hip-Hop Group presented to the group by Harlem's 369th Armory in early 1984.

That night, a young teenage girl with braces approached Debbie D and voiced her admiration for Us Girls in what Debbie describes as a "squeaky voice."

Her name? Shanté.

Chapter Three

THERE'S A WAR GOIN' ON OUTSIDE

IN LATE 1984—JUST A FEW MONTHS AFTER *BEAT STREET* HIT theaters—Roxanne Shanté pulled off the greatest marketing stunt in hip-hop history. At the time, Brooklyn's U.T.F.O. (Untouchable Force Organization) was pushing their record "Hanging Out," an R&B-leaning track with a B-side called "Roxanne, Roxanne," where the rap crew chides a woman named Roxanne for denying their multiple advances. The name "Roxanne" predates U.T.F.O.'s mention, of course. In 1978, The Police's song "Roxanne" details a sex worker being urged by Police frontman Sting to quit her business in the name of love. U.T.F.O. simply continued that thread of hypersexualizing with their fictitious Roxanne. The B-side dipped on the group's priority scale, as radio stations were looking to abolish hip-hop music based on the success of Mr. Magic's *Rap Attack* with Marley Marl, since hip-hop was perceived as a threat to other genres. Magic and Marley's radio show was both an artistic breeding ground and prime rap real estate. Kids would tape the episodes on their stereos and play them back like they were albums. If you didn't have the latest episode of *Rap Attack* recorded, you weren't cool at all.

Rap Attack first aired on New York's WHBI, an FM station on which DJs paid to air their shows. The radio show was later picked up by WBLS in New York, where money poured in, per Tyrone "Fly Ty" Williams, *Rap Attack* producer/engineer and founder of Cold Chillin' Records. Once the coup was staged by New York radio stations to remove rap from the airwaves, the team of Mr. Magic, Marley Marl, and Fly Ty was offered beaucoup bucks to retain positions at WBLS, absent hip-hop. They declined and moved back to WHBI, where they continued to pay their own money to keep hip-hop going. It took a financial toll on them.

U.T.F.O. was looking to drift away from standard rap music, focusing their efforts on "Hanging Out," but when they brought the record to Mr. Magic, he insisted that "Roxanne, Roxanne" was the bigger hit. "'Regular radio isn't playing rap anymore,' [U.T.F.O.] told us," Fly Ty recalls. Both U.T.F.O. and their manager Steve Salem were still pushing "Hanging Out." Never one to listen to what other people told him, Mr. Magic played "Roxanne, Roxanne" instead, and it was a hit. To thank Mr. Magic and his team, U.T.F.O. agreed to perform at a show for free so the *Rap Attack* guys could make some money, which they desperately needed. All they had to do was pick a day and a location. "I pick a venue called Broadway International," Fly Ty says. When Ty brought the information to Salem, he told Ty the show was off. KISS FM, a rival station, had added U.T.F.O.'s record, so they no longer needed Mr. Magic. "The bottom dropped out from under me," Fly Ty says. Christmas was right around the corner and the money from that show was their only shot at buying gifts. When Ty got to the station and broke the news to Mr. Magic and Marley Marl, they were all rattled. With nothing but the power of their radio presence, something had to be done.

"We used to drop Marley off at Queensbridge," Fly Ty recounts. "We're standing outside of Marley's building, talking rather loudly about what U.T.F.O. and their manager had done to us. A little girl hears us. She walks up to us and says, 'Why don't you let me make a tape dissing them?'" Ty wanted nothing to do with her offer, but Magic saw an opportunity. Marley, who lived above the same laundromat where the young girl did her laundry, asked her to come upstairs and rock over the "Roxanne, Roxanne" beat. Marley worked at the Sergio Valente jeans factory, so while she was hoping to break through as an MC, she was also looking for the denim hookup. Little did she know how much that moment would affect her entire life.

Ty still wasn't convinced, until he returned to work a day later. "The next night at the station, Marley says, 'Ty, remember that little girl? Listen to this.'"

Lolita Shanté Gooden was a native of the now infamous Queensbridge housing projects in Long Island City, Queens, and the gumption she exhibited by walking up to a group of guys and forcing her way into their conversation would become her reputation. She had already made a name for herself among her peers as a small-time battle rapper, though she leveled up when she propositioned Mr. Magic and Marley Marl. The product of her efforts was a song called "Roxanne's Revenge," where the then fourteen-year-old Gooden assumes the role of "Roxanne." The song is a retort to U.T.F.O.'s track, as Shanté shames the group for attempting to make moves on her when they aren't of her caliber. She calls them all by name, acknowledges that she jacked their beat, and runs through a list of grievances about why they have no business trying to talk to her to begin with. Oh yes, and she says they're broke. Picture that: a teenager barking at a group of men for attempting to put her down for not accepting their advances. It's the sonic equivalent of verbally destroying a catcaller in front of all his friends. A star was boldly about to be born, and she wouldn't take shit from anyone.

Ty suggested she use the name Roxanne Shanté, with "Roxanne" moving into a ranking title, similar to how "Grandmaster" was used for men. "Roxanne's Revenge" premiered on *Rap Attack*, and the episode was recorded by fans and passed around. Early tapes even include the "*Rap Attack* World Premiere" drop at the beginning. After swiftly selling five thousand copies, the song led to a cease-and-desist from U.T.F.O. for Marley Marl's uncleared use of a sample of their instrumental track. A new beat was quickly recorded, and the song went on to sell close to 250,000 copies.

A switch was inevitably flicked between 1977 and 1984 as it pertained to women in the rap space. Prior to this moment, a spot on a flyer hardly led to money on the table. But once Shanté hit the radio, things changed. The playing field was no longer level. Gone were the days of a bunch of kids having fun. Hip-hop was a business, and the bargaining chip was named Roxanne. Instead of adding to her appeal, she had to be stopped, or topped. Enter Brooklyn native Adelaida Martinez, who would assume the moniker "The Real Roxanne" (with a whole song about it in tow). She was pretty and had lighter skin than Shanté. Martinez was U.T.F.O.'s secret weapon in the battle of Roxanne domination. There was another Real Roxanne chosen, though U.T.F.O. didn't think she had the looks Martinez had, so one woman was swapped for another under the same name. This was the first move in hip-hop history to present women as figureheads cloaked in anonymity, considering Roxanne Shanté was not only being challenged for her remarks but for her identity. By creating a whole new character sharing the same name, U.T.F.O. was stripping Shanté of the game-changing move she had made by assuming her rap name to begin with. After all, Shanté gave a face to the anonymous "Roxanne" at a time when the comfort zone was to regard women simply as the "plus one," "ladies," or "girls." The "Roxanne Wars" were launched; over eighty response records blasted the moving target known as Roxanne. It's hard to even fathom anyone else owning the name Roxanne now, but that was not without hard work from Shanté. "You'll never have the Roxanne phenomenon again," Roxanne Shanté told *VICE News* in 2017. "I made one song, and had eighty-three songs made about me, specifically where they said 'Roxanne Shanté.' No other artist has ever had that."

Many tried to challenge Shanté during the Roxanne Wars, but there wasn't a worthier opponent for her than Brooklyn's own Sparky Dee. Born Doreen C. Broadnax, Sparky was rapping as part of the group the Playgirls. She was tuned in to *Rap Attack* the night "Roxanne's Revenge" first aired. "When the clock struck midnight, [Mr. Magic] played the world premiere, which was Roxanne Shanté," Sparky remembers. She was sitting with her then boyfriend, rapper and producer Spyder-D, who suggested she respond to Shanté for targeting U.T.F.O. "Being that U.T.F.O. lives in Brooklyn, and I'm from Brownsville, I said, 'I'm going to take her on for U.T.F.O.,'" Sparky says. Her track "Sparky's Turn (Roxanne You're Through)" was a tough-as-nails response record, where Sparky fired verbal darts at Shanté. Sparky pokes fun at Shanté's lawsuit for the jacked beat, calls her conceited (among other things), and claims it was U.T.F.O. that made her famous. The biggest takeaway was that Sparky was assuming the position of "chief," and that she was the superior MC. Sparky even makes fun of Shanté's rhyming pattern on "Roxanne's Revenge," adding an "-a" to the ends of the words. It was vicious, it was pointed, and it kicked off a battle that traveled from the studio to the stage and made people a lot of money.

The battle between Sparky Dee and Roxanne Shanté became notorious. "We didn't like each other," Sparky admits, their animosity a combination of borough loyalty and plain adolescent personality conflicts. "We knew of each other, we did shows, but no—it wasn't an act at all." At the behest of Mr. Magic, Spyder-D, Marley Marl, and Shanté's manager, Fly Ty, the two opted to work with each other to "make some money together." The record "Round One, Roxanne Shanté vs. Sparky Dee" was released, with the cover art displaying the two together with their dukes up, boxing gloves touching as they glare into the camera. Animosity grew, though, as Shanté had a calculated upper hand. "[Roxanne Shanté] went on for sixteen extra bars, and she wasn't supposed to," reveals Sparky. The tacked-on bars included some venom from Shanté:

> I'll bust this shit here, Sparky Dee
> When it comes to rhymes I say
> You can't hang with me, Miss Shanté

"I was mad at my record company because that's not what she's supposed to do," Sparky says of Shanté's lengthy verse. "And at the time, I was told as an artist not to curse." But the teenage Shanté sure did. Still, the two toured together, promoting the battle even when emotions were high. "Mr. Magic taught us, and this is something I'll never forget," Sparky recounts. "We were doing our first battle in North Carolina, Raleigh-Durham. We sold out. Roxanne Shanté and myself on the bill. No one else. We weren't speaking to each other, it was so much tension. It was really, really bad. Mr. Magic said this: 'You have Larry Bird from the Boston Celtics, and you have Magic Johnson from the Lakers.' He said, 'Look, they don't like each other, but they go play basketball.'"

The best way to view their traveling battle was like a sport, with spectators watching as the two traded bars. But having Shanté close the battle with an extended verse on their record placed her at an unfair advantage, despite Sparky telling me she still thinks she was a better rapper.

These were chess moves indicative of the fact that Roxanne Shanté was driving the zeitgeist of the era for women in hip-hop, yet her success and skill posed a threat to men. The New Music Seminar's MC Battle for World Supremacy, started in 1980, deflated any shot she had of achieving the top spot in hip-hop. The music networking event turned battleground showcase for optimal visibility was the stuff of legend, and a prime location for talent to be cultivated. In 1985, the finalists came down to Busy Bee Starski and Roxanne Shanté, who was the only girl competing. Shanté was blasting through her opponents in every round, spitting off the top of her head and taking no prisoners. "That was always a problem for anyone battling Shanté," Fly Ty says. "Because they had written rhymes. Shanté would take what you just said and flip it back on you and have the crowd going crazy." Then she faced off with Busy Bee. Described by Fly Ty as a "party rocker," Busy was more concerned with getting the crowd going, which was his forte. Shanté was chasing punchlines and insults.

Busy opened with lines from his "Busy Bee's Groove," including:

> *Two weeks ago at the place to be*
> *They was standing in line to see who? Busy Bee*

Shanté returned with her own rhyme about getting hit on by a guy in the projects:

> *He said you're fly from behind to the guys, don't know why*
> *And there ain't a guy who can't pass you by*
> *I looked at him and I said, "No lie."*

Somewhere in the middle, Shanté got fired up and started directly targeting Busy Bee, claiming they made a deal backstage that she would keep it chill. Well, she reneged on that premature peace treaty.

> *What is a bee? It ain't cool with me*
> *I'll stomp that shit in a 1, 2, 3*

As the battle went on and the opponents breezed through each of their timed responses, it was clear that Shanté had a real shot at taking home the crown. But when it came down to the judges' scores, hip-hop sexism reared its head. Buff Love and the Fat Boys gave both Shanté and Busy a 10. Whiz Kid gave Busy a 9, Shanté a 10. Afrika Bambaataa gave Busy a 9, Shanté a 10. Kool DJ Red Alert gave Busy a 10, Shanté an 8. Then came Kurtis Blow, who gave Busy a 9 and Shanté a 4. The final score? 47–42. Busy Bee was the winner. The battle was rigged. Why would Kurtis, a fellow member of the Juice Crew with Shanté, do that to her? Per Fly Ty, it was over Kurtis's annoyance that Shanté had called out her crew affiliate on a rhyme: *Run-DMC? Kurtis Blow? Where they come from? I don't know.*

"Shanté dissed everybody, though," Ty says with a laugh. Kurtis Blow remembers Shanté's calling him out: "I was furious! When [Shanté] got out there, I wasn't really too supportive, to tell you the truth. I regret that now, but her whole thing was listening to Mr. Magic—and I hate to say it, rest in peace, but he was like a troublemaker almost, and he put her up to those lyrics."

Days before the infamous battle, Kurtis was in Los Angeles, judging a whole other showdown. "I'm far away from home in LA at a club called Carolina West. I did a show, and then I was the judge of a rap contest," Kurtis says. "Here comes this light-skinned guy with a ponytail, and he gets on the mic, and he starts cursing up a storm. I'm totally against that, totally against cursing on the mic. He's calling women b's and, 'betta have my money, I'm a pimp, I'm a hustler, I'm a gangster,' all this stuff. I'm like, 'Oh my God, we can't have this in hip-hop. We're never gonna go anywhere with this kind of rap.'" Kurtis wanted to give him a 2, but "the crowd was going crazy." Added to that, Kurtis was out of his element. "I thought about it, and was like, 'If I give him a 2, I might not get to make it back home.'" He gave the rapper a 10, which made him the winner of the contest. "Three years later, I find out that Ice-T tells the same story. He's the guy with the ponytail! He went on to say that him winning that contest inspired him to keep rapping and go on and make his career."

Back to the Battle for World Supremacy. Kurtis leaves Los Angeles and is in New York City on friendly turf, ready to judge. "And here's Roxanne Shanté against Busy Bee. Busy Bee was my friend; we used to hang out frequently." While Shanté was part of Kurtis's crew, she was introducing a different spirit to the battleground. "This was the first time you heard somebody in a rap contest disrespect the other rapper. You know how the battles are now, where they talk about you from head to toe? She was the first one to do that. To Busy Bee! I'm like, 'Oh my God, this is crazy.'" While he couldn't put his foot down in Los Angeles, he certainly could at home. "I said, 'Look, I'm not going for it,'" and he gave her the 4. Roxanne lunged for Kurtis, but Fly Ty pulled her off. "She was crying," Kurtis says. "I felt so bad. But you know, that was sort of a little revenge that I got because of that record that she made that was on the radio. I told her—I said, 'Look. This is hip-hop. This battling stuff, I don't believe in that. You can't disrespect people from head to toe and win a contest like that. You've gotta show your skills.'" Through her tears, Roxanne said to him, "I was just listening to Magic! Magic and Ty told me to do that." Kurtis apologized, but still got to celebrate. "The night after that,

[Busy Bee] and I went up to the Disco Fever and partied all night with his trophy."

Kurtis says his decision to lowball Shanté was lyrics-driven above all. "And Magic was my best friend at the time," he says. "But we used to argue and debate about the future of hip-hop." Using a teenage girl as the driving force to make a hard switch, especially on the battlefront, wasn't something Kurtis was down for. To him, it was for shock value, so he wielded the power of the point system. Others, however, including her opponent himself, viewed it as his blocking a woman from leading the charge for hip-hop's next phase. "I think they weren't ready for a female to take the helm," Busy Bee explains to me over thirty years later. "No one ever heard a female do or say the things she said. In my opinion, I won, but she was good." Busy refers to that moment as a potential changing of the guard, since a female MC got so close to the finish line. So what would've happened if that new guard had been led by a woman? That 4 from Kurtis Blow had a crippling effect on everything Roxanne Shanté could have been. Even Sparky Dee had to agree.

"I mean, they would knock the girls out," Sparky explains. "They would have seven guys on the show and barely have a female on the show to perform." The ladies were often invited onstage to perform as last-minute, unscheduled, and unpaid special guests, after the men had already been booked in advance and paid to be there. "It was very hard to get a job because of all of the guys," she continues. "Just like Kurtis Blow knocked out Roxanne Shanté, because she was supposed to win [at the NMS], but because that was Busy Bee, and she was a woman, they were like, 'Nah, this can't happen.' That's their mentality."

In 2015, Tom Silverman—founder of Tommy Boy Records and cofounder of the New Music Seminar—was asked in an interview if Busy Bee was the winner of the first MC Battle for World Supremacy. Silverman deflected, citing how 1985 was the year the

New Music Seminar changed venues to the Marriott Marquis and shouting out Busy's now infamous "Squirrel and the Nut" rhyme. Even the person who started the battle couldn't answer that simple question.

But it wasn't all in vain, really. "She put the females on the map from that point on in hip-hop," Busy Bee notes. "It was all guys at that time. You gotta remember she was young; we was grown men. There was no ladies our age doing it, so she was the one. But she was just too young at the time." So in essence, Roxanne Shanté won that battle, and after three decades, it's finally recognized. "She should've won," Kurtis Blow says regretfully. "She should've gotten that ten like Ice-T. The crowd definitely loved her, and she did the best that night. I still feel bad today about that."

Maybe that's Roxanne's real revenge.

Chapter Four

WILL THE REAL ROXANNE PLEASE STAND UP?

I WOULD NEVER THINK, 'OH, THIS GIRL HAS JUST BEEN BEATEN UP.'"
I'm sitting at a restaurant on Lafayette Street in New York City, a few blocks shy of the Bowery, where the legendary CBGB nightclub once stood and where veteran hip-hop photographer Janette Beckman has had her studio for over thirty-five years. Beckman is known for taking some of the most iconic hip-hop photographs of the '80s, including the infamous pic of Slick Rick grabbing his crotch with a Fendi bag at his feet and a bottle of champagne in his hand.

We're scanning pictures that she's taken of Roxanne Shanté over the years, searching for signs of distress. Across the street from us is the location where Beckman first shot Shanté, adjacent to a parking garage that's still standing decades later. Shanté is in a tracksuit, scowling at the camera. Her hair is slicked back into a ponytail. She looks like a menacing child who could pop off at any moment, yet here her mouth is firmly shut. In Netflix's *Roxanne Roxanne* biopic, there's a scene in which a female photographer commands Shanté to smile. She can't. In the film, her jaw had been broken by her boyfriend, yet she attempts to keep her face straight for a photo. Following the biopic's release, Beckman's photo resurfaced as the real-life image from the film's traumatic scene, but Beckman isn't convinced that it's hers. "Look at how swollen her jaw is," I say to Beckman, pointing to Shante's jawline in Beckman's iconic photo. "Her eye looks swollen, too." Beckman shows me a second photo, this one quite the opposite of the first, and she believes this was from the same photoshoot on the same day. Roxanne is wearing a pale-pink outfit with a giant deep-pink bow on her head. She has a red Fila sneaker on each hand, with the soles against her ears like headphones. She's smiling wide, her braces in full view, though her bite is a bit crooked. "Look how happy she looks in that picture!"

Beckman argues that maybe it was just her younger face that looked so puffy and unsure. She shows me another photo she shot of Shanté a few years later, where Shanté has her arms resting on the shoulders of two bent-over individuals, each sporting a denim jacket with her image airbrushed on the back. Shanté is wearing a bare-midriff top, semi-concealed by a denim jacket. Her wedding ring is in clear view. Here she looks more confident and self-assured; her eyes look like she's lived a million lives in just a few years. It's all confusing, to say the least, and Beckman is irked that one of her most famous hip-hop portraits is now the subject of this kind of debate. "I probably would've gone, 'Oh my God! Are you okay?' And gone to the kitchen and gotten an ice pack for her," she says of that day. The shoot would've been a wrap. "We never would've done it."

Roxanne's jaw was allegedly broken by a punch from her older, drug dealer boyfriend (whom she later married). Fly Ty, who was still managing Shanté during that time, says he only saw Shanté physically assaulted once, and it wasn't by the man that Shanté accused.

According to Ty, Shanté would vanish from time to time, especially before a commitment. He recalls one very specific incident. "We have a show in Milwaukee, I'm looking for Shanté everywhere. I can't find her. I'm looking all over for her. At the time, I'm twenty-seven, twenty-eight. She's maybe fifteen, going on sixteen. Earlier, I used to take Marley [Marl]'s older sister Belle with us to be the matron for Shanté. I always thought, 'A woman's gotta be with us. Little girls have little girl problems that a man don't need to be a part of.' So anyway, I'm looking for Shanté everywhere. I go to Belle's house. Belle says, 'Ty, I saw her with Chris.' I'm like, 'Who the hell is Chris?'" Belle explains that Chris is a drug dealer around those parts. "'What? A drug dealer?' And he's thirty-two years old. Mind you, I'm like twenty-seven, and I'm her guardian, so immediately I call the police. I'm in Marley's house, because they all live in the same little area in Queensbridge. I have the police meet me there. Two police officers come, I take them to the building across the way—to Shanté's mother's house." The cops arrive at her mother Peggy's house and tell her that Ty says her teenage daughter is running around with a grown man. "Her mother says, 'I know. They left here together.'" If her mother's consenting to that behavior, then what could Ty really do? "That's when I pull out my guardianship forms. I had to carry them with me all the time." Since he was managing the career of an artist who was still a minor, Ty had become her guardian, because it was against labor laws to take an underage child over state lines for business. As Shanté's guardian, Ty had the upper hand at this point, and demanded that they find the teenager regardless of her mother's approval of the relationship.

"Peggy is being no help." Meanwhile, the cops are doing their intake, getting a description of Shanté, etc. Marley Marl and MC Shan are there while Ty talks to the cops. "One cop is in the doorway, one is in the kitchen with me," he recalls. Ten minutes go by, then the officer in the doorway walks up to Ty and the other officer and describes a girl to Ty, asking if she fits Shanté's description. She does. "He steps out of the way and Shanté is standing behind him, with a big bouquet of roses. Smiling." Presumably, the flowers were from her drug-dealing paramour. Her DJ isn't pleased. "I ain't deejaying for her no fuckin' more" is what he tells Ty.

"He isn't her DJ no more, because he is secretly her boyfriend," Ty reveals. "He's mad as hell. You see the steam coming out his nose. That was the first time I've ever punched him, because he smacked Shanté. He smacked her so hard, it left an imprint of a ring in her face, and I punched him in his face." Mr. Magic's thirteen-year-old son, Lucky, was the replacement DJ for that Milwaukee show, and that was the first and last time Fly Ty ever witnessed Shanté being abused. "Chris adored Shanté," Ty says of Shanté's older boyfriend. "There's nobody at Cold Chillin' or in that Juice Crew who was around—whether it's [Big Daddy] Kane, Biz [Markie], [MC] Shan—who could tell you that Shanté had any altercation with Chris." Chris has since passed away, making Ty even more upset that his legacy has been reduced to this questionable series of events, wedged into one short biopic. "Shanté is slick," he says. "She tried to plant the seed—'Remember when Chris used to hit me?'" to which Ty would reply no.

I point to the biopic as circumstantial evidence to patterns of abuse. Plus, there's no trace of Ty in the film, though a turbulent character named "Ray" is Shanté's de facto manager, a figure who in the film took advantage of Shanté in many ways. "She wants to galvanize women to support her," Ty says. "But at the stake of what?" So, what about Ray? If Ray was theoretically Ty, then Ty was no better to her, right? "She knew not to say my name. In her mind, 'I didn't do nothing to you, Ty, because I said it was some guy named Ray,'" he responds. "Everybody knows I was her manager, but also everyone who knows I was her manager knows my love for her, knows how I took care of her." According to Ty, Shanté took his son and daughter to the film's premiere to gauge their reaction. "My daughter was furious. My son [said], 'Dad, the people who are gonna see that movie don't know you. She didn't say your name. They're gonna look for somebody named Ray. We know it's not you, and you know Shanté.'

"Yeah, I know Shanté," he adds.

With a past of fabricating stories, including her PhD ("She has a doctorate in game, is what I tell people," Ty says with a heavy laugh), it's hard to really figure out the truth. I tried numerous times, to no avail, to speak with Roxanne Shanté for her to comment on these controversial footnotes, especially now, when a younger generation can watch this story as the only account of what went on in her personal life throughout her rap career. But does this apply to her musical legacy? Not entirely, though hip-hop can certainly be seen as the root of all the turbulence in her life. Further, maybe Chris was a stand-up guy in front of everyone else, but behind closed doors, he was a different person. Maybe Shanté's experiences shouldn't be up for debate, since they're all her own and she was guided by a team of men to be their moneymaking pit bull.

Maybe we should just get back to the music.

It's hard to really process just how young Roxanne Shanté truly was, and also how so widely accepted it was to disrespect her. After all, she was barely eighteen when Boogie Down Productions dropped the heinous line "Roxanne Shanté is only good for steady fuckin'" on "The Bridge Is Over" during the height of the beef between the South Bronx and Queensbridge. Shanté later responded to BDP on "Have A Nice Day," but even before that incident she was treated like an undisciplined child by everyone perplexed by her success, especially when she was the first female rapper in history to really aim for the jugular of men who attempted to benefit from a song on disrespecting women. She herself was barely on the cusp of womanhood; in a sense, she was still an undisciplined child, albeit an outspoken and gifted one.

Shanté attributed her "rap like she's speaking" rhyming style to a song she would listen to as a kid with her mother, "The Name Game" by Shirley Ellis:

> *Shirley, Shirley, Bo-ber-ley*
> *Bo-na-na fanna, Fo-fer-ley*

Shanté never wrote down her lyrics before recording her records. It all came from her head in the moment. "Shanté would come down to the studio with a shopping cart with her mother's laundry in it and her little sister because she always used to have to babysit," Fly Ty remembers. The studio was a few blocks from her house, and she would stop there on the way to the laundromat. In one take she would record a track. He recalls one session in particular: "One time I said, 'Shanté, rap about how you got started.' She said, 'Okay!'" Shanté stood before the mic and started rapping about how she was listening to the radio, heard about a contest, and knew she would win it.

That song later became "Queen of Rox (Shanté Rox On)," one of many songs she recorded off the cuff, though none would match the power of "Roxanne's Revenge." At that point, it didn't matter. Shanté's stage performances kept her in demand, touring with grown adults and quickly moving into big arenas. But she was still a kid both in age and at heart. She still sucked her thumb in her teens, and at times when she didn't want to get onstage, she would retreat to a corner with her thumb in her mouth. Her team would try to force her to perform, and a tantrum would ensue. "That's when I learned when Shanté was mad, it made her better," Ty says. The anger would charge her up, and every show became the best one of her career. "You wanna talk about somebody who was built to perform? She was built to perform," he adds. "The stage became a part of her. I've never seen anybody—male or female—rock a stage like Roxanne Shanté."

Other acts on the bills weren't always feeling her popularity. By 1985, Shanté had finished her tour with Sparky Dee and had already moved on to larger-scale performances, even landing the coveted R&B tours—a feat for rap artists at the time. She was too big to open the shows, too "hip-hop" to close them, so they would wedge her in the middle, much to the chagrin of the R&B acts before and after her on the lineup. Shanté was damned if she did, damned if she didn't. "The way they would talk about this child, I couldn't believe it," Ty recalls. "'I ain't goin' on before that little bitch.' Nasty stuff! Grown-ass people talking about somebody that could've been their daughter." Despite being fans of the artists talking about her, Shanté took her hurt feelings to the stage. "It seems like she would always catch a whiff of what they said. When she would get on that stage, she would talk about them." One time she had the whole Spectrum arena in Philly chanting "Fuck New Edition." The crowd bowed before the shrine of Roxanne Shanté, especially when many assumed she was a Philly native because her record label at the time, Pop Art Records, was based in Philadelphia. Eventually, her most noteworthy songs lost priority on her setlists, in exchange for more off-the-cuff improv. Shanté's knack for impromptu battles was her greatest selling point, regardless of the opponent. Her performances had a new itinerary: "She had to diss a girl, diss somebody in the audience, and diss somebody on the show," Ty says. "That's what the audience wanted. She became the foulmouthed little girl that could rap all day."

Emphasis on the "little girl." Shanté was classifiable as a child star, complete with a fan base that was her own age. And Shanté loved impressing her fans. She would think nothing of rolling up into a fast-food restaurant and buying all the kids value meals with an invite to her show (another smart marketing tactic to boost concert attendance), but there was also a part of her that just wanted to hang out. Disguised in a hoodie covering most of her face, Shanté would go to the arcades at skating rinks before her hip-hop performances and play games with the kids, or sit cloaked in the audience to watch her favorite artists perform before her when she was out on tour. Sparky Dee even recalls Shanté pulling a similar stunt when Sparky boldly performed on Shanté's turf in Queensbridge. "She paid her way to get in to see me perform," Sparky says. "She had a hood on her head." The fun never lasted, though. "I would walk up to her and beckon her with my finger, like 'C'mere,'" Fly Ty adds. "She would walk over, but make sure they would all see it was her, because she would take the hood off." Pandemonium would ensue, and her bodyguard would pick her up, put her on his shoulders, and walk her away.

While Roxanne Shanté had a steady reign of live performances, her recorded music didn't connect to her audience in the way it had when she was first introduced on the radio. Her official debut album, 1989's *Bad Sister,* released on Ty's Cold Chillin' Records and distributed by Warner Bros., was met with a lukewarm reception. Madonna had released her epic second album *Like A Prayer* via Warner Bros. earlier that year, so Shanté was far from a priority. The shame there was that record labels didn't take female rappers seriously until Roxanne Shanté arrived, yet now she was feeling the effects of pop music over hip-hop. "It became a job for her," Ty says, and so it simply stopped being fun. Kids like to have fun.

"I used to say rap was like gymnastics back then," says Ty. "By the time you're eighteen, it's over. A whole new set of girls were coming."

THE *CLASS OF '88* PHOTO

Thirty years ago, *Paper* magazine hired Janette Beckman to take a photo of the female rappers on the scene in 1988 for a "Class of '88" feature. Beckman's friends had started *Paper* in 1984, highlighting all the popular trends on the downtown New York City scene. Beckman shot for *Paper* during the publication's first five years of existence, and considering her work with hiphop artists, her coverage of this growing phenomenon of women on the mic was destiny. The photo was intended to showcase the most promising female rappers in New York, along with the singer Millie Jackson. Millie was known for her edgy songs and performances, and had toured with Roxanne Shanté. Perhaps she was added because, like the rest of the women in the room, she was causing a stir among the men of the music industry with her less-than-timid vibe.

"We all met at this Mexican restaurant in Soho," Beckman recalls. A lot of the girls came with their boyfriends, and the guys were eventually asked to leave so the shoot could take place without them distracting the girls. "So it was just a room full of women. And everybody was chatting. It was a great atmosphere." The photo includes rivals Roxanne Shanté and Sparky Dee, along with MC Lyte, Ms. Melodie (wife of KRS-One at the time), MC Peaches, and E-Vette Money, known for her song "E-Vette's Revenge," a response record to LL Cool J's "Dear Yvette." There was also Sweet Tee [Toi Jackson], Synquis (of Finesse & Synquis), and Millie Jackson. Sparky Dee's two dancers were there as well, bookending the sides of the photo.

The work is arranged like a real classroom photo, where the front row of women are seated with another row standing behind them. Millie Jackson is posted in the middle, flexing her arms and sticking out her tongue. Everyone else appears to be having a good time, looking noticeably happy in the picture. Did they love each other? Probably not. But they all knew what that photo was about. "We all went into the room, we all spoke together, Janette took the picture," Sparky says. "We all knew it was business. That's the one thing back in the day . . . It's easy for us to go into the room." There wasn't noticeable drama, "but you knew it was tension."

No chaos happened that day, but per Sparky, the battle for the upper hand came down to their outfits. "I had a Gucci dress on, and my two dancers had on a Fendi and a Louis Vuitton [outfit]." Synquis was also sporting a Fendi outfit. "We knew who we were, we believed in ourselves, and we knew we were going to be the flyest ones there," Sparky says of herself and her dancers. "We still came in there like, 'Yeah, we're the shit. It's us.'" Her opponent didn't arrive with any delusions of grandeur or expecting to leave with a new squad. "Roxanne Shanté knew they wasn't really her friends, and she wasn't really my friend. I knew we weren't going to fight or anything." Still, Sparky Dee and Roxanne Shanté didn't speak to each other that day.

The irony of the *Class of '88* photo is that as soon as 1988 closed out and 1989 began, a whole other group of girls were coming up in New York City and beyond. Salt-N-Pepa, though not included in the photo, had already been making significant strides, as well as MC Lyte (who just made the "Class of '88" cut). Lyte, along with Ms. Melodie, made history as part of the release of the Stop the Violence Movement's collaborative song "Self-Destruction" as a means to stop the spread of violence within hip-hop and the Black community. The song was the first number one single ever on the Billboard Hot Rap Songs chart, staying at the top for ten straight weeks.

More talent would enter the scene shortly thereafter, especially as the reign of Roxanne Shanté came to a close. The photo is monumental, though, for placing a group of women in rap together in one big photo to show just how many were out there, even if some faces were missing. It was one of the first (and presumably last) times that a group of female MCs showed up together, talked, took a photo, and went home.

Ten years later in 1998, both *VIBE* and *XXL* released their own sort of classroom photos for their magazine covers, though theirs were coed. *XXL* re-created the iconic 1958 Art Kane photograph *A Great Day in Harlem,* which was a snapshot of the greatest jazz musicians of that era for *Esquire* magazine. *XXL*'s photo was titled *A Great Day in Hip-Hop,* shot by Gordon Parks. The photo spanned generations of hip-hop artists, from Kool Herc, Fab 5 Freddy, and Naughty by Nature all the way to Wu-Tang Clan, The Roots, and A Tribe Called Quest. A handful of women were included, including Debbie Harry, Da Brat, Heather B., Paula Perry, Queen Pen, and Nikki D. In the photograph, most of the women are huddled up. "If you look in the back of the photo against one of the walls, you'll see most of the women in the picture are together," remembers author Nelson George, who was in attendance that day. "They kind of posse'd up, and it was very interesting because that was a very male cypher, but it was also a really great day. In light of all of the shenanigans that happened with female rappers, [the photoshoot] showed how much of a team they were, how supportive of each other they were, and how they were having a good time together." While no real rivals were present that day, it still was a moment where women found each other in a swarm of men.

The cover of *VIBE*'s "Rap Reigns Supreme" issue, on the other hand, had both Lil' Kim and Foxy Brown, still at the heart of a beef that had carried over from the year or two before, right after their solo debut albums dropped. Shot by photographer Lorenzo Agius, the cover features Method Man, LL Cool J, Busta Rhymes, and Master P, with a fold-out featuring Lil' Kim, Lauryn Hill, Missy Elliott, and Foxy Brown. Seeing both Kim and Foxy on a magazine cover side by side was a total surprise, especially since they hadn't been photographed together like that since their *Source* magazine cover in 1997.

Per Agius, Kim and Foxy agreed to be in the same room together for the shoot, but had to sit far away from each other, especially during hair and makeup. The two sat on opposite ends of a long makeup counter, about fifteen feet apart. Some snide remarks were exchanged (even one involving potentially stealing the other's purse), but that was the extent of the beefing, that day, at least.

"Sometimes a bit of rivalry leads to a better show. Girls trying to outperform each other is always a good situation," Agius says now, twenty years later. His perspective is interestingly in line with Sparky Dee's take on her "Class of '88" shoot. There was more to that day, though, than worrying if a fight would break out between Foxy and Kim. "The real queen of the shoot was Lauryn Hill," he remembers, a very true point, since 1998 was Lauryn Hill's year. "The nicest and most interesting was the amazing Missy [Elliott], who kind of looked lost but super cute, fun, and professional." Missy was just a year into her solo fame coming off 1997's *Supa Dupa Fly*. "Kim and Foxy were amazing, too, working it. In the end, everyone was cool and professional and knew they had to deliver. Four very different ladies doing what comes naturally."

The most dynamic aspect of that *VIBE* shoot was that Lil' Kim and Foxy Brown got into a room together at all, the same way Roxanne Shanté and Sparky Dee had done one decade prior. They all had a similar goal and achieved it at a moment when most felt like it couldn't be done. Sometimes (though very rarely), emotions are put to the side, and it really is just about the business—at least for women. Take two male artists who are mortal enemies and ask them to smile for a photo. Would it happen? Probably not.

II

Class Acts

Chapter Five

A NEW DAY

"THIRTY YEARS," MC LYTE YELLS INTO HER MICROPHONE AMID background screams of joy. "We have grown up together."

The rap veteran is standing before a packed crowd in the smoky Sony Hall, located in Midtown Manhattan, addressing them all warmly for their consistent support over three decades of successful hits. Nearly fifty years old, Lyte looks younger now than she did back in 1988 when she unleashed her debut album *Lyte as a Rock*, becoming the first solo female MC to release a full-length studio album. The crowd surprisingly spans all ages and races. Lyte, born Lana Michelle Moorer, reminds everyone in the room that while kids might know her as the voice of the BET Awards and others know her as Kai Owens from the sitcom *Half & Half*, the real fans know her as MC Lyte. On this particular evening, it was all MC Lyte, lyrical beast and living legend. As she traveled down memory lane through her own eight albums punctuated with guest appearances on other artists' hits, it was surreal to witness. So many hip-hop artists throughout history are flashes in the pan—typically with one or two singles that temporarily shapeshifted something or other—but the span of their success is limited. Not so for Lyte, a woman who came into her own from the moment we first met her.

Some might call it the post–Roxanne Shanté era, despite Shanté still being active on the scene (and not even releasing a full-length album until 1989), but a foundation was laid following the "Roxanne's Revenge" radio debut. Something was percolating, and the labels wanted in. Now, however, there was female talent emerging from everywhere. In 1985, Salt-N-Pepa (then called Super Nature) released a response record to Doug E. Fresh's "The Show," titled "The Show Stoppa (Is Stupid Fresh)." On the Hurby "Luv Bug" Azor–produced track, Brooklyn's Cheryl James (Salt) and Queens's Sandra Denton (Pepa) refer to themselves as "The Salt and Pepa MCs," and once the record hit radio rotation, the name stuck. Following Salt-N-Pepa's newfound popularity came their debut album, *Hot, Cool & Vicious*, in 1986, later armed with the unstoppable single "Push It." Initially the B-side to their "Tramp" single, "Push It" wasn't on the original version of their debut album but was added a year later, which drove both the single and the album to platinum status. That same year, Latoya Hanson, the original Spinderella, was replaced by Deidra Roper. Roper was in eleventh grade when she was approached by a friend about the opportunity to DJ for an all-girl group, not knowing who it was. "I said, 'Okay!' and they had a conversation and set up a call. Hurby called me that night. So I auditioned and then I got it." The rest was history. "At the time, the formula was 'the girl next door' speaking the language of young women," Spinderella explains. "Salt-N-Pepa was talking to them about 'pushin' it' and having fun, shakin' that thing, having a good time. Visually, we had a look to us. The folks identified with us. The music was fun, the look was colorful." In 8-ball jackets and matching outfits reminiscent of early rap pioneers like Mercedes Ladies, Salt-N-Pepa charted new territory for all-female rap groups. They had sequenced dance routines, something that had never been successfully combined with rapping before on a mainstream level (Spinderella even started out as a dancer), along with an energy that translated impeccably well from the record to the stage.

A year later, J. J. Fad would adopt a similar sound and aesthetic, releasing their classic "Supersonic." A month afterward, Salt-N-Pepa dropped their follow-up album, *A Salt with a Deadly Pepa*, which featured the single "Shake Your Thang." The video depicts the duo being arrested for "dirty dancing," perfectly timed with the film *Dirty Dancing* that had released the year before, along with the censorship war being waged on hip-hop, beginning with Tipper Gore's "Parental Advisory" crusade. Self-expression in hip-hop was a priority for the artists, and a bane for the government to stop. Was sexuality so offensive? And was it more horrific coming from women? If male rappers used their podium for whatever they wanted, why couldn't women?

In the May 21, 1988, issue of *Billboard* magazine, journalist Bill Coleman penned a piece called "Female Rappers Give Males [A] Run for Their Money," crediting the platinum success of Salt-N-Pepa's debut album with creating a new lane for female rappers. Coleman spoke with the program director of Pittsburgh station WAMO, who says of "Push It," "Because of the different style, a lot of people didn't view it as rap." Further, the program director of KZZP in Phoenix said, "The female rap songs are novelties. Some of them, like 'Push It' are a little more of a song, while the others are a little more novelty. I hope the trend continues, but I don't want to see a glut of product." Things were moving forward quickly for women, yet skeptics circled overhead, still questioning the validity and stability of their presence. Apparently, the only way for women to win at rap was to not let their audience know it was rap. In the same article, MC Lyte is commended for moving 75,000 copies of her debut album "with virtually no airplay." She praises Salt-N-Pepa in the article, stating, "They've come a long way and are still progressing."

"I loved MC Lyte," Spinderella says. "She was a girl from Brooklyn, just like me."

MC Lyte had been rhyming since she was a preteen (originally under the name Sparkle) and made her way through the ranks of the New York City streets, known for her astonishingly intricate wordplay at such a young age. Working multiple jobs while still in school, Lyte was a true student of the game. She was inspired by Salt-N-Pepa, practicing her rhymes in their style to hone her craft. Quickly she became the top female MC among her peers. She grew up with brothers Kirk "Milk Dee" Robinson and DJ Nat "Gizmo" Robinson, who, as the group Audio Two, were known for their 1987 hit "Top Billin'." Their father, Nat Robinson, formed a record label for his sons called First Priority Music, signing Lyte as well. When Atlantic Records took an interest in First Priority, Nat brokered a deal with Atlantic to include Lyte.

Also in '87, Salt-N-Pepa's producer Hurby "Luv Bug" Azor dropped *The House That Rap Built,* a compilation album featuring his artists, including a female rapper named Antoinette. Audio Two were supposed to record a track for the album called "Top Illin'" (an alternate spin on their single), but it never happened. Instead, Antoinette came through with something very similar. Her track, "I Got an Attitude," sonically leaned on Audio Two's "Top Billin'" and included some subliminals aimed toward MC Lyte. Antoinette made some slick remarks about MC Lyte's deeper-toned voice, claiming that Lyte really wasn't all that hard. It was simply for effect. The real target (at that point, at least) was Audio Two, since Antoinette had taken what was supposed to be their slot on the album. There had to be retribution, but how?

Much like Mr. Magic had with U.T.F.O., Audio Two wanted to get back at Hurby for slighting them and choosing his signee for the compilation, but the duo didn't want to make a diss track about a girl. MC Lyte was up for the challenge, especially when she had been tangentially thrown into the fire. So Lyte in turn released the Audio Two–produced "10% Diss" and so began one of the greatest battles in hip-hop history. The song features one of the most classic rap openers, frequently reused by rappers down the line:

> *Hot damn ho, here we go again*
> *Suckers steal a beat when you know they can't win*

She called Antoinette a sucker and a nerve plucker, while back-door dissing Hurby as well. It was intense from the jump, and while the title was "10% Diss," Lyte kept it 100%. When it comes to the etiquette of rap battles, "my standard is Lyte and Antoinette," Monie Love explains. "When Lyte and Antoinette were beefing, nobody got involved. It was them two going back and forth." The battle intensified, as Antoinette then retaliated with "Lights Out, Party's Over," reusing Lyte's opener, but calling her a ho in turn. She even goes as far as saying that MC Lyte reminds her of her dead dog. Lyte then bluntly released "Shut the Eff Up! (Hoe)." On this one, she compares the heat from her "10% Diss" to a microwave (with Antoinette's head inside), but the next one would be in a blender. On top of all that, she questions the whereabouts of the father of Antoinette's child.

The back-and-forth spread like wildfire for nearly three years (from 1987–1990), as the fandom for the diss tracks spread to the artists themselves. Everyone was tuned into what was going to happen next. "Girl, we would anticipate it," Monie says. "We would be on pins and needles, can't wait until Friday night or Saturday night when [New York City radio staple] DJ Red Alert's show comes on or Mr. Magic comes on, to see if there'd be a brand-new Lyte answer-back to Antoinette or Antoinette answer-back to Lyte. Do you know what I mean? It kept us charged. It was dope. We loved it. We loved hearing it. 'Lights Out, Party's Over'! 'Shut the Eff Up.' Oh my God, it was awesome!"

Antoinette in turn dropped "Unfinished Business," but the business was already finished by then. At this point, MC Lyte was securing a legacy as both a battle rapper and a hitmaker. Rarely do the two meet in one artist, even today, but Lyte made it happen. During the height of her beef with Antoinette, Lyte released two albums, with the diss tracks wedged in the track listings among other solid cuts. *Lyte as a Rock* had standouts, like the lead single "I Cram to Understand U (Sam)," along with "Paper Thin" and the title track. Her follow-up, 1989's *Eyes on This,* had "Shut the Eff Up! (Hoe)," but also the game-changing "Cha Cha Cha," which earned Lyte a number one song on the Billboard Hot Rap Singles chart.

It was evident that while she was lyrically gifted, MC Lyte had her eye on a bigger prize. The war with Antoinette was kept on wax and never escalated to anything more, especially when Lyte was destined for far greater things. She had already cross-genre collaborated with Sinéad O'Connor, at the time a bubbling college-radio fixture, on 1988's "I Want Your Hands On Me," at just eighteen years old. O'Connor's star was on the rise, and due to Lyte's steadily growing track record, she reached out to collaborate. "She wanted me to rap on her song and say 'shut the fuck up,'" MC Lyte told *Rolling Stone* in 2018. "She was like, 'Don't leave that part out. I need you to say that part.' And so I arranged some lyrics that said that part."

With her third album, 1991's *Act Like You Know,* led by the single "Poor Georgie," Lyte secured her spot as a great storyteller. On the track, Lyte paints a picture of a deep romantic tragedy: Girl meets boy, girl falls for boy. Girl realizes boy is a rebel, yet can't seem to turn away. Boy has a drinking problem, and on top of that is diagnosed with both colon cancer and lung cancer. Boy crashes his car and dies. It's a lot to take in, especially considering the youthfulness behind the pen that wrote the song, but MC Lyte was wise well beyond her years.

She became known as a "rapper's rapper," where her lyrics came first and all else followed. But her bluntness had given her carte blanche to tell any story, really, since day one. She wrote "I Cram to Understand U (Sam)," a song about falling in love with a drug addict, at just twelve years old and recorded it at fourteen. She painted the most painful poetry, thinking "Sam" was cheating on her with someone named Miss C and trying to figure out why the object of her affection has his eye on someone else. In the end, his addiction wasn't to another woman, but to drugs: "Miss C" was actually crack.

In 2011, journalist Keith Murphy spoke with MC Lyte for *VIBE,* where she dissected her own catalog, including "I Cram to Understand U (Sam)." The song was inspired by one of her cousins being addicted to crack, but also her witnessing the widespread addiction happening in New York City at the time while sitting at her mother's job. "My mother used to work at North General Hospital in Harlem," Lyte said in the interview. "Whenever I would go, there would be a slew of heroin and crack addicts and everybody there at the rehabilitation center that was a couple of floors down. I would have to come into contact with these addicts and I would think, 'Wow, what a jacked up way to be.'" The song is a direct descendant of "The Message," released in 1982 by Grandmaster Flash & the Furious Five, in which Melle Mel goes into detail about the ills of New York City living, from drugs to violence to poverty.

By 1988, the United States was in a downward spiral, and the switch from Ronald Reagan to George H. W. Bush as president did little to boost the economy in the continued aftershocks of Reaganomics. The AIDS epidemic had reached its height, and in the inner cities, drug addiction and destitution still went hand in hand. It's proof that in the eye of the chaos, hip-hop was still the only watchdog relaying what was going on to the public. Starting at age fourteen, Lyte carried that torch, with her own messaging and knack for lore that would transcend generations of hip-hop. Her rhymes were potent but relatable, no-nonsense but full of heart. It's a charm she carried with her from the booth as a teenager to the stage, even thirty years later.

"MC Lyte made me want to rap," remembers Grammy-nominated North Carolina native Rapsody. "Seeing 'Poor Georgie' and her ability to tell a story with words, that was my first time hearing that. For me to see a woman who wasn't timid with it and the pictures she painted? I fell in love with it all."

MC Lyte and Salt-N-Pepa were different, yet cut from the same self-expressive cloth. Their artistry was clearly indicative of something evolving in hip-hop, a cross-genre phenomenon with women at the helm. In November 1988, British pop magazine *Smash Hits* profiled Salt-N-Pepa and referred to the trio as a "dance group" on the verge of major stardom. "I didn't see that as a problem," Spinderella says. "We didn't set out to do it, but it was an added advantage. We made music and people just happened to dance to it. That just means our music was crossing the regular standards, crossing lines. Which is always good." Their popularity went global, led by a sound that was both pop and hip-hop at the same time. Lyte, on the other hand, was inserting her graduated level of lyricism into the mainstream. It was a lesson in coexistence as hip-hop's sound was expanding, and with the level of female talent brewing, there was plenty of room for diversity.

There was nowhere to go but up.

Monie Love and Queen Latifah, the architects of "Ladies First."

Chapter Six

RIOT GRRRLS

"OH, SHE'S CUTE, SHE'S GOT A CUTE ACCENT."
That was the knee-jerk reaction from male rappers during the late '80s when they first met Monie Love.

"No, I'm not cute," Monie Love declares to me emphatically, her faint British accent accentuating her point. "That's why I shaved my hair off. I taped the boobies down. Not cute. I'm a mess. I'm a deadly, venomous mess on this microphone. Do not sleep on me."

In the spring of 1988, Simone "Monie Love" Johnson left London, England, at the age of seventeen to pursue hip-hop full-time in New York City. Having already secured some entry-level success in England, Monie arrived ready to rock. By then, Def Jam was dominating the scene, as their acts—including LL Cool J, Run-DMC, the Beastie Boys, and Slick Rick—were all enjoying significant success, along with outsiders like Big Daddy Kane and Eric B.

& Rakim (signed to Island Records). Def Jam wouldn't sign their first female rapper, Nikki D, for another year, and Nikki wouldn't release her debut album, *Daddy's Little Girl*, until 1991. The market was saturated with male talent, so for a new girl, getting some mic time in was tough to do. It was '77 all over again.

"You know, it's just passing [the mic] around to men to men to men. So finally, I'd have to tap somebody on the shoulder and be like, 'Yo, I've been standing here. Can I get on the mic?'" Monie explains of the boys' club. "They'd all be looking at me like, 'What?' Then, when they gave me the mic, they're all looking at me with their mouths to the floor. Like, 'Holy crap!'" With Salt-N-Pepa on their second album and MC Lyte dropping her debut, 1988 was a big year for women. Men, however, were in the throes of leveling up. In 1988, DJ Jazzy Jeff & The Fresh Prince released their second studio album *He's the DJ, I'm the Rapper* with the colossal single "Parents Just Don't Understand." (There was a fresh princess in the Smith family too, Will's sister Ellen, who also rapped, though she didn't hit the mainstream like her brother.) South Bronx trailblazers Boogie Down Productions (comprising KRS-One, D-Nice, and DJ Scott La Rock) came through with their groundbreaking follow-up *By All Means Necessary*, released after the death of the group's DJ/producer Scott La Rock in 1987. Run-DMC was on their fourth album, *Tougher Than Leather*, as N.W.A changed rap as we know it with *Straight Outta Compton*. No two artists sounded alike, and all were winning at their own game, though with no small amount of ego. This time was looked upon as the start of hip-hop's Golden Age, one that would extend well into the '90s.

For Monie Love, being new to the territory, cute, and with an *exotic* accent, she entered a meat market, not a battleground, when she first walked into the club. All the A-list rappers tried hitting on her; she replays for me some of their pickup lines, with a heavy sigh. Her personal goal was to turn them all down, because it only took one romance to change the popular opinion of the men in the mix. Hip-hop was becoming an undeniable moneymaker, and the male performers would rather have "the girl from England" on their arm than beside them onstage. "What you all need to be clear on and flattered about is that you and the culture that you exude has touched outside of where you're from," Monie remembers thinking. "You have touched other countries. That's really what you should be focusing on when you look at me." The solution was to conceal everything but her lyrics. With a shaved head, taped-down breasts, and baggy clothes, Monie demanded respect for what came out of her mouth, since everything else was an unfortunate distraction. Her skills were undeniable, with syllable flips that made her rhyme patterns feel like lyrical hopscotch as she breezed through her verses. There was no one on the scene like Monie Love, and while there was still room for women to grow, the true strength of their power came in numbers. The best defense was to unify.

Before Monie Love moved to the States, she met a young American artist named Queen Latifah, who was on a mini tour in England. Born Dana Owens, Latifah was a New Jersey native who started out as a beatboxer for a trio named Ladies Fresh, while dividing her time with singing at her local church. Ladies Fresh surpassed their Irvington High School fame and began traveling the local circuit. Meanwhile, Latifah hung out with a small crew of new rappers and creatives who later became Flavor Unit. Producer The 45 King was one prominent member of Flavor Unit, and other acts would eventually be managed by the entity, including Naughty By Nature, Black Sheep, Nikki D, and many others. There was something special about Queen Latifah, though, and like her demo track, she was the "Princess of the Posse." *Yo! MTV Raps*'s Fab 5 Freddy caught wind of the Jersey girl's cut, and it wasn't long before Latifah locked a record deal with Tommy Boy and delivered her first single, "Wrath of My Madness." Her style was direct and commanding, sealing her fate as one of the strongest voices of women in hip-hop out of the gate.

A friendship with Monie Love was immediately forged. They stayed in touch after Queen Latifah left England. "Then we had the discussion during one of our friendly conversations that we should do a song, and we should make some type of song that's an anthem for women," recalls Monie. It took about eight months for the two to actually record "Ladies First," though once Monie reached New York City for good, it was on. The two met up in Queens to get the track done. "It was really a fun session," Monie says. "The Flavor Unit guys were there, and of course, Mark 'The 45 King.' Latifah would be on one side of the studio, and it was like we'd write a couple of rhymes, we'd show them to each other, and we'd be like, 'Yo, cue the song.'" They would volley their product back and forth. "[Latifah would] do the lines she wrote," Monie recalls:

> The ladies will kick it, the rhyme that is wicked
> Those that don't know how to be pros get evicted

"I'd be like 'Yo, that's dope!' Then I'd do the lines I wrote":

> Slick and smooth throwing down the sound, totally a yes
> Let me state the position: Ladies first, yes?

"And she'd go 'Yo, that's dope!'" Then they'd retreat back to their corners, write some more, and check back in on their progress. "The whole session went like that. It was so funny. It was so much fun." Unbeknownst to them in the moment, they were changing the face of hip-hop for women everywhere. "We didn't realize that we were making a song that was going to be so socially packed and such an anthem for women," Monie says. "We did not realize the seriousness of what we were doing. We were having so much fun, but we were also so proud of what we were saying."

The song was released as a single and appeared on Latifah's 1989 debut album *All Hail the Queen*. In the music video, images of recognizable figures from Black American history flash before the screen, as Queen Latifah moves pieces around a large chessboard and Monie Love shimmies in front of project houses in the distance. Other female rappers like Ms. Melodie make cameos, and Queen Latifah harmonizes on a special hook for the music video version.

"It was just perfect, and it was the right timing," Monie adds, since 1989 was a monumental year for hip-hop music. The Recording Academy had just begun to recognize rap as Grammy-worthy, so that year, a Best Rap Performance category was added to the awards ceremony. The nominees included DJ Jazzy Jeff & The Fresh Prince for "Parents Just Don't Understand," LL Cool J for "Going Back to Cali," Salt-N-Pepa for "Push It," J. J. Fad for "Supersonic," and Kool Moe Dee for "Wild, Wild West." The hip-hop community staged a massive Grammy boycott, however, because their award category wasn't televised. Even the winners, DJ Jazzy Jeff & The Fresh Prince, weren't in attendance, though Kool Moe Dee did attend; when he presented the award for Best Male R&B Vocal Performance, he rapped a freestyle about how hip-hop wasn't going anywhere.

It was the first stroke of rebellion that hip-hop would introduce to the mainstream, pushing to show just how strong a force both the culture and the music had become. Never to be muted, hip-hop continued speaking up. Knowing they could easily be marginalized, female rappers were charged up. In 1990 Monie Love debuted her first full-length album, *Down To Earth*, which included her hit single "It's a Shame (My Sister)"—a song that made it onto both the rap and dance charts—as well as "Monie in the Middle" and "Ring

My Bell." Salt-N-Pepa's third album, *Blacks' Magic*, sealed the trio's fate as seductive rhyme spitters, where songs like "Let's Talk About Sex," "Do You Want Me," and "You Showed Me" combined sexuality with social awareness.

With "Let's Talk About Sex," the title foreshadowed a bigger discussion of not only removing the stigma from conversations about sexual intercourse but also introducing a greater acceptance that young adults were, in fact, having sex. Further, with the AIDS epidemic still in full force, stressing the importance of safe sex was urgent. Salt-N-Pepa smashed through the barrier that sex talk was taboo, and their status as both celebrities and artists made their input even more important. "When you grow up and things are going on around you and you see how it affects people, you have an opportunity to motivate people in directions that will help a cause or inspire," Spinderella says. "We were growing up, and we were facing things." The group, like other female acts, had the will and drive to speak out, while men at the time were often reveling in their own success stories. That's not to say men were completely quiet. Slick Rick was developing a strong track record of rhyming fables with a moral at the end (which began in 1988 with his debut album, *The Great Adventures of Slick Rick*). But there was something about how women were finessing this narrative and weaving in their own truths. For men, it was taking a step back to address issues involving women. Female artists spoke from experience, only intensifying the message. After all, it wasn't the men being assaulted, it wasn't the men getting pregnant, and it wasn't the men being reduced to objects with pretty exteriors.

Queen Latifah brought her second album, *Nature of a Sista'*, in 1991, with the dynamic "Latifah's Had It Up 2 Here." Hip-hop was growing for women as a means to express themselves in ways that were new and boundary-pushing. While so much of the time at the dawn of the art form was spent simply legitimizing their very presence as active participants in the music, now it was using that opportunity to deliver much-needed messages. Times were changing, women in rap were speaking up, and, for what felt like the first time, the wider audience was listening. Sexism was still everywhere, including in the DJ community.

"From my standpoint as a DJ, [sexism] was happening most of the time," Spinderella says. "People look at you because you're cute, they look at you because you're sexy, and it just totally takes away from the talent that you bring. I've dealt with that: 'Oh, she can't DJ.' 'C'mon let's battle.' 'You cute, but it's all a gimmick.' For me, it only pushed me farther to show those naysayers what it was that I could do." There are some perks to that uphill battle. "You can use it to your advantage, though," she continues. "When you're doing something different from what the norm is, you take that and let it be the fuel to catapult you. At the end of the day, your talent is going to speak for itself. If you showin' them boys out, they're gonna hate that. And they're gonna hate it even more when you're cashing those checks."

While the fight against sexism continued to be a problem, there still wasn't some tight-knit community of female rappers propping each other up, despite them all having a similar goal in mind. "I want to be fair by saying that there was beef amongst us back then," Monie Love says. "Sometimes when people say, 'Oh, girls back then all got along.' No, we didn't, and I like to be honest about that because I don't want to demonize the current women for whatever qualms they may have with each other. The one thing we knew for sure is that hip-hop was not a fully respected genre, and we were all so busy fighting and trying to get back to being respected that trying to shut somebody else down behind closed doors was not ever a thought that crossed any female's mind." Women were just looking to get ahead in the race, unaware of who could be undermining whom amid the whispers.

Per Monie, "What did cross our minds was . . . girls on the East Coast, we felt like we had lyrics." Out West, J. J. Fad had "Supersonic," but a slim few were considered worthy competition. "Girls from the West Coast, aside from Yo-Yo and [later] Lady of Rage, just had spandex and body parts. That's all we saw," she continues. "We were like, 'Y'all girls can't rhyme. J. J. Fad can't rhyme. Oaktown's 357, y'all can't rhyme. Y'all just showing your body and the California sun and the spandex. Like, we really got the lyrics over here. We're in the trenches rhymin' for real. So there was that dislike, in all honesty."

Years later, though, Monie saw it differently. "It's funny, because I apologized to 357 in [my] adult years. I was like, 'Girl, you guys are significant. I can't look back and not see you guys now. There had to be a you. There had to be a J. J. Fad. There had to be an Oaktown's 357," Monie says. "'We had to have you because if we didn't have you, then our representation of women in hip-hop in whatever way, shape, or form wouldn't have existed in L.A. We needed to have your presence.'" J. J. Fad was rooted in the heart of the goings-on of L.A. hip-hop, particularly with N.W.A. J. J. Fad's debut album, *Supersonic*, was executive produced by Eazy-E and included production from Dr. Dre, DJ Yella, and Arabian Prince. Over in the Bay Area, Oaktown's 357 was formed under the eye of MC Hammer, who was swimming in the success of "U Can't Touch This" off his third studio album, 1990's *Please Hammer, Don't Hurt 'Em*. Both J. J. Fad and Oaktown's 357 did provide a necessary female component to the male energy emitting from the West Coast, no matter how pop their sound skewed. But another female artist from the west would come through with both lyrics and demands for respect from even the most misogynistic of men.

Compton's own Yolanda "Yo-Yo" Whitaker made her introduction on Ice Cube's "It's a Man's World," by correcting him that it wasn't:

First of all, let me tell you my name. It's Yo-Yo
And downing a girl, first offense, and that's a no-no

Somebody had to speak up about the widespread woman-bashing that was blanketing the Los Angeles hip-hop scene at the time. "Really, it had gotten a little out of hand," Yo-Yo says. With N.W.A ushering in gangster rap, along with Ice Cube's chart-topping success as a solo artist, misogyny was rampant.

Comparatively speaking, the West Coast's bashing of women in song was more apparent than on the East Coast, where it was more implied. Ice Cube was a major component of a trend in West Coast rap fueled by anger toward the system, the police, and, yes, women. Still, he gave Yo-Yo a platform to bite back.

"I think it was the power, the relationship that I had with Ice Cube," Yo-Yo says of her immediate exposure. "N.W.A was very powerful here on the West Coast—underground and getting to become really mainstream. To be the first woman out of Ice Cube's camp, after he left N.W.A and went through all of that? It just really came naturally."

Despite being a member of Ice Cube's crew and a mouthpiece in the growing West Coast hip-hop scene, Yo-Yo still had to earn respect. "I hung out with the boys; I battled them all," she recalls. "I battled Tupac. I battled the whole Digital Underground camp. I was on the road with Too $hort, and so many other artists—Scarface, Geto Boys. I think the respect came because I wasn't afraid to battle. I really was a rapper." In 1990, Yo-Yo was profiled by the *Los Angeles Times*, alongside Queen Latifah and MC Lyte, in an article about breaking into the men's club of rappers while traditionally being seen as "sex objects" or "gold diggers," per the profile's author, Dennis Hunt. "In some ways, their effort is a repeat of what female rockers went through in the '60s and '70s," he wrote. When asked about her then unreleased record's mission, Yo-Yo explained, "What I want my record to do is push women rappers up the ladder even closer to men. We've got some catching up to do, some more barriers to break down, some more minds to change. And we're doing it—fast."

Yo-Yo's 1991 debut album, *Make Way for the Motherlode,* reached number five on the Billboard Top R&B/Hip-Hop Albums chart and delivered the anthem "You Can't Play with My Yo-Yo," which inevitably became her battle cry. She may be named Yo-Yo, but she's not one to be played with like a toy. Her intent was made clear as she proudly stood up for intelligent Black women everywhere, but also aimed to uplift all women. Yo-Yo was bringing a new age of feminism into hip-hop, starting with that single.

"You Can't Play with My Yo-Yo" and her other single from the record, "What Can I Do?" both featured Ice Cube, solidifying that she was gangster rap–approved, which offered her an opportunity to add her flair to the growing number of voices speaking out in West Coast rap about the ills in their respective neighborhoods. "It was really intense on the West Coast, more so of a perspective, so [N.W.A's] 'Fuck The Police' . . . We felt that," Yo-Yo says. "We had a lot of harassment by the police. The crack-cocaine game was really big on the West Coast, so they had a gang task force. I mean, whether you're in a gang or not, they stereotyped everybody. If you're Black, you were in a gang. When I came on the scene, I really didn't realize all that was happening at that time. I was just a young girl, who was an entertainer who loved music."

But what Yo-Yo wouldn't do was compromise her authentic self, especially at a time when it was crucial to remain on brand. "I remember writing 'Bonnie & Clyde' [with Ice Cube], and Cube got to his verse. He went, 'Got me a down bitch on my team.' I said, 'Wait, wait, wait. You can't call me a bitch.' So he changed it to, 'Got me a down girl on my team,'" Yo-Yo recalls. "And I was still able to keep 'Got me a down-ass nigga on my team.'" Suggestions about her style would be offered and politely rejected, even in the years to come when the movements of Lil' Kim and Foxy Brown would have their female rap predecessors questioning a stylistic switch into potentially sexier territory. "Of course, you have all of these guys in their cliques, and they want you to perform a certain kind of way," Yo-Yo says. "A lot of guys come to you. They say, 'Hey, Yo-Yo, I think you should write a rap about this.' I remember Tupac said, 'You should write a rap like, I'm in love with my best friend's man.' I was like, 'No! I could never do that. I would never be in love with my best friend's man.'"

Looking to the East Coast, Yo-Yo saw the immediate potential in her own uprising on the rap scene, as the block in LA grew hotter by the day. The work of the girls on the opposite coast fueled her to do more on her own stomping grounds. "[East Coast female rappers] really motivated me," she says. "And hearing Monie Love, with that English accent, it really motivated me. Like, 'Wow, women are really doing it.' Here I was on the West Coast protecting women and creating my own Intelligent Black Women's Coalition and trying to stand up for women. It was just something that . . . it's always been in me."

The riot was only just beginning.

REVENGE ON ROXANNE

In 1992, Roxanne Shanté released *The Bitch Is Back,* attacking the next generation of artists under her on the venomous track "Big Mama." She starts with rehashing her beef with The Real Roxanne and Sparky Dee, namechecking them for no apparent reason but to add to the body count. Her next set of victims includes Queen Latifah and Monie Love. She collectively bullies them about "Ladies First," flipping the script to remind them that she's the first lady, though she takes it a step further. With Latifah, it's the insertion of R&B into her rhymes, which theoretically set a tone for generations to come (if Roxanne Shanté only knew what the future would hold). With Monie Love, she challenges having a hit single over being a one-hit wonder, despite the fact that Monie had a whole healthy career long before and after "Monie in the Middle."

Then came MC Lyte's turn, followed by Yo-Yo's, Salt-N-Pepa's, and even Isis, the Corona, Queens, X-Clan affiliate later known as Lin Que. Using words like *slut, butch, bitch,* and *ho,* Roxanne was bringing a different energy to the space, one that could be viewed as self-aggrandizing, given the number of insults she was hurling toward the generation she had inspired. The track has gone down in rap history as one of the most murderous disses, and when Shanté targeted all the female rappers on the rise by name, it was only a matter of time before most of them returned the favor. By then, they were the ones in demand, and Shanté's diss track felt like sour grapes. Still, she indisputably paved the way for them all and had no qualms about reminding them of that. In the true spirit of competition, their responses were inevitable.

Queen Latifah dropped "I Can't Understand" on her *Black Reign* album in 1993. The smooth album cut is laced with jabs, as Latifah addresses the elephant in the room: that Roxanne Shanté's career was long past its prime. Meanwhile, MC Lyte titled her Shanté response, released on 1993's *Ain't No Other,* "Steady Fucking" after the Boogie Down Productions line against Shanté from "The Bridge Is Over." She even uses the line as a sample on the track. A seasoned battler from her war with Antoinette, Lyte pulled no punches, telling Shanté to quit trying and then threatening to hit her with her car (a Land Cruiser, to be exact). Salt-N-Pepa joined in with the *Very Necessary* album cut "Somebody's Gettin' on My Nerves," simply stating that Shanté was jealous of their success.

"This is what Kurtis Blow was saying," Debbie D says of Roxanne Shanté's battle with the new class. "You don't just start dissing other people like that. It's about the rhymes and having substance in your lyrics." If the only substance to your rhymes is an insult, then a layer of negativity is automatically added to your whole aesthetic, a characteristic which now dominated even Shanté's live performances. But like Kurtis Blow said, that contribution to the art form set a new standard for what battle rap would become, for better or for worse. When jabs are your trademark, that leaves little room for diversifying. Shanté's animosity for the artists who followed her was indicative of her short-lived success story. Here was an artist who, in one fell swoop, took on the whole rap industry by not only boldly challenging a prominent group but landing right on the radio when most rap artists couldn't. She had the success, saw the success, and felt the success, but then lost the success. Times were changing, and like so many girls before her, Shanté was shuffled to the back to make way for the new group of artists on the come up. That didn't sit right with her, clearly, so her response was to bark back in really the only way she knew how: with her lyrics. Did it do much for her career besides adding another diss track notch to her belt? Not really, but it did prove she still had the fire in her.

While her peers didn't exactly credit her for the success of their contributions, years later, Roxanne Shanté was acknowledged as a major influence by female rappers, and is still referenced today. In Foxy Brown's December

1998 cover story for *VIBE* magazine, she praises Shanté. "Roxanne Shanté! She's a pioneer for the type of shit I'm doing," she tells *VIBE* editor in chief Danyel Smith in the piece. "I swear by her. She was a bitch back in the day—for having skills. She was stepping out of limos with full-length minks. Diamonds. She was like, 'I'm that bitch. I'm here, and these are my niggas, and this is how we roll.'"

This cycle would take place again and again, as artists from one generation took umbrage over the next not crediting them for passing the baton. We saw it with Lil' Kim and Nicki Minaj, and later with Nicki Minaj and Cardi B. While it could be argued that Roxanne Shanté was setting a tone for what other female rappers would do in the decades to follow, it was more reflective of the threat of losing the place she had worked to fill. Roxanne Shanté stood in between two worlds: she was the first female rapper on the radio, but one of the last of her peers to release a physical album. By then, radio airplay was par for the course, so her milestone had lost its luster. Undeniable behind the mic, her skills felt reserved for the stage and nowhere else. It was a symptom of hip-hop evolving so quickly that Roxanne Shanté had no time to catch up. This would all be a moot point if she were a male, as acts like Eminem have made a whole career out of constructing lyrically sharp parodies and puns, yet Shanté couldn't, despite doing it first.

Maybe Roxanne Shanté was still too young to accept that she was now a predecessor, or maybe she was just so used to being the one and only solo female rapper on the scene that she didn't take kindly to the new class. Whatever the case, at the age of twenty-three, Roxanne Shanté essentially retired from rap.

Chapter Seven

TIME FOR
SOME ACTION

ONCE DUSTED A TLC CASSETTE FOR LEFT EYE'S FINGERPRINTS.
True story. They were performing at East Side Park in Paterson,
New Jersey, promoting their debut album, 1992's *Ooooooohhh . . .
On the TLC Tip*. I wasn't allowed to go to the show because I was
young, it was too late at night, and East Side Park was a hot spot for
violence. My friend Tracy's father, Tim, was working security at the
event, and while guarding TLC's trailer, he had them autograph a
poster for his daughter and a cassette tape for me. I used this conve-
nience store detective kit I had to dust the cassette for prints, in the
hopes that there was a trace of Lisa Lopes on the plastic wrapper
engulfing what would soon become my favorite album of the early
'90s. I still have that cassette to this day, along with a pair of glasses
with one lens covered in green Saran Wrap because I didn't know
what a prophylactic even was and therefore couldn't successfully

nail Left Eye's signature condom-on-her-glasses look. A for effort, I suppose.

Even as a preteen, I was tuned into the messages coming through the pipeline from TLC, as the boys' club was slowly breaking up and women's voices were truly being heard. It was more than a time to speak up; it was the time to finally learn how to do it effectively. TLC cast a wide net with their fan base; we came for the aesthetic, yet stayed for the messaging.

Politically speaking, 1992 is regarded as the Year of the Woman, due to the significant jump in female representation within the Senate. The boost was not so coincidentally timed with Anita Hill's sexual harassment allegations toward then Supreme Court nominee Clarence Thomas in 1991. The social climate in the United States was changing, too. That year, the National Center for Victims of Crime issued a statistical study titled "Rape in America: A Report to the Nation" revealing dramatic statistics about sex crimes in America, considering that 1,871 reported rapes were happening per day. Tori Amos dropped her folk-pop solo debut album, *Little Earthquakes,* a self-healing classic about her overcoming the devastating effects of her own rape. The third wave of feminism was growing, along with punk rock's Riot Grrrl movement. That revolution started at Evergreen State College in Olympia, Washington, after Bikini Kill frontwoman Kathleen Hanna learned that her roommate had barely escaped a potential rape right in their apartment building. She stood before her classmates chanting the rhythmic spoken word poem "The Middle of the Night in My House," informing everyone of what happened.

Concurrently, the Rodney King verdict sent Los Angeles into a downward spiral, giving way to the LA riots and being the first true example of exactly what groups like N.W.A and Public Enemy had warned us about when it came to the intersection of racism and police brutality. Four cops were caught on videotape nearly beating a Black man to death. His name was Rodney King, and when Los Angeles learned that three of the four police officers were acquitted (the fourth lacked a true verdict), a riot ensued, lasting for six straight days.

This whole period of American history would become the perfect storm for female rappers, as the combination of gender and race crossed paths in a way that could only be reported through the microphones of Black women. The many men of hip-hop were contributing more to the problem and not the solution. This was the year Boogie Down Productions dropped *Sex and Violence,* complete with the controversial track "13 and Good" about having sex with a criminally underage girl. Dr. Dre dropped his solo debut album, *The Chronic,* significantly upping the "bitches and hoes" quotient in rap lyrics. Sir Mix-a-Lot dedicated a hit single entirely to a woman's backside that same year with the now infamous "Baby Got Back," as Oakland, California, rapper Too $hort was on his seventh album about pimpin', aptly titled *Shorty the Pimp.* Female groups like duo BWP (Bytches With Problems) were willing to take a stand and bark back at all of the jokiness about women in men's rhymes by having a little fun of their own. With a twist on N.W.A's acronym mixed with the lewdness of acts like Florida's 2 Live Crew, BWP caused a stir, evidenced by their 1991 album *The Bytches* and its lead single, "Two Minute Brother." The potency came and went, unfortunately, as major labels (like their own, Columbia) were still reticent to allow women fully expressive free reign without proven marketability. If misogyny pays, then it still gets the upper hand when it comes to the bottom line.

Of course, there were other corners of rap balancing out the sexploitative saturation with different kinds of sounds, like the poppier Kris Kross's *Totally Krossed Out,* House of Pain's eponymous debut album (which birthed the whitewashed wedding favorite "Jump Around"), the Beastie Boys' *Check Your Head,*

Pete Rock & CL Smooth's *Mecca and the Soul Brother,* Eric B. & Rakim's *Don't Sweat the Technique,* and Arrested Development's *3 Years, 5 Months and 2 Days in the Life Of . . .*

Without a doubt, a mixed bag of male-driven hits was filling up, indicative of the fact that most male performers were more preoccupied with their growing success stories than returning to rap's rarest (yet most important) form as an agent for change. It would be the year in which female rappers recharged, only to strike harder come '93. But the one female hip-hop group who had an open lane in 1992 was TLC. The group began in 1990 in Atlanta, Georgia, when a young girl by the name of Crystal Jones was formulating a hip-hop-meets-R&B group of girls with the help of a local producer named Ian Burke. Tionne Watkins and Lisa Lopes responded to the casting call, and the group was formed under the name 2nd Nature. They cut a demo with Rico Wade and Jermaine Dupri, but lucked out on an audition with Perri "Pebbles" Reid, who was interested in working with them. She changed their name to TLC (an acronym of the group members' first names), and TLC was quickly auditioning for Pebbles's then husband, Antonio "L.A." Reid, and Kenneth "Babyface" Edmonds, who ran the label LaFace Records. Crystal ultimately left the group she started and was replaced by a dancer named Rozonda Thomas. The girls all got nicknames: T-Boz (Tionne), Left Eye (Lisa), and Chilli (Rozonda), keeping the TLC acronym intact.

Ooooooohhh . . . On the TLC Tip was equal parts Public Enemy and Salt-N-Pepa. T-Boz, Left Eye, and Chilli were animated yet activated; their music was zany and hyper, yet attached to each story, woven within the high-powered music, was a moral. Many viewed their debut album as an entrée into pop music. This wouldn't be fully manifested until their second album, 1994's *CrazySexyCool*— and particularly with the song "Waterfalls." However, it was impossible to box a group that accessorized with vibrant colors to make a visual statement, along with inserting poignant messages and mixed styles of singing/rapping into their sound. So the pop title was granted as the easiest category, despite the group being rooted in hip-hop thanks to Left Eye. Ken Tucker of *Entertainment Weekly* called TLC "a perfect pop group for the times" in his 1992 review of their first album. It was an ill-fitting descriptor to say the least, a half-baked classification for a group that didn't need to be classified at all.

As the primary cowriter on the project—alongside Dallas Austin, Marley Marl, Jermaine Dupri, L.A. Reid, and Babyface—the late Lisa "Left Eye" Lopes was the strongest mouthpiece of the Atlanta-based trio. Yes, their Cross Colours clothing was all checkered with condoms, neon Band-Aids, and giant pacifiers, making them appear almost cartoonish, thanks to Pebbles Reid, whose vision was for TLC to be the female answer to groups like Kris Kross. Left Eye's giant hat and suspenders gave her an added Flavor Flav aesthetic, but her lyrics were brutally honest and cut through the sexually charged hooks and melodies like a knife. Popular singles on the album like "Ain't 2 Proud 2 Beg" and "Baby-Baby-Baby" were rooted in expressions of sexuality, while "What About Your Friends" tackled loyalty and distrust. All three singles broke the *Billboard* Hot 100's top ten. Despite its overly enthusiastic sound, "Hat 2 da Back" carried a strong sentiment of remaining authentic and dressing as what some would regard as a "tomboy," baseball caps and all. Left Eye even flips the script, highlighting how some men dress categorically "effeminate," with finger waves, earrings, and tight pants, to no issue.

"His Story" highlighted sexual assault set to the backdrop of the controversial Tawana Brawley rape trial of 1988, while "Bad by Myself" discussed living independent of a man. The group's fan club was called TLC's Proud 2 B Me, and there was no better means to summarize exactly the mission TLC had in mind. They were simply proud to be themselves.

Their potency in hip-hop would inevitably be derailed by the success of the single "Baby-Baby-Baby," which landed them the number two spot on the Billboard Hot 100 and topped the Billboard Hot R&B/Hip-Hop Songs chart. The completely sung R&B love song about being romanced properly featured Left Eye only on the backing harmony, leaving no room for one of her signature raps in the middle. From that point on, Left Eye would be pushed further and further into the background, evidenced in 1994 by the removal of her classic rap, arguably the heart of the song, from the radio edit for "Waterfalls":

> I seen rainbow a yesterday
> But too many storms have come and gone
> Leavin' a trace of not one God-given ray

A rap for Left Eye was tacked on to the music video version of TLC's "No Scrubs" off 1999's *FanMail.* As Left Eye's involvement was becoming less visible, she began lashing out, though was she the one changing, or was the group's direction causing her to change?

Either way, Left Eye's bad-girl image began developing in June 1994 after she set fire to her then boyfriend Andre Rison's mansion. Rison, an Atlanta Falcons wide receiver, was allegedly cheating on Left Eye, and when he came home from a night out, she challenged him for buying himself sneakers and none for her. He slapped her and tried sitting on her, eventually leaving the house. Left Eye placed a pair of his sneakers in the bathtub and lit them on fire. Then, she walked outside, cracked the windshields of his cars with the pipe from a vacuum cleaner, and stuck around to watch the house turn to ruins. She was arrested, released on $75,000 bail, sent to a halfway house, and received five years' probation plus a $10,000 fine. Though she also checked herself into rehab, her rebellious reputation became her defining characteristic. In the November 1994 issue of *VIBE* magazine, TLC is on the cover, dressed in firefighter uniforms. "TLC Fires It Up: Burning Up the Charts, Burning Down the House" is plastered across the cover, which became one of *VIBE*'s hottest-selling issues, pun fully intended. The cover story is dedicated almost entirely to Left Eye's rap sheet. "The hardest thing about being in TLC is accepting the fact that I am Left Eye," she tells journalist Joan Morgan, who penned the story. "I have to act a certain way according to what people expect." And what people expected at the time was a loose cannon, partially praised for the group's growing popularity, partially written off as a liability.

Still, she managed to flex lyrically when she could. On the soundtrack to the 1995 film *Panther,* women in both hip-hop and R&B gathered together for two songs titled "Freedom" (a sung version and a rap version). The rap version boasts a lineup including dancehall queen Patra on the hook, Queen Latifah, Yo-Yo, Salt-N-Pepa, MC Lyte, rhythmic rhymer Meshell Ndegeocello, and of course TLC. In the video, Left Eye is the one standing front and center, flanked by T-Boz and Chilli. Their arms are extended, fists up, as Left Eye delivers a thought-provoking rhyme:

> Whoever said these are the things that you can do
> And the things you ain't supposed to?
> So am I further when I think I'm getting closer?

Left Eye launches into a charged-up verse, attacking the system, saying her life choices should never be questioned, alluding to the conservative/religious stance on abortions. She concludes with a comparison of how America's bald eagle is treated more delicately than the lives of Black people. She's not having it:

> A bird is never more important than my people
> I guess we didn't need him so I took away his freedom

As she finishes her rhyme, she rolls up her shirtsleeve, revealing a tattoo of an eagle on her arm.

As a group, TLC delivered socially conscious pop, but as a soloist, Left Eye continued to evolve her hip-hop art with her witty, poetic lyricism. She appeared on Lil' Kim's remix of the *Hard Core* track "Not Tonight," alongside Missy Elliott, New York City Radio icon briefly turned rapper Angie Martinez, and Chicago rabble-rouser Da Brat. In Left Eye's verse, she makes light of her fire-starting, as she rhymes: "I be the one to blame as the flames keep risin' to the top, and it don't stop." In 2001, her solo debut album, *Supernova*, displayed her progression as a lyricist, along with musical anecdotes about her life and journey through self-awareness. The song "Untouchable" includes a posthumous verse from Tupac Shakur. Before her passing in 2002, Left Eye joined Suge Knight's controversial Death Row Records label, with the new moniker N.I.N.A. (New Identity Not Applicable). She was slated to release an album of the same name the year that she died. There was so much more for Left Eye to do, both with TLC and as a soloist. Thanks to Left Eye, TLC brought a renewed spirit to outspoken female hip-hop artists. The year after their debut, many of their peers followed suit.

With the release of Salt-N-Pepa's *Very Necessary* in 1994, the group's commercial appeal was at a record high, and the aftereffects would be felt for decades to come. The project's lead single, "Shoop," helped Salt-N-Pepa reach a milestone as their first top-five single on the Billboard Hot 100 (at number four), and also hit number one on the Hot Rap Songs chart. In 2003, Ellen DeGeneres quoted the lyrics to "Shoop" during her *Here and Now* comedy special, a testament to Salt-N-Pepa's reach. Their single with En Vogue, "Whatta Man," became their biggest hit, reaching number three on the Billboard Hot 100 (and also hitting number one on the Hot Rap Songs chart). The album's third single, "None of Your Business," won them their first Grammy in 1995 for Best Rap Performance by a Duo or Group, and Salt-N-Pepa made history as the first female rappers to take home the Grammy in that category (Queen Latifah also made history that year as the first female rapper to win Best Rap Solo Performance for "U.N.I.T.Y."). They released a final single, "Heaven or Hell," that covered everything from police brutality to prostitution. It was packaged as a maxi single with a reworking of "Let's Talk About Sex" titled "Let's Talk About AIDS," with lyrical changes to reflect the still rampant spread of HIV and AIDS. As their platform grew, so did the priceless value of their messaging. "The whole 'Let's Talk About Sex' turning into 'Let's Talk About AIDS' . . . I think [late *ABC World News Tonight* anchor] Peter Jennings was the one who fronted that whole situation," Spinderella recalls. In 1992, Jennings hosted a special program called *Growing Up in the Age of AIDS,* a pioneering show that spoke directly to the youth. Fourteen years later, ABC aired *Out of Control: AIDS in Black America* with more filmed commentary from Jennings (who had died the year prior in 2005).

"This was really about what was going on in the community and what the fears were. We were addressing the fears from our standpoint, and just researching it and getting information," Spinderella continues. "When you're blowing up, you come out to just give messages, but these messages come through you . . . if you allow it. It was just our responsibility to our audience to address things that were going on around us."

The contributions of women were pinging on the major labels' radars, and they were searching for new female rap talent to add to their rosters. Sure, many of the executives weren't discerning about the female artists they signed, but luckily there was some quality in the quantity. Arriving on the heels of Yo-Yo's success came another West Coast female rapper by the name of Bo$$. Born in Detroit, Michigan, Lichelle "Bo$$" Laws gained her rap pedigree in Los Angeles as one of the first female rappers regarded as a true gangster rapper. Her debut album, *Born Gangstaz,* in 1993 yielded two intense singles, "Deeper" and "Recipe of a Hoe," both of which grabbed the number one spot on the Billboard Hot Rap Tracks chart.

In the video for the album's third single, "Progress of Elimination," Bo$$ is walking around a hazy morgue and driving through the California streets in a lowrider. Bo$$ was aesthetically the polar opposite of her West Coast peer Yo-Yo. While Yo-Yo donned long blond braids, tight pants, and bomber jackets, Bo$$ wore bandanas and Carhartt jackets with her eyes permanently concealed by pitch-black Locs sunglasses. She resembled the male gangster rappers in both style and delivery, reaching the eyes and ears of Russell Simmons, who signed Bo$$ to his then newly minted (albeit short-lived) label Def Jam West. Another dynamic aspect of Bo$$'s first and only album was that it was primarily produced by New York beatsmiths including Erick Sermon, MC Serch, Def Jef, and even the late Jam Master Jay of Run-DMC.

Queen Latifah's double-edged podium came later that year with the debut of her sitcom *Living Single* and the release of her third studio album, *Black Reign.* She was already building up her film résumé, with movies like *House Party 2* and *Juice* under her belt. She also had a role in the 1993 film *My Life,* starring Michael Keaton, but would gain her greatest traction on the silver screen as Cleo in the 1996 urban classic *Set It Off.* As Queen Latifah was becoming more and more mainstream, she pulled no punches lyrically on *Black Reign.* On the Grammy-winning lead single, "U.N.I.T.Y.," she posed the powerful question: "Who you callin' a bitch?"

In the music video, Vin Rock from Naughty by Nature plays a gropey passerby who grabs Latifah's ass, the play-by-play told through the lyrics. The result of his efforts (and use of the B-word) is a black eye. Enough said.

Her other single off the album, "Just Another Day . . . ," brought to light everyday life in the streets of New Jersey, in a similar vein as Ice Cube's "It Was a Good Day," weaving inner-city scenery with social commentary as Latifah rhymes about kids selling guns to police detectives, only to get arrested, and the all too frequent carjackings happening in her neighborhood, since Newark, New Jersey, became the car theft capital in 1992.

Black Reign also marked a shift in Queen Latifah's personal life, as she lost her brother, Lance Owens, to a motorcycle accident a year before the project was released. Her video for "U.N.I.T.Y." provided subtle homages to her brother—including her clutching a necklace that bears his motorcycle key at the start of the video and riding a motorcycle in the visuals. The album's closer, "Winki's Theme," is a tribute to Lance.

It was also during this time period that Queen Latifah changed her record label, making the switch from Tommy Boy to the higher-profile Motown. Life and the music industry had matured a then twenty-three-year-old Latifah quickly, and *Black Reign* showed the evolution. The work was more refined and structured than her previous releases, yet still uncompromising, even when Latifah was on the brink of diving headfirst into Hollywood.

During an interview with *Billboard* in 1993, Queen Latifah was asked if she felt the music industry was showing more respect toward female rappers. It was a fair question, considering the growth of female rap talent was proof alone that women had just as much skill as men. The charting successes were just an added bonus, and Latifah in particular was head of the class. So were women more respected?

"Hell no," was her reply.

WHO YOU CALLIN' A BITCH?

There's a long-standing debate over the word "bitch," one that's carried over into generations of hip-hop. At times, even the word *female* can sound pejorative, depending on the vocal inflections of the man saying it, but *bitch* has had its own controversial history. In the late '80s when Yo-Yo aligned with N.W.A alum Ice Cube, he was coming off a track record of songs like "A Bitch Iz a Bitch" (from N.W.A's 1987 compilation project *N.W.A and the Posse*), where misogyny was not only understated in tone, it was overstated in lyrics as well:

> Now the title bitch don't apply to all women
> But all women have a little bitch in 'em

Still, Yo-Yo felt conflicted about the word *bitch* and its targeted usage.

"I remember doing one interview where the journalist asked what do I feel about [men] calling women bitches? I said, 'Well, they're talking about those types of girls,'" Yo-Yo said. "So when [N.W.A] said 'A bitch iz a bitch,' [Ice Cube] was talking about the one that only wanted to use the guys for their money. Drug-dealin' type of girls. So we associated the word 'bitch' to that type of woman." She likened it to the phrase "gold digger," which was something she didn't identify as anyway, so it didn't mean much to her if the term was used.

Da Brat had a similar philosophy, breaking it down in the 1997 documentary *Rhyme & Reason*. "When guys say 'bitch' or 'ho' it don't bother me because of the simple fact that, one, they're not talking about me," Brat explains. "And where I'm from, the West Side of Chicago, we could see our homegirls and be like, 'Wassup, bitch?! Shut the fuck up, you stupid.' It's all in fun, and it really depends on how you say it. You know when somebody's saying it wrong. You know when they're trying to be derogatory about the shit." She compares it to the N-word, where its level of appropriateness is contingent upon the person who is using it. In the same documentary, Lauryn Hill describes a whole other perspective. "I'm not really big on that," she says. "I happen to think that if we hold the women in higher respect—and the women who have the children of these men who are calling the women 'bitches' and 'hoes'—will treat their children with more love and raise up stronger individuals."

Bitch would come to mean something more like "difficult woman" as hip-hop evolved, since the financial success of hip-hop grew and female rappers were afforded the luxury of being high-maintenance. Lil' Kim owned the word in 1996, referring to herself as "queen bitch, supreme bitch" on her *Hard Core* album cut aptly titled "Queen Bitch." She would abbreviate it to Queen B, with the double meaning of Queen Bee. Miami rap vixen Trina would later emerge with the tagline of "The Baddest Bitch."

The self-identification of the "bitch" became the new wave, taking the sting out of the word, as a greater awareness developed in the minds of the female rappers as they grew up. Suddenly it wasn't as cool as it once was to shrug off the word when it came from a man.

"Until you started looking at and hearing women call themselves bitches and hearing Too $hort say, 'Bitch!' And you're like, 'Oh, wait a minute. Hold on,'" Yo-Yo says. "The feminist movement didn't really take place until we started being more aware of who we were growing up."

The "bitch" discussion is now almost a moot point in hip-hop, especially when, for the most part, the word is back to being embraced by female artists. Maybe the sting has been removed, or the argument's been exhausted, at least for the younger generation.

After all, one bad bitch doesn't ruin the bunch these days. She makes it that much better.

Chapter Eight

ARE WE THERE YET?

MARIANA "MARY" VIEIRA IS IN HER ZONE, CLOAKED IN HER alter-ego, Ladybug Mecca, and rocking onstage for adoring fans with a passion that radiates like it's her very first time behind the mic. After she finishes her set with her group Digable Planets at UK's Barclaycard Arena in Birmingham, she stands at the back of the stage to watch Lauryn Hill perform. It's *The Miseducation of Lauryn Hill* 20th Anniversary Tour, and Digable Planets are the opening act. While Mecca is awaiting the arrival of Ms. Hill, there's a tap on her shoulder. It's Lauryn Hill herself. The two give each other the warmest hug, and then Lauryn Hill hits the stage. "It's been years since we've seen each other," Mecca tells me, though their initial arrivals in hip-hop were simultaneous. That moment between Mecca and Ms. Hill was more than just a greeting; it was a survivors' embrace.

Between 1993 and 1994, hip-hop's sound was rapidly expanding. The golden age was well under way, and during this period, some of the most prolific and influential debut hip-hop albums would surface, along with second and third endeavors from artists who had already hit their stride and had zero plans of stopping. The release of Tupac's follow-up album, *Strictly 4 My N.I.G.G.A.Z. . . ,* would propel him to stardom. Onyx released their aggressive debut album, *Bacdafucup,* along with Mobb Deep's debut, *Juvenile Hell,* and Souls of Mischief's laid-back introduction, *93 'til Infinity.* Run-DMC leveled up with their sixth album, *Down with the King,* as Snoop Dogg brought his debut album, *Doggystyle.* Wu-Tang Clan introduced themselves on *Enter the Wu-Tang (36 Chambers),* and A Tribe Called Quest dropped their critically acclaimed third studio album, *Midnight Marauders.*

Women were shining in new and expansive ways. Queen Latifah delivered *Black Reign,* armed with her most successful single to date, the respect-commanding "U.N.I.T.Y." Change was on the horizon, considering the song hardbody drilled the question "Who you callin' a bitch?" into our brains, and men and women alike loved it. Then MC Lyte brought *Ain't No Other,* with the Grammy-nominated single "Ruffneck" that challenged men who didn't fit the rough-and-rugged bill. Salt-N-Pepa were *Very Necessary* with their fourth studio album and the aforementioned successes of "Shoop" and "Whatta Man." Monie Love came through with *In a Word or 2,* as Digable Planets dropped their debut album, *Reachin' (A New Refutation of Time and Space).*

By 1994, Digable Planets were on their follow-up album, *Blowout Comb,* as The Fugees came out with their debut, *Blunted on Reality,* Gang Starr dropped their fourth studio album, *Hard to Earn,* OutKast released their debut, *Southernplayalisticadillacmuzik,* not to mention Nas's game-changing debut, *Illmatic,* along with The Notorious B.I.G.'s groundbreaking debut, *Ready to Die.* Da Brat released her debut album, *Funkdafied,* along with Method Man's solo debut, *Tical*. The list goes on and on and touches various regions and territories across the nation where hip-hop was not only fully immersed in the major label machine but experimenting with sounds and styles, and within a few short years would land in consistent pop-radio rotation with a mainstream audience.

It was dubbed the "Golden Age" for good reason. We were leaving the fog of the gangster rap takeover, and more artists were trying to lighten the air with soulful music while remaining impactful and keeping social consciousness within the hip-hop frame of reference, or at least trying to. It was also the peak of the boom bap production style, a divine combination where the kick meets the snare in studios filled with Timberland boot tracks. This was perhaps the first time in hip-hop's then two-decade history where you couldn't pick a song or two and use them to accurately define "hip-hop" by a singular sound. Album sales were on the upswing, as Tribe's *Midnight Marauders* reached over 500,000 units sold a year after its release, and Wu-Tang's *36 Chambers* reached platinum two years later. It's also indicative of the slow-burning replay value of the works released, where projects were being discovered and rediscovered—almost in record time. All eyes on everyone, if your audience was right.

For the female artists, there was a new challenge approaching. Overdiversification meant figuring out where they fit within a rapidly growing environment. "It was really exciting," Ladybug Mecca recalls. "Really fast. Everything was new—meeting lots of new people, traveling to new places. It was mostly a positive experience in the very beginning." A group like Digable Planets arrived in the heart of this sonic expansion, complete with jazzier production that wrapped itself around the trio's sharp lyricism. Visually, the group dressed as what Mecca defined as a jazz-influenced ensemble, where even she donned trousers, button-down shirts, and hard-bottomed shoes. Mecca stood petite yet proud, with short, slicked-back hair, parted on the side. She was pegged as a tomboy, a title that she openly embraced at eighteen years old, though not everyone was as welcoming of that tomboy swag. "Before the first album came out, we were meeting with a stylist, and she's also a clothing designer," Mecca explains. "And she did some sketches . . . Really nice lady, but she tried to put me in a catsuit or something. And that just was not me. I was a tomboy. I was still that rebellious teenager that hated the fact that men lusted over my body, and I was prepared to fight you. So, there was no way I was about to throw on a catsuit and get onstage or do music videos. Not at that age. Not at that point in time."

Over time, the subtle sexist nuances became more glaring for Mecca. "I think as I just became more aware of just how ingrained sexism is in hip-hop and the world in general and just how much [the] patriarchy has a grip on even those that are closest to you . . . That was tough, because [the hip-hop community] is a real family for me, outside my own family. And little by little, I just started experiencing really disrespectful things from men in the industry. Just shit like that is very shocking when it happens. It just wakes you up." Here was an artist who once rhymed, "Rip it till dawn, kick it till dawn / Hip-hop is the fix or else we be gone," on *Reachin*'s album cut "Where I'm From." Yet that love of hip-hop was becoming less of a "fix" and more of a poison in the midst of a growing gender divide.

It was a lesson in patience, but also in maintaining self-control, especially when respect for the music and respect for the women making it were not in harmony. "I had to learn how to maintain my personality," she says, "but at the same time strengthen that commanded respect. Because there are men out there that will really test that shit."

Digable Planets secured their success with their first single, "Rebirth of Slick (Cool Like Dat)," which earned them a Grammy in 1994 for Best Rap Performance by a Duo or Group and hit number one on the Billboard Hot Rap Singles chart. The trio spent the next few years touring and releasing more music before going on a lengthy hiatus. They reunited in 2005 for the release of a compilation project titled *Beyond the Spectrum: The Creamy Spy Chronicles*. Mecca's solo debut album, *Trip the Light Fantastic,* arrived that same year. Ladybug Mecca took a break from the business from 1995 to 2005. Her life took her to other places, and she was mainly focused on being a caregiver to her parents. But the short-lived collective success of Digable Planets could perhaps be attributed to just how fast hip-hop was evolving during that time.

The geographical landscape was expanding, no longer relegated to the East and West Coasts, where even the neighboring cities outside of NYC and LA had their own je ne sais quoi. Take Philadelphia, arguably a truncated version of the New York City rap scene, considering its artists were consistently straddling a line between street and soul.

In 1993, an artist emerged from the belly of Philly with a perfectly coifed Afro that stood like a crown. Her name was Bahamadia, and she was making waves locally with the release of her single "Funk Vibe." Her voice was gruff yet slick, and she would smoothly lure her audience in when she rhymed. Influenced by fellow Philly radio jock turned rapper Lady B, as well as Salt-N-Pepa and Queen Latifah, Bahamadia continued the progression of authentic female voices, creating her own lane in her local hip-hop scene.

In 1994, she aligned with Brooklyn duo Gang Starr to release the single "Total Wreck," produced by Gang Starr's rhymesmith Guru. That track would later appear on her 1996 debut album, *Kollage*. While 1996 saw an influx of female rappers with male mentors, it wasn't widely known that some of the men were ghostwriting for the women they were pushing. Don't get it twisted; men had ghostwriters, too, though the code of conduct was like Fight

Club or *omertà*. No one spoke on that, yet they were freely rocking back and forth on their heels when it came to taking credit for the ladies. Bahamadia had her head too deep in her own rhyme book to even notice. "I wasn't even aware that some people had people writing for them," she says, noting that she always created her music with her own pen. "That's why I focused so much on my lyrical content, because I felt like that was the measuring stick that I had to adhere to." Born Antonia D. Reed, Bahamadia entered the music industry as a quiet force, looking to align with like-minded female rappers to keep the growing going in the culture-based genre. "Remember in *The Source* magazine back in the day, they used to have those pictures in the back and you would see all of these artists and they would be hanging out?" she asks, with a slightly embarrassed laugh at herself. "I found out one time at an industry party that this stuff was staged. I thought that it was a community, and everybody's cool. Yo, my heart was broken when I realized it was staged, a lot of it. That was the business of music, though. That wasn't the culture of hip-hop."

After that realization, Bahamadia learned to navigate rather fluidly through hip-hop, while establishing some bonds with her female peers. "Mecca from Digable Planets was the first female that I met in the industry that I actually built a genuine camaraderie with to this day," she says. "She was the one that showed me the ins and outs of the business. She was the first one that I disclosed to that I was going to name my first project *Kollage,* and she was the one that told me, 'Do you realize that you can create your own cover art?' I didn't know any of that. She showed me the ropes and stuff."

Bahamadia toured with everyone from Lauryn Hill to Lil' Kim and even Da Brat. While she lived in a similar space as Lauryn, Bahamadia managed to balance the heightened sexiness of Kim and high-powered energy of Da Brat, thereby proving she could coexist with like-minded peers while still offering a much-needed contrast to other female artists. "It was an interesting dynamic for me, too, because I would do pop stuff still and then I would turn around and do some underground stuff, and then I would do some electronica stuff," she says. "It was always diverse for me, and I always thought that the common thread, particularly with us as women musicians in hip-hop, was that it was always a segregated element there. I don't know if that was mainly coming from the women, or was it coming from the teams behind the women? Especially the ones that had the major deals at that time." Recognizing the split between men and women in hip-hop, Bahamadia elected to keep her skills at the forefront and everything else second.

"For me, even when I got my hair cut and had that Afro, that was about me showing my independence, saying, 'This is my hair, and I have every right to wear my hair how I want to wear it.'" She even deepened the tone of her voice for her music. "I was like, 'You know what? I'm going to have to put on a hard shell, because that's me. That's my protective shell,'" she says. "I didn't want them to look at anything about me except for myself and my talent and my business acumen or what I thought I had at the time developed. To get me by, I felt like I had to do that. I shouldn't have had to do that just so I could survive. I shouldn't have had to do that."

Bahamadia sat in between the two worlds of underground and mainstream hip-hop that existed between the 1990s and early 2000s, a complicated space, to say the least. There was this all-or-nothing manifesto permeating the hip-hop industry. Either you surrendered to Puffy's Shiny Suit Era and tailored your sound specifically for the mainstream with boisterous samples and pop-standard BPMs, or you slid to the polar opposite—the indie scene fueled by labels like Rawkus Records that pledged an organic sound that emanated from artists rocking Triple Five Soul hoodies. Few could live in the middle, but Bahamadia was willing to try to forge a success story there, amid the constant comparisons thrown her way.

In one breath she was compared to indie titans like Jean Grae (known earlier as rapper What? What?), and in another to the iconic Lauryn Hill. In 1997, she changed the game by rapping over house-infused production on the track "New Forms," a risky move since there was little experimentation during this period; you were either syrupy in the mainstream or stripped of any flair in the underground. Not Bahamadia. Collaborating with British producer Roni Size of the drum-and-bass collective Reprazent, she set a new standard. That rhyming pattern would find its way into hip-hop years later, primarily through Timbaland's own work and his work with Missy Elliott, though it was Bahamadia who first took the leap. "I remember one time, I think it was in an interview with Timbaland or something, and he was asked how he came up with that style, sonically," Bahamadia says, "and I think he said something to the order of, he made a mistake on the drum pads or something. But that style, we had been doing that like five years or something prior."

While her debut had been released via EMI, in 2000 she went indie with her follow-up, *BB Queen*. "I remember I bought Donald Passman's *All You Need to Know About the Music Business* for twenty-five bucks," she recalls, "and I highlighted the book. I would take it to meetings at the label. That's how I did it." No manager, just a label. "I was going to do my second album with [EMI]. I was going to have all A-list producers and the whole nine," she recalls, "and then EMI folded. They got broke, but I was fortunate, though, because a lot of [artists] went to subsidiary labels, but I actually got the option to leave if I wanted to leave, or stay. I decided to leave because I felt like the team of people weren't going to be there that understood my direction and who I was as an artist and as an individual. That's when I started touring Europe and stuff like that."

Meanwhile, a doe-eyed hurricane named Lauryn Hill was slowly making her way into the public eye as a recording artist. In 1993, Lauryn starred opposite Whoopi Goldberg in the *Sister Act* sequel *Sister Act 2: Back in the Habit*. *Sister Act* had been a box office smash, grossing over $139.5 million in the US alone. *Sister Act 2* grossed only $57 million domestically, though it proved that Lauryn Hill was a triple threat of actor-singer-MC. In the film, she plays a troubled teen named Rita Watson who both sings and raps and wants a fair shot at stardom, much to the chagrin of her mother (played by Sheryl Lee Ralph). Though the film's success was flimsy, it bolstered Lauryn's popularity, and in 1994 she made her debut as L-Boogie, one-third of the New Jersey–bred group The Fugees. Their debut project, *Blunted on Reality*, was sonically uneven, as the group was still finding their identity. The first single, "Boof Baf," was a hyper introduction, followed by the far more subdued (and much more successful) follow-up single "Nappy Heads." In the music video, the group is dancing on the steps of the Low Memorial Library at Columbia University, where Lauryn was a student. The Salaam Remi remix to the album's third single, "Vocab," became one of the tracks on the project where Lauryn Hill's potential for greatness came into clear view. However, Lauryn had her own solitary moment on the album on a song called "Some Seek Stardom," which would later be the reference point at which it was neatly proven that L-Boogie could deliver and thrive as a solo artist.

She possessed both girl power and the "little sister" vibe in her crew of guys, or at least that's what was portrayed in the early days. When she joined Bahamadia and a handful of indie rappers named Precise, Treep, and Uneek on DJ Big Kap's "Da Ladies in Da House" in 1995, it became one of the most classic female rapper posse cuts, mainly because their collective presence was such a rarity. "Everybody has a song that gets you where you need to be, and when we did the 'Da Ladies,' we all just celebrated with each other," recalls Precise, now an award-winning producer and songwriter for acts like Pink and New Kids On The Block. "We were all like, 'Oh, you killed it. Oh, you did this! You did a great job!' I remember talking to Lauryn. She was such a sweetheart. It was such a good time."

The hip-hop expansion was vast and wide, stretching down south to where Atlanta was crafting its own little niche. The ATL scene was heating up, stylistically hugging a funkier production, where in just a few short years the likes of OutKast and the rest of the Dungeon Family would be introduced. Producer Jermaine Dupri was young but hungry, introducing us to the backward-pants-donning duo Kris Kross and their hit single "Jump," off 1992's *Totally Krossed Out.* Dupri was on a mission to find more raw talent, and he got more than he bargained for when he met a Chicago-bred "brat" named Shawntae Harris.

Shawntae—better known as Da Brat—was securing success on a local level, and was known for her speedy yet sharp rhymes. A rap contest sponsored by *Yo! MTV Raps* landed her on the radar of Kris Kross after Brat won the grand prize. By then, Kris Kross's success had made them a household name. The two introduced Brat to Jermaine Dupri. In 1993, Kris Kross dropped their follow-up, *Da Bomb,* and featured Da Brat on the title track. A year later, Da Brat released her solo debut album, *Funkdafied.* The project leaned on soul samples, particularly on the title track, where Da Brat struck a balance between hyper and laid-back. Laced with weed references and nods to "pimpin'," Brat was like the female answer to Snoop Dogg, complete with a funk slant and smooth delivery, even name-checking Parliament-Funkadelic on her "Funkdafied" verse. She was flanked by Dupri in the video, and while Brat possessed star power, she was placed like an accessory on her own track. That would soon change. Brat saw the game through a different lens; perhaps it was because she wasn't in a hip-hop hub like New York

City, or maybe she saw the roadblocks before everyone else did. Either way, she was far from quiet.

While her debut project was certified platinum, it also made history as the first platinum album by a solo female rapper (and the second female hip-hop act to go platinum, after Salt-N-Pepa). Da Brat rose up the ranks quickly, and immediately she was stacked against her female peers. She was candid from the jump, and in an early interview in 1994 with the *Atlanta Journal-Constitution,* she cleared up a rumor that she didn't want to be categorized among her female peers. It wasn't about lacking in sisterhood; it was the notion that if the "female rapper category" was going to be that limiting, then she wanted to be regarded like any talented male rapper.

"Please print this," she told the interviewer, Sonia Murray. "People keep on misinterpreting what I say about that. What I'm saying is females don't get the notoriety that males get." She uses the example of how Will Smith was able to premiere his music video on NBC during his *Fresh Prince of Bel-Air* sitcom, but Queen Latifah couldn't on Fox during *Living Single.* "Guys just get a lot of hype and the females don't," she continued. "That's why I was saying hype me up just like the fellas." Her early aesthetic placed her in between both genders, as her oversize denim, braids, and bandanas spoke exactly to her desire not to be sexualized, to the point where some were even confused about her gender altogether. To Brat's point, however, what was the allure of holding the title of "female rapper" if proper respect still wasn't being given? On her follow-up, 1996's *Anuthatantrum,* Brat would assume greater creative control of the project, still working with mentor Jermaine Dupri, but seen less as an addition to his production and hype-man duties and more of her own person. The lead single "Ghetto Love," featuring TLC's T-Boz on the hook, reached number twenty on the Billboard Hot 100.

Out west, a new queen was emerging, and she was bearing two Afro puffs.

The year was 1992, and all of Death Row Records showed up in New Orleans for the Black Radio Exclusive Convention (better known as the BRE). This was the very same event that ended up plastered across news headlines when a fight broke out and two people were stabbed, leaving Suge Knight, Dr. Dre, and The D.O.C. arrested. "Everybody from Death Row goes to the BRE," producer Chris "The Glove" Taylor remembers. At the time, Chris was a part of Ruthless Records R&B group Po' Broke & Lonely?, on the verge of signing with Death Row. Chris was there to perform with his group alongside other R&B acts like R. Kelly. Death Row was heating up, thanks to Suge, who was bubbling out west. His growing enterprise functioned as part record label, part gang experience, considering that his Blood ties didn't end in the streets—they trickled into every part of his business acumen. We would learn just how toxic his energy would get in later years once he and Dr. Dre parted ways and Tupac was shot, though at this point in time, Death Row was merely a crew of musical tough guys willing to pop off at any given moment. When the Death Row artists toured, they would go by the name the Death Row Inmates, if that's any indicator of their stress-delivering abilities.

Back to the BRE.

"After the event, a fight ensues," Chris recalls. "It was a riot." Men are attacking each other left and right, and in the middle of it all stood one woman: The Lady of Rage. "In the midst of this riot, I see Rage manhandling cops," Chris says with a laugh. "Then she hit a horse, right in the face, like in *Blazing Saddles*." The Lady of Rage didn't just talk about it, she was about it.

Born Robin Yvette Allen, Rage first appeared on Dr. Dre's solo debut album, *The Chronic,* on the cuts "Lyrical Gangbang" and "Stranded on Death Row," along with the "Doctor's Office" skit and "The Roach" outro. The following year she appeared on Snoop's *Doggystyle* on the "G Funk" intro and "For All My Nig-gaz & Bitches." The time was coming for Rage to stand on her own and show just how lyrically potent she could be. And that's how it was for women in predominantly male crews. You got your starter verse on one of the guys' tracks. Then you got another, and maybe another. If the steam rose, your album would come eventually. If it didn't, you stood in their music videos nodding your head. Rage didn't have to wait that long for her lyrical fury to come full force.

In 1994, Rage dropped her solo debut single, "Afro Puffs," on the *Above the Rim* soundtrack. With Snoop Dogg on the ad-libs, Rage delivered a womanifesto for the times: a declaration of show-ing how one woman can be both tough and unfuckwitable, even with her hair in two perfectly coifed Afro puffs. With an adjust-ment of her bra strap, Rage delivered her tough and raw rhymes like a seasoned pro. She didn't fit the mold of female rappers at the time; she broke it. Gangster rap lyrics with a confusingly cute coif, The Lady of Rage wasn't playing any games.

The video depicts Rage commanding the room in a black leather jacket with a black lace bra peeking out from underneath in one scene, and in an open-stitched black vest with a cowry shell necklace in another. Black gloves were a must, as if she were about to commit a crime and wanted to leave no trace on the scene. Her energy was unique, a necessary addition to the roster Death Row was building in the waning gangster rap era, which would inevita-bly close just a few years later with the murder of Tupac Shakur. But Rage was something special, a beast on the mic with commercial appeal. "She laid everything down in one take," Chris remembers of the "Afro Puffs" studio session. "Rage sounds like she sounds. It wasn't hard to mix her. I recorded her. There was nothing to it. She has such a smooth voice." While the song didn't chart incredibly high on the Billboard Hot 100 or the Hot R&B/Hip-Hop Songs chart, it reached the top five on both the Dance Club Songs and the Hot Rap Songs charts, the former indicative of Rage's reach in spite of the gangster rap peg.

"What I didn't like was how nothing else happened after that," Chris says of Rage's career. For one, reviews of her single chose to home in on Dr. Dre and Snoop on the "Afro Puffs" extended remix, and *Billboard* referred to her rhymes in a 1994 review as "brassy bragging." Her solo debut album, *Necessary Roughness,* wouldn't release until 1997, long after the reign of her hit single and the Death Row dynasty had faded. The album landed within months of The Notorious B.I.G.'s passing, and close to a year after the death of Tupac Shakur, when hip-hop was already transitioning out of the gangster rap sound. Jay-Z had arrived a year earlier with 1996's *Reasonable Doubt,* and its follow-up, 1997's *In My Lifetime, Vol. 1,* sonically changed the genre. The fans' tastes followed. Rage's debut album also marked the very last release on Death Row Records. Too little, too late.

"She just disappeared," laments Chris Taylor. "I think with everything else heating up, she got lost in the mix. Another Death Row inmate."

III

Only Female in My Crew

Chapter Nine

DIVIDE AND CONQUER

THERE'S NO MANDATE THAT SAYS WE HAVE TO ALL GET ALONG."
Rah Digga is seated across from me at a restaurant in
Montclair, New Jersey, breaking down her philosophy on "the Sex
Kittens vs. the Nubian Goddesses." The descriptors shouldn't be in
direct conflict, though by the mid-'90s, it sure felt that way. Lyrics
and looks were mutually exclusive, meaning sex appeal couldn't
exist where real bars were present, and vice versa. So, the Sex Kittens exuded the sexuality, while the Nubian Goddesses did not.
Sex Kittens could have lyrical skill, though that was overlooked by
their form-fitting clothing. If the Nubian Goddesses showed cleav-
age, it was like, "Hey, you! Cover up!" Nubian Goddesses didn't
have the luxury of showing off their beauty or their bodies, especially when it was assumed that their music was the main priority of their brand. "I noticed when the Nubian Goddesses make
attempts to show off our goods, people actually get mad at us,"

Rah Digga says. "Like, 'Oh, what are you trying to do?' Last time I checked, I'm still a woman. Women do women things. It doesn't mean I'm about to go sliding down a pole or anything. Don't worry, there's no sex tape coming, I promise. It's ninety degrees outside. I want to show some skin."

Sex Kittens didn't seem to mind their title, though. When Lil' Kim spoke with MTV's *RapFix Live* in 2011, she discussed Puff Daddy's early image of her: "Puffy looked at me as like the little sexy kitten one," she says, "because that was me." She still rocks with that title. "I was a kid when I released my first album," she told me in an interview for *Billboard* in 2018. "Now I'm like this woman, this sex kitten, a sexy kitten that knows myself."

There was also something to be said about how the Nubian Goddesses wore their hair naturally and embraced pro-Black beauty, while the Sex Kittens subscribed to the European standards of beauty. It was no coincidence where the unfair bias landed, though it was Lauryn Hill who eventually changed that, especially following the release of *The Miseducation of Lauryn Hill,* when she embraced her fuller post-pregnancy body, yet still killed it musically. "She made good music, and she actually made the Nubian Goddess sexy," Rah Digga reflects. "Brown-skinned women with natural hair actually became a thing of beauty," she said, describing them as "Bantu girls," a nod to African roots. "It wasn't just light-skinned, weave, blond hair, long hair. She made Bantu girls and brown skin sexy."

A self-identified Nubian Goddess, Rah Digga is known for her growl behind the mic that could cripple opponents of any gender. "I think I'm the sweetest person on the planet, but I've met so many people that said, 'Oh, wow. You're really nice. Like, I didn't know what I was walking into,'" she tells me. "Just because I was so cutthroat and sharp and just so slick with my tongue, like, 'Who want it? Dudes, females, who want it?'" She still looks almost exactly as she did when we got our first real glimpse of her, hopping off a stagecoach with her crew, the New Jersey battle rap outfit Outsidaz, and Lauryn Hill in The Fugees' music video for "Cowboys." Rah was the sole female member of Outsidaz, though she felt like one of the guys. "I never looked at myself as a female rapper to be objectified," she says. "I was so oblivious to everything. Like, if there was anybody making passes at me, it was totally going over my head. All my girlfriends now tell me like, 'Girl, you don't remember when such-and-such was trying to holla at you, and you blew them off?' I wasn't picking up on any of that. My mission was, 'Can I get on the record?'"

Hip-hop would change forever in 1996, a landmark year for the genre. Tupac Shakur released his last album while still among the living, *All Eyez on Me*, on February 13, 1996. The Fugees released their follow-up, *The Score*, on the same day. Jay-Z released his debut, *Reasonable Doubt*, in June, and Nas released his follow-up, *It Was Written* (featuring Lauryn Hill on the intoxicating "If I Ruled the World"), in July, along with A Tribe Called Quest's *Beats, Rhymes and Life* and UGK's *Ridin' Dirty*. In August, OutKast released *ATLiens*. Then, Tupac was killed on September 13 and had his first posthumous release, *The Don Killuminati: The 7 Day Theory*, less than a month later, under the name Makaveli. The Roots released *Illadelph Halflife* on September 24, with Wu-Tang Clan's Ghostface Killah dropping *Ironman* on October 29. Then came the back-to-back releases of Lil' Kim's *Hard Core* and Foxy Brown's *Ill Na Na* in November (*Hard Core* on November 12, *Ill Na Na* on November 19). Queens duo Mobb Deep dropped *Hell on Earth* the same day as *Ill Na Na*. In the same year, Bahamadia dropped her debut album, *Kollage*, Da Brat dropped *Anuthatantrum*, and MC Lyte dropped *Bad as I Wanna B*, anchored by the single "Cold Rock a Party," which featured a young artist named Missy Elliott singing on the hook.

It's an overwhelming list of releases, to say the least. Hip-hop was playing a game of numbers, mainly because record labels were growing more and more terrified of what was to become of the growing genre. After Tupac passed (followed, six months later, by The Notorious B.I.G.), the growing trend was to find *air quotes* safer rap acts to invest in, to make the money without being accessories to what felt like a growing body count. All the while, artists were aggressively releasing their catalog so as to not dip on their fans' radars, since so many acts were on the scene. This space of both "safety" and "skill" became The Fugees' playground, tempering it all with showing up everywhere to keep reminding the world that they were on the path to domination.

The Fugees were fixtures in the budding New Jersey hip-hop scene, previously occupied by artists like Queen Latifah, Naughty by Nature, and Redman. Meanwhile, in the underbelly of that scene lived groups like Outsidaz. "In the Outsidaz space, it was serious," Rah Digga remembers. "All they cared about was having the best verse. So just imagine being in a room with a bunch of guys. Not only was it a competition to be the best, it was also a competition to finish the verse first. You didn't want to be the quote-unquote 'Sucka MC,' and let everybody else go and try to study what everybody else was doing." It wasn't for the faint of heart. "No matter how insecure you may have been in that moment, you didn't want to be the cornball who told everybody to get out of the room so you can have your privacy to record. It's like, 'No, come in. Have a party. Listen to me spank these guys.'" The Fugees, however, were different. "They were more of the artsy, musical types," Rah Digga explains. "Wyclef plays every instrument under the sun, and his cousin Jerry ["Wonda" Duplessis] is an engineer and a producer, as well."

And then there was Lauryn.

Having already secured her status as a lyrical beast with star potential, her real opportunity to show out would be on *The Score*. The Fugees' previous album, *Blunted on Reality*, moved a reasonable number of units (around 120,000), though their parent record label, Sony, wasn't impressed. The reality was, the group had yet to discover who they were. They needed some time to figure it all out (with the help of producer Salaam Remi, who would later mentor Amy Winehouse), and once *The Score* was in progress, they were ready to rock with a structured identity. "The Fugees were finally focused on being this hybrid pop/rap group that they were formulating when they were making the first record," Joe Nicolo, co-owner and president of Ruffhouse Records, told me in 2016 during an interview for *Pitchfork* on the twentieth anniversary of *The Score*.

They returned to work with Salaam Remi, who, at this point, was growing his own track sheet of hits even outside of the group. "My position with The Fugees, in general, was bringing out my potential and for them, the same thing," Remi told me in 2010. "Bring forth the potential of what they could be to the point where during our sessions I started calling [Lauryn] Madam Potential." In a later freestyle, Lauryn would reference Salaam's nickname for her: "Madam Potential, I'm deadly with a pencil."

Remi was already sitting on "Fu-Gee-La," as it had been recorded prior to *The Score*, though the beat was originally intended for Fat Joe. Lauryn was in rare form on this project, perhaps subconsciously aware of where it might take her. As the only woman on a team full of men—from the business to the creative—she fought for her voice in every sense.

"There was a time when we were recording, and every once in a while, she'd be like, 'You know what? There's too much testosterone here,'" Remi told me. "Because we were always going back and forth. I was the person that would not challenge her, but I would go back and forth with different lines. Like 'Oh, you know, I really like that one a lot. But if you would just say this part like that and say this part like that.'" She wanted everything to be on point and fit her criteria. "On the very first record we did, there are three different vocals released," he said. "There's one vocal performance in the video. There's another vocal performance on the radio CD singles, and another vocal performance on the 12-inch. People can't hear the difference. Most humans can't hear the difference. But she could tell the difference. She did it over a million times until she was satisfied with it." He called her "Madam Potential" in the studio ad nauseum. "And then probably after the twentieth time I said it, she was like, 'Potentially what? Potentially what?' And I was like, 'Potentially the greatest artist of all time, if you stick with it.'" While Salaam Remi didn't have a heavy hand in the production of *The Score*, he was their creative confidant on the project.

The Score broke down all sorts of barriers as they pertained to what starkly defined the lines of hip-hop music. Using live instrumentation, soul samples, and carefully placed lyrical patterns, the album was regarded as a crossover masterpiece. The sound was elevated, along with their live sets, which drastically changed from the first album to the second, eventually becoming the most treasured aspect of the group.

"Their presentation in 1993 was just a little bit different some three years later in 1996," The Roots' Ahmir "Questlove" Thompson recalls of The Fugees' early days. Back then, Questlove was interning at The Fugees' label, Ruffhouse Records; actively performing with his later Grammy-winning Philadelphia-based band, The Roots; and releasing their projects. During the last week of his internship (before being replaced by their next intern, Santi White—better known as Santigold), Thompson was approached by Ruffhouse cofounder Chris Schwartz, who asked if The Fugees could open for The Roots. "They were big on lighting incense. They were real coffee-shoppy," Questlove says. "They were doing Haitian rituals and that sort of thing," he says of their early aesthetic. "It was weird." Their sets changed, arguably after opening for The Roots, who devised a segment of their shows called Roots 101, dedicated to covering rap classics. The Fugees picked it up from The Roots, later claiming they were the first hip-hop band. "You'll be the first person that I have ever publicly admitted to that the last line in verse one of [The Roots' song] 'What They Do' . . . we definitely had The Fugees on the mind when we added in 'Joke's on you, you heard a bitin'-ass crew' because we felt some sort of way at the time," Questlove tells me. "Once they started getting platinum love and the cover of *Rolling Stone* and all that stuff, then it was just like, ah man, the gods are against us."

The two groups' creative differences dissipated enough to hit the road together, again. The Roots embarked on a tour with The Fugees and Atlanta's Goodie Mob (responsible for the success of group member and former Gnarls Barkley frontman CeeLo Green), in early 1996, right around the time of *The Score*'s release. "During that tour, that was like one of the most fun times of my life," Questlove recalls, citing water balloon fights and other road shenanigans. "Which is weird now, because our relationship is so strange with [Lauryn Hill] now and so guarded and so eggshell-ish." It was on this tour that The Fugees became a household name. Within weeks of the start of the tour, *The Score* became the centerpiece, where the audience shifted from knowing only the singles to reciting even the album cuts verbatim. "I will absolutely say everybody benefitted from that tour," Questlove says. "The Fugees definitely brought audiences that otherwise probably wouldn't have come seen us in the first place and exposed them to that."

By the spring, the tour reached the next level, and Lauryn Hill was the star. It was April Fool's Day 1996, and The Roots were performing with The Fugees in Los Angeles. "It was the most surreal night of my life," Questlove remembers. "Number one, we are in

the thick of Bad Boy vs. Death Row." He's referring to the gigan-
tic eruption between The Notorious B.I.G.'s Bad Boy and Tupac's
Death Row that ultimately claimed both their lives. It was the Soul
Train Music Awards weekend—almost exactly a year later, The Notorious B.I.G. would be murdered two days after his appearance on
the 1997 Soul Train Awards. "You're already hearing stories of like,
Pac with his middle fingers up in the air in a Hummer and passing
Biggie, and a shootout at Roscoe's Chicken and Waffles, and Puffy
buying out the entire Hotel Nikko, so now we gotta go to another
hotel, you know, it was so high-tensioned," Questlove continues.
"And so on April first, 1996, we were the only game in town. Everybody and their mother was trying to get in to see The Fugees
perform." Acts like Natalie Cole, TLC, Faith Evans, and even Tupac
were in attendance to witness The Fugees live onstage, but most important, to see Lauryn Hill. This was the same show where Questlove would meet both D'Angelo and Erykah Badu for the very first
time, both of whom he would later work with extensively. Badu
and D'Angelo had recorded a duet earlier that day, a cover of Mar-
vin Gaye and Tammi Terrell's "Heaven Must've Sent You" off the
High School High soundtrack. "That's the show where I famously
used our show as my audition for D'Angelo," Questlove says with
a laugh, "because D'Angelo and Erykah were literally dead center,
like some king and queen shit, on the upper balcony watching the
proceedings. That whole J Dilla choppy style that I'm known for
now?" he says with a pitch, referring to his now legendary high-
energy stuttering drumming style. "I debuted it that night." An
argument arose among The Roots in their dressing room, as Questlove was questioned over why he was "drumming all fucked up." It
escalated, so he left.

"And when I'm in the hallway, it's Tupac, Suge Knight, and
Warren Beatty. Yo, the joke premise couldn't be funnier." The
strange trifecta was waiting outside Lauryn Hill's dressing room,

which was set apart from Wyclef's and Pras's. Warren Beatty was holding a bouquet of flowers. "He was literally pitching her the *Bulworth* idea that night," Questlove says of Beatty. "That's why he was there." It was more than just a random group of people showing up to adore the newfound marvel that was Lauryn Hill. Something bigger was happening for The Fugees as a whole. "In my head, I was just like, 'Yo, they are the new Beatles. They beat us to the punch,'" he adds. "Because Warren Beatty is waiting outside of her dressing room with the world's most dangerous man in hip-hop, and it's not even fazing him. That's how famous Lauryn Hill was in April of 1996. After that, their stardom just kicked into high gear."

The Score was six times platinum by the year following its release, and earned two Grammys: one for Best Rap Album and the other for Best R&B Performance by a Duo or Group with Vocals for "Killing Me Softly." That single would be the gift and the curse for both Lauryn and the group, in a sense. The song was initially a hip-hop-leaning track, with Lauryn rhyming on it. The "Killing me softly with his song" hook was reworked, as Lauryn sang a reggae-inspired version where instead of "killing me softly," she's "killing a sound boy" while "strumming dub plates."

When they attempted to clear the song with its songwriters, using this new rap version, they were turned down. "[The Fugees] wanted to change the lyrics [to 'Killing Me Softly'] to make the song about anti-drugs and anti-poverty," Roberta Flack told me during my *Pitchfork* interviews for *The Score*'s twentieth anniversary. "They were all about politics. Given their name and all, the (Re)Fugees, it made sense. It was more Norman [Gimbel] and Charlie [Fox] [the songwriters behind 'Killing Me Softly with His Song'] that wanted their song to not be changed."

A remnant of that original song (the "killing a sound boy" verse) is found on the introduction to the album version of "Killing Me Softly," and it was later leaked as a remix. While the cover was the most successful Fugees single to date (and more than likely the last), it thrust Lauryn Hill into a wave of gender-driven controversy. Animosity in the group was already brewing before *The Score*'s success was even realized. "Once you read the magazine, it says the girl should've went solo. The guys should stop rapping, vanish like Menudo," Wyclef rhymes on *The Score*'s album cut "Zealots." It became more and more apparent that tensions were building, even absent the tumultuous relationship between Lauryn and Wyclef that we wouldn't even learn about until years later, though *The Score*'s final track, "Manifest/Outro," where Lauryn details unrequited love and wanting to harm herself, may give an inkling of it. "You see I loved hard once, but the love wasn't returned / I found out the man I'd die for, he wasn't even concerned," she opens her verse, closing it with, "I was God's best contemplating death with a Gillette / But no man is ever worth the paradise manifest." There was clearly a lot going on, though her struggles were layered and we wouldn't fully understand them all until years later.

"Being a woman in the industry is not very easy. For some reason, the industry has a tendency to think there's always some male puppet master—some puppeteer—pulling the strings," she told MTV during her episode of the short-lived *Masters* series. "All we do is 'diva'; to this day I don't know what that really means." During her interview run with The Fugees, she would feel the gender divide the most. "I remember doing interviews with the guys, and the interviewer would be like, 'Now, Wyclef, tell us about your thoughts on the world. Pras, what do you think of hip-hop as an industry? Lauryn, what is your favorite color of lipstick?'"

Lyrically, she was unstoppable, further evidenced by the release of *The Fugees*' remix album *Bootleg Versions* that arrived in November 1996. Lauryn was rapidly evolving as a lyricist in spite of the critiques that she teetered as a hip-hop artist because her biggest track was mostly singing. It was on the *Bootleg Versions* project that she proudly flexed her bars over remixes of their existing hits. Her references began to change; Lauryn was flipping verses about politics and religion. Take her bars on the album cut "Don't Cry Dry Your Eyes"—a reworking of their cover of Bob Marley's classic "No Woman, No Cry"—which combine elements of religion, race, and the prison system as she closes with the lines:

> So, teach the youths they got more rights than Miranda
> Tell 'em this whole shit is propaganda

In one breath, she alludes to Rastafarianism; in another, she's referencing the Miranda rights. Her complexities within her rhymes became more apparent, as she was showing just how potent she could be with a microphone in hand.

Lauryn rose to prominence as a rapper, especially in the midst of the dramatic shift in styles coming down the pipeline. She struck a balance with her singing and rhyming, as her sound was a stark contrast to her groupmates, though similarly about self-expression.

"Some of the young ladies have to become themselves. They have to learn how to stop being what a man wants them to be and start realizing who they are and what they are," Lauryn said in *Rhyme & Reason*. "If they wanna wear the short skirt, if they wanna wear the baggy jeans, do whatever it is that they wanna do."

While Lauryn appeared on Wyclef's solo debut, *Wyclef Jean Presents The Carnival*, in 1997, she was ready for solo takeoff, with a pregnant belly in tow. A superstar had been on the rise two albums prior, and that star was about to blow up rather quickly.

"Years later, she was like, 'Yeah, I guess I really am Madam Potential now,'" Salaam Remi says. "I was like, 'Yeah, I guess you are.'"

Foxy Brown in 1999, smiling for the cameras . . . and the haters.

Chapter Ten

LET YOUR
FREAK FLAG FLY

DON'T LOOK NOW, BUT LIL' KIM IS SITTING RIGHT AT THAT TABLE over there."

It's the winter of 1998, and I'm at a TGI Friday's in Hackensack, New Jersey, with my friends Christina and Paul. Tupac had passed away in September 1996, Biggie in March 1997. Lil' Kim was still at war with Foxy Brown, by far the most prominent beef among the women in hip-hop, though many feuds were still bubbling beneath the surface. And there sat Kim, at a long dinner table with a bunch of her friends, Junior M.A.F.I.A. member Lil' Cease being one of them. We wouldn't hear her follow-up album, *The Notorious K.I.M.*, for another year, though she kept us fed with guest spots on Puffy's "All About the Benjamins" and Mary J. Blige's "I Can Love You," among others. With her long blond hair and camel-colored velour jumpsuit, Kim was regal. She was a superstar. There she was, sitting at a table with a Friday's Three-For-All appetizer sampler, and I was going to say hello.

I carried a keychain of a license plate with an Italian flag on it and the words "Queen Bee" embossed over the plating. I pulled my keys from my purse, the tiny license plate dangling as I nervously walked up to Kim's table. "Excuse me, Lil' Kim," I said rather boldly (for someone who was about to faint). "I'd like to offer my condolences on the passing of the Notorious B.I.G. Also, I'm the other Queen Bee." I waved my keychain in front of her. She looked up and smiled, pulled out her chair, and stood up. She stretched out her arms upward; with her tiny frame, her hands met my height. With a big hug, she told me to sit down and have dinner with her. I had already eaten, but she didn't know that. "Whenever you see me, you always have a seat at my table," Lil' Kim told me that night. I started working in the music industry a year later, based on the strength of Lil' Kim's humility when she could have politely asked me to leave. After all, she had been to hell and back for three straight years, yet still found it in her to smile.

The Notorious B.I.G.'s 1994 debut album, *Ready to Die,* quickly solidified that Biggie was in the running for the one seat New York City was looking so desperately to fill: the King of New York. Prior to the arrival of artists like Biggie, Nas, Jay-Z, and later 50 Cent, the concept of a "King" was an afterthought in NYC in the '70s and '80s. Back then, it was all about whose borough was the baddest. But by the mid-'90s, that had all flown out the window. Now it was who was the wealthiest, individually, as crack was replaced with cocaine and the rap dominators were cutting up that coke for a nice profit—before jumping into the rap game . . . and sometimes even during it. Money, power, and respect were the keys to life, along with loyalty from your "family." The rap business became a mafia in every sense of the word. And every mafia needs its First Lady.

As Biggie's career was just taking flight, he made the early decision to bring his friends along for the ride. Kimberly Jones was a street soldier from the Bedford-Stuyvesant section of Brooklyn. She moved weight for her boyfriends, worked menial jobs, and did anything and everything to keep her head above water. She was on the edge of eighteen when she met Biggie, who was then almost twenty years old. By this point, his localized fame was growing thanks to an "Unsigned Hype" column feature in a 1992 issue of *The Source* magazine. He was already cultivating his team, composed of longtime friends who would collectively be known as the Junior M.A.F.I.A. Meeting Kim was serendipitous, as a female was a much-needed addition to *la famiglia*.

"Whatever her situation was, she wanted to be out of that situation," recalls award-winning filmmaker and writer dream hampton. "Later we learned that her father was abusive and all of the things that I wouldn't have known about her at that moment." Hampton was one of Biggie's closest confidants, while also a top-tier journalist for the likes of *The Source, Rap Pages* (where she was editor in chief), the *Village Voice,* and *VIBE*. "I didn't know her well, but I remember the optics of her changing, and everyone saw that," Hampton says of Kim. "I remember Big and Un having a conversation about Kim, and I remember pushing back in that moment. They were talking about Inga [Foxy]—because they were thinking about her being in the crew—and they were like, 'Let's fuck with Shorty.'" *Shorty* was their nickname for Lil' Kim. "Big was like, 'But you know, we want her to look like a girl we wanna fuck. Not one of these dyke ass bitches.' And by that he meant Bo$$, Da Brat. I mean I had a Caesar haircut and fuckin' Timbs; it could've been me." Kim's style was functional like most women in the Northeast. "The way that women dressed in New York City was to get around and ride trains and not have rats walking over your feet and not splash in some urine puddle. Thank you, Biggie and Un, for introducing really impractical fashion to hip-hop." Hampton even remembers traveling with B.I.G. and Un to buy Kim a unitard for a performance without Kim being present. ("I was there in protest," she jokes.) It didn't matter, really, considering Kim was down for the transformation, and as hampton mentions, it was to escape something far worse than some fashion choices.

In a scene from the Biggie biopic *Notorious*, we witness Biggie developing the Lil' Kim character. While Kim wants to rap like the guys, it's at B.I.G.'s discretion that she sexes up her bars, since men don't want to hear such lyrics fly out of the mouths of women. "She'd put her hand over the mic in a certain way so that her voice would be extra deep," Lil' Cease told *VIBE* back in 2011. "I remember Big told her not to do that. He said, 'I want niggas to drool over you. Don't be too hard.'" In the same *VIBE* story, DJ/producer Clark Kent revealed, "Lil' Kim was created. She was told exactly who to be: 'You are going to be a pretty little Biggie.'" Various versions of that story have floated through hip-hop history, yet the sentiment remains intact: Biggie developed her image, but Kim possessed the talent. That skill would be realized with Junior M.A.F.I.A.'s 1995 debut album, *Conspiracy*, particularly on the singles "Player's Anthem," "Get Money," and "I Need You Tonight," featuring the late Aaliyah (though Faith Evans was originally on the track). Kim's undeniable prowess sans Junior M.A.F.I.A. was on full display in 1996 when she appeared on the soundtrack to *Don't Be a Menace to South Central While Drinking Your Juice in the Hood*, on a song called "Time to Shine" featuring Mona Lisa (Kim still shouted out Junior M.A.F.I.A. throughout the song). A lyrical switch was flicked; Kim's combination of seduction and the lavish life were introducing something entirely new to the landscape. If female rappers thought they were categorically "edgy" before, Kim was challenging the parameters of that descriptor.

While other acts like Salt-N-Pepa and even TLC were inserting sex into their rhymes, rarely did they go into detail of the *how*, the *where*, the *when*, and the *why*, as well as the *how much*. Theirs was more of an acknowledgment of the physical act, if anything—a PG-13 depiction of what women did behind closed doors, maybe even flirting with rated R. Lil' Kim jumped straight to X-rated under Biggie's tutelage. She talked about oral sex, throwing the word *pussy* around like it was currency, something entirely new for female rappers. While Biggie wanted her to remain feminine, he gave her masculine vulgarity. Somehow, it worked. Her battle-cry track "Queen Bitch" on *Hard Core* was proof of that:

> *I am a diamond cluster hustler, queen bitch, supreme bitch*
> *Kill a nigga for my nigga by any means bitch, murder scene*
> *   bitch*
> *Clean bitch, disease-free bitch*

Sex, violence, and of course money were the key components of Lil' Kim's credo, as she became the star member of Biggie's squad, almost the yin to his yang. At four feet eleven, she stood tall, petite and beautiful and ready to hide the drugs and grab the guns at any moment.

Across Brooklyn, a brown fox was roaming the streets. At fourteen years old, a young Inga Marchand, from a crew called Rotten Candy, was rhyming in the Lyricist Lounge scene under the name Queen Nefertiti. She would soon transform into Foxy Brown, staying on the rap circuit and participating in local contests and shows, with an early mentor being local buzzing rapper Smoothe da Hustler. One night when Foxy was sixteen-going-on-seventeen, she was declared the winner of a contest in Park Slope where Brooklyn production duo Tone and Poke of the Trackmasters witnessed her skills in real time. Foxy landed a coveted slot on the remix to LL Cool J's "I Shot Ya" alongside Def Squad's Keith Murray, the late Prodigy of Mobb Deep, and Fat Joe. Her bars made the room blink twice:

> *Wanna creep, on the light raw ass cheeks*
> *I'm sexin' raw dog without protection, disease infested*

"In the very beginning of what would become Junior M.A.F.I.A., Glenn 'Daddy-O' Bolton—who was one of the orchestrators of Junior M.A.F.I.A.—had Foxy going into Junior M.A.F.I.A.," Clark Kent told me in an interview back in 2016. It didn't pan out, as Lil' Kim joined the group, though Clark Kent was Foxy Brown's cousin and introduced her to Jay-Z. "He was my artist and was doing his thing and was dope," Clark explained. "She was my cousin and she was dope. I didn't have to convince [Jay], I just had to call him like, 'Yo come to the studio. [Foxy] didn't even know what she was coming for.'" Foxy Brown's brand was building, with labels vying for a shot at taking her career to the next level. Def Jam won the war, and 1996 became Foxy's golden year. Her appearance on the *Nutty Professor* soundtrack gave her more leverage, particularly thanks to Case's "Touch Me, Tease Me," and "Ain't No Nigga" with her new mentor Jay-Z. Jay-Z was readying his debut album, *Reasonable Doubt,* that year (on which "Ain't No Nigga" also appears).

Chris "The Glove" Taylor recalls the studio session for Nas's track "Affirmative Action" off 1996's *It Was Written* (months before *Ill Na Na*), where Foxy sat in a dimly lit studio scribbling her lines. Often accused of not writing her own rhymes (claiming her mentor Jay-Z was the real genius), Chris says, "I didn't see her writing . . . I heard her writing," as the sound of scribbling from her marker filled the room. This is the same track where Foxy was challenged for getting the math wrong in her cocaine-cutting verse, another indicator, per Chris, that she wrote it herself and without the help of Jay-Z or anyone else. "No drug dealer would have ever gotten that math wrong," he jokes, alluding to Jay-Z's past as a drug dealer.

While Foxy appeared to come with a home-grown image, it was Jay-Z who sharpened her edges. Her exotic look and gruff vocals were in perfect contrast, as the self-proclaimed "Ill Na Na," first introduced on "Touch Me, Tease Me," demanded the finer things in life, and if her man messed up, there was a price to pay:

> *Nigga you fuck around*
> *I'll have your loyalties and your joints*
> *Nigga your royalties and your points*
> *So what the deal is?*

Brooklyn was quickly becoming the hub for New York City hip-hop. With Jay-Z and Biggie both making their careers and developing others, the sky was the limit. Both Foxy Brown and Lil' Kim were steering the new era of the female MC, a rap vixen, or the aforementioned "Sex Kitten," christened by their male counterparts and peers alike.

Foxy Brown and Lil' Kim showed the world their collaborative potential when they appeared on the remix to Bad Boy's female R&B trio Total's single "No One Else" with Da Brat. The music video shows both girls alongside Brat and Total (with Biggie in the mix) plotting a bank robbery, on par with the hijinks happening in the 1996 film *Set It Off*, starring Queen Latifah. Kim and Foxy were friends, maybe not *close*, but friendly enough at that point.

"Foxy is wearing my shoes in that video," Kim remembered during a 2011 MTV *RapFix Live* interview. "Those shorts she was wearing were for me. [Puffy] had those for me with the little cropped shirt. [Foxy] whined and she whined, so I gave her that outfit. I literally helped dress her." Her reasoning? "I want to see the next girl fly," Kim said in the interview. "As a matter of fact, I like to be amongst beautiful women."

It was the perfect storm, really, headed for a tsunami. While Lauryn Hill was occupying a whole different side of the rap space with The Fugees, there was a new type of lady being thrown into the mix, and the world was waiting for what would happen next.

November was the month it would all begin. The hip-hop industry was still spiraling from the unexpected violent death of Tupac Shakur, despite still being unaware of what March 9, 1997, would bring for The Notorious B.I.G. A shift was entering the atmosphere, something to move the focus off the East Coast vs. West Coast war and onto something less volatile, though equally shocking.

Lil' Kim's debut album, *Hard Core*, arrived on November 12, 1996, via the Atlantic/Big Beat Records imprint Undeas Recordings, led by Biggie's longtime friend Lance "Un" Rivera. The project is a shocker from the start, as the "Intro in A-Minor" features the audio of a man at a theater watching a porno of Lil' Kim while masturbating with the lubricating assistance of popcorn butter. By the follow-up track, "Big Momma Thang," with Jay-Z and Junior M.A.F.I.A. star Lil' Cease, Kim is going full throttle, counting the number of times she wants to cum—up to twenty-four, like the carats in her diamonds. Jay-Z chimes in with what, in hindsight, are some suspiciously predatory lines: "How B.I.G. and Un trust you in the studio with me? / Don't they know I'm tryin' to sex you continuously?" Of course, Kim's opener isn't exactly for innocent ears, either, talking about her previous fear of the dick, but now she welcomes it with open mouth. On this track, Kim also explains her gratitude for B.I.G. giving her this shot, where she started out hopping from man to man and was taken by Biggie and given a better life. Now she's platinum.

It was a significant switch in the dynamic between men and women on a track, where the intentions were blatant and nuance was out the window. Inhibitions didn't pass over the welcome mat from that point on.

Where groups like Salt-N-Pepa and even TLC crystallized the concept of tackling sex even remotely explicitly in their rhymes, it still had the idea of love embedded at its core. Not here, and not anymore. Lil' Kim wasn't rapping love songs, even though we learned she was madly in love with the person helping her craft them. If Salt-N-Pepa and TLC were discussing making love, then Lil' Kim was talking about fucking. There's a difference, and it's a framework that's remained intact ever since Kim said, "I used to be scared of the dick, now I throw lips to the shit" on "Big Momma Thang."

There was an edginess to Lil' Kim, arguably raunchy, and at times she definitely treaded into that territory. In an interview with the *Guardian* in 1997, titled "The Lil' Things in Life," the writer Emma Forrest makes the distinction of why Kim's content seems so much more suggestive than, say, Foxy's. Forrest chalks it up to Kim's tiny frame. "Foxy Brown is making much the same kind of music," she writes, "but people seem more aghast at Kim, maybe because of her stature." In fact, the subheading of the article reads, "She's only four foot seven in high heels, but Lil' Kim's hip-hop rhymes make Snoop sound like Mother Teresa."

There's a reason her album was titled *Hard Core*, after all.

The album's lead single, "No Time," featured Puff Daddy, and became Kim's first solo platinum single, with the album as a whole achieving double platinum status. "No Time" was, at its core, a declaration that hip-hop was about to jump tax brackets, and Kim was the first to announce the spending habits that would follow. In one verse alone she name-checked Ivana Trump, Zsa Zsa Gabor, Demi Moore, and Princess Diana, calling them all "rich bitches." In addition, she tosses around designer labels such as Prada and Dolce & Gabbana as if they're everyday fabrics and brags about riding in a Mercedes E-Class (apparently the S-Class wasn't yet within the realm of possibility). But that laundry listing of braggadocio became a signature Kim move that many artists later adopted, including Jay-Z himself.

It was a mix of many things that made Lil' Kim so alluring. Besides being a sexual provocateur, she had a boldness about accepting no nonsense and maintaining a stance of mafia-driven loyalty. When she wasn't being sexploited on her own songs (see the previously mentioned Jay-Z verse), she was emasculating men left and right, often diminishing them into sex objects themselves—a powerful reversal. Kim flipped Biggie's song "Dreams," which detailed sex with female R&B singers, to male R&B singers in her own version. Even when a reference track for "Queen Bitch" surfaced years later, proving Biggie wrote the song, it didn't matter. It was Lil' Kim's hard-hitting delivery that made her so vital and her debut a masterpiece.

The album would go through some transitions, even following its release. The album version of "Crush on You" features only Lil' Cease on the verses and Biggie on the hook (it was later revealed that Cease's verses were written by Harlem rap leader Cam'ron). The remix adds Kim back in and was released a year later with Kim's "Not Tonight" remix, titled "Ladies Night." In the "Crush on You" music video, Kim dons multicolored wigs with matching furs, conversation pieces that would in turn define Kim's luxurious style as a whole. She was beloved by her growing fan base, though the greater public launched a campaign against Kim for her uncensored lyrics and entire aesthetic, starting with the album's marketing plan.

The promotional poster for the album (as well as a photographic insert on the inside album cover) showed Lil' Kim squatting in a leopard print bikini and diamond-studded heels, legs spread. In 2017, she told Hot 97's *Ebro in the Morning* about the now infamous poster's concept and the backlash that followed. "I went into the pose naturally, and the photographer [Michael Lavine] was like, 'Keep that! Keep that!' When we got the photos back, Biggie actually picked that photo." It became an often-imitated signature pose for Kim, yet a controversial one. "Don't forget, I was seventeen," she explained to Ebro in her interview. "People don't understand that; they don't get that. They had to market me like I was mature because I was seventeen and I'm talking like this and I'm dressing like this." Critiques ran high, as words like *slut* were used to describe Kim, yet it only fueled her fire. "But the more they did that," she said, "the bigger I became." The poster found its way to prison walls and the bedrooms of horny teenage boys. Lil' Kim was becoming an icon, much to the chagrin of conservative society.

Foxy Brown's debut album, *Ill Na Na*, dropped a week after *Hard Core*. While it sold more in the first week than *Hard Core* (109,000 copies to *Hard Core*'s 78,000), *Ill Na Na* sold half of Kim's numbers nationwide. Both were certified platinum.

Ill Na Na possessed a similar level of sex appeal coming from Foxy Brown, though her style and delivery were different from Lil' Kim's on *Hard Core*. Besides Foxy's deeper voice on the project, the Def Jam release was arguably more rooted in traditional hip-hop, as Foxy reworked LL Cool J's "Rock the Bells" on "Foxy's Bells" and the legendary NYC fixture Kid Capri even checked in on "Fox Boogie." There were also mainstream hits like "Get Me Home" with

Blackstreet and "I'll Be" with Jay-Z. Mafia loyalty was still present, as Foxy's aligning with Nas's crew The Firm was building, first introduced on the opener "(Holy Matrimony) Letter to The Firm," where Foxy makes her vow to the collective, saying that she'd even go to the electric chair in their name, if she had to.

Foxy's angle on her project was more laden with tales of drug dealing than sex, though equally explicit, especially when her album title (and her nickname) referenced her vagina. With the album's second single, "I'll Be" (featuring Jay-Z), garnering her highest chart position (number seven on the Billboard Hot 100), Foxy cleverly wove innuendos within her smooth wordplay:

> *I saw your little thing now I'm swayin', OK'in*

Foxy Brown was in a league of her own. Her full-bodied voice came in a petite frame with a face of Trinidadian and Chinese features. Her style at the start of her career was simple—darker tones and big floppy hats over her long, straight tresses with consistently manicured pro-nails. Not only did Foxy Brown sound completely unique, she physically looked it with her Asian features. Plus, her delivery was sharp, despite residing on the Sex Kitten side of hip-hop's division.

In 1996 during an interview with BET's *Rap City*, Foxy Brown sat with Jay-Z beside her and declared 1996 "The Year of the Ladies." Host Joe Clair asked, "Why is it now, though?" Foxy's answer: "I think females are just not havin' it this year. It's like, more flavor—not to say they didn't have flavor back in the days, but—" Joe Clair interjected, saying, "Hip-hop used to treat [women] like second-class citizens," to which Foxy replied, "I think more so because they don't think that females can hang with males or either it was stereotypical, like you had to be hardcore, [in] hoodies, Timbs, fatigues. You had to be hard or you weren't trying to get noticed. Now we're adding more class, sex appeal, sassiness back to hip-hop."

Both Foxy Brown and Lil' Kim epitomized a shift for female rappers, though on their first projects, their mentors' influences were glaring, right down to their grunts in between bars. Take Kim, whose lyrics co-penned by Biggie were often crude and direct, with far less subtlety, much like Biggie's strong style within his own work. Foxy, on the other hand, had the heavy pen of Jay-Z in her lyrics, making them punchy and layered, just like Jay's.

The messaging was similar: two women, dedicated to their respective crime families, who loved sex, violence, and designer fashion, the latter so much that they would either kill or fuck for it. Here was a far cry from the demanding of respect we'd heard from the women of years prior, though to Foxy's point in her *Rap City* interview, the new era was simply proving that they could hang with the men as women, not as "one of the guys." Hip-hop purists took umbrage at the fact that not only were Foxy Brown and Lil' Kim shredding the fiber of the meaningful fabric from which hip-hop was woven, but they had arrived with their mentors in tow who were doing the exact same thing on the male side. The "golden age" was reaching its close (with 1998 marking its historical end), replaced by a new guard that would completely reverse everything the previous era had stood for. While over the years, a lot of the blame for killing the golden age would fall upon Puff Daddy, as well as on Jay-Z, a considerable amount of that blame was also launched at Lil' Kim and Foxy Brown.

What the end of the golden age did was create an even greater gender divide, since now it rang abundantly clear that women had an entirely different duty within hip-hop. Certainly, the mega-success of Kim and Foxy created more options and openings for skilled female rappers, but at labels big and small, Kim and Foxy would become the go-to archetypes of how to revive even female rap legends' careers. The message was simple: women rappers now had to be sexy—the dirtier the better. The Nubian Goddess was dropping in demand. This moment would forever change hip-hop as we knew it, a business model that was on the verge of blowing up even bigger than any player or observer ever fathomed.

And it was only the beginning.

THE LEGEND OF THELMA AND LOUISE

Thelma and Louise are surrounded by the police, who are anxiously waiting to take them down. Louise loads up her gun and revs up the engine of her turquoise 1966 Ford Thunderbird, as Thelma looks at her with both amazement and confusion. They're near the edge of a cliff, and their only options are to give up and go to prison, or drive straight ahead. Then, the moment of clarity arrives. They know what they have to do. No retreat, no surrender. Engulfed by the dust of desert clay, Thelma and Louise kiss, and the car accelerates forward at full speed, plummeting over that cliff into the Grand Canyon and cinematic history.

That's the final scene of the 1991 film *Thelma & Louise,* a movie about two women who flee the law after Louise murders a man who attempts to rape Thelma. Often referred to as a road flick, the two friends have completely contradictory personalities, yet together, they're a force.

Thelma & Louise is also the title of an album that Lil' Kim and Foxy Brown were set to record together, though it never happened. Their war became one of hip-hop's greatest mysteries, about which even the deepest insiders only have speculations to offer. In 2016, I penned a piece for *XXL* attempting to get to the root of the problem, and just as expected, it was a complex, tangled mess.

When Lil' Kim and Foxy Brown arrived in tandem with their solo debut albums in November 1996, it felt like a no-brainer that the two would somehow join forces. After all, they were both shifting the scope of women in rap into a new arena filled with sex, violence, money, and unbridled self-expression. They were both from Brooklyn, and rumor had it that they shared mutual friends and at one point briefly attended the same high school, Brooklyn College Academy. In addition, Foxy's mentor was Jay-Z, and Kim's was The Notorious B.I.G. Their Brooklyn-bred teachers had appeared together on the song "Brooklyn's Finest" on Jay-Z's debut album, *Reasonable Doubt,* six months before Kim and Foxy dropped their respective projects. Jay-Z appeared on Lil' Kim's album and on Foxy Brown's. They all had Clark Kent in common, since Clark was Foxy's cousin, Jay-Z's producer, and The Notorious B.I.G.'s DJ. It was a family affair, though not quite.

Foxy and Kim appeared on the cover of *The Source*'s February 1997 issue in matching white outfits with white boas, their shoulders touching. The cover splashed "Sex & Hip-Hop: Harlots or Heroines?" The feature was penned by journalist Michael Gonzales, who followed the two around at separate intervals in 1996. For Kim's portion, it was during a Junior M.A.F.I.A. tour stop in Washington, DC; Foxy's was in the midst of the *Ill Na Na* craze, and Gonzales chased her through an album signing in Brooklyn. Kim and Foxy were still on speaking terms at the time of the cover shoot, since they posed together for a magazine cover. On the title track to *Ill Na Na,* Foxy even raps about how she's looking forward to what Kim's got cooking:

> Shakin' my ass half naked, lovin' this life
> Waitin' for Kim album to drop, knowin' it's tight

"All of a sudden, they just weren't cool," Clark Kent told me in 2016. "It was like, What the fuck happened? How did they become uncool? Who said what? Who did what?"

There was some speculation of residual beef over their album cover art. On the inside covers of both *Ill Na Na* and *Hard Core,* Foxy and Kim are wearing the same taupe jumpsuit with black trimmings and black chaps. Was it a coincidence? Purposeful biting? When Kim told MTV that Foxy "whined" until she gave up her outfit for the "No One Else (Remix)" video, this would fall in line as pattern behavior. "Foxy used to call Kim all the time, and then she would [turn around and] dog Kim out to people," Monica "Shaka Don" Dopwell told *VIBE* in 2011. Shaka Don was Kim's friend and road manager, also the woman blowing cigar smoke into the camera in the "No Time" music video. "Kim finally told me to call [Foxy] and tell her to stop calling her phone," Shaka Don continued. "It seemed like everything Kim would do, Foxy would do it right after. Kim bought a Land Rover. Foxy bought a Land Rover in the same color. Kim colored her hair. Foxy got the same color." More rumors suggested Foxy wanted whatever look Kim was going for at the moment, and whatever Kim had, Foxy wanted—minks, money, everything.

Of course, this is just one side of the argument, and there was obviously mutual animosity that appeared to arrive rather quickly. But as fast as the conflict began, so did the desire to unite the two vixens under one project. It was Lyor Cohen who first suggested the *Thelma & Louise* album when he was CEO of Def Jam. His offer was for a million dollars, to be split evenly between Foxy and Kim. All the women had to do was show up to the Hit Factory and get in the booth to record. The contract was waiting to be signed; Biggie and Un would force Kim's hand (or rather, attempt to), and Jay-Z, along with Don Pooh, Foxy's manager at the time, would try the same with Foxy. Everyone arrived at the Hit Factory for the moment in question. Everyone, that is, except for Foxy Brown and Lil' Kim, who both pulled their phones off the hook so they couldn't be contacted. Welp.

In the midst of this war, each was dealing with a lot personally, so this dream collaboration could have also dipped on their priority scales. It was no secret that Lil' Kim struggled with the concept of beauty, dating all the way back to her childhood. "Her father told her she was ugly," Michael Gonzales remembers of his *Source* interview with Kim. "And [Kim] said her father dealt with his own abuse when he was a kid because he was so dark. No matter how cute the rest of the world perceived her, she always thought of herself as ugly. The plastic surgeries she's had over the years [have] been a response to that, I guess." Her relationship with The Notorious B.I.G. was equally abusive. In 2017, when she talked to Hot 97, Lil' Kim explained one incident in particular, in which Biggie pulled a gun on her in front of Jermaine Dupri and Usher during the recording session for Usher's "Just Like Me" track, which featured Kim. Biggie was there writing lyrics, and Kim arrived upset because Biggie had had sex with one of her family members. She was too riled up to lay down her verse. A fight with B.I.G. began that poured out of the studio into the hallway, where he almost grabbed his gun. He might have shot Kim that day; it wasn't the first time their blowouts had turned volatile. "We did have a very violent relationship," Kim confirmed in her interview. "I hate that, for a while, that was all I attracted, was like, violent guys." On top of that, he was controlling, showing up to that Usher studio date on his own accord. "He put himself there," Kim said in her interview. "He just wanted to make sure I wasn't having eyes for Usher or Jermaine." Biggie's relationship with Kim was toxic, keeping her on the side during his marriage to Faith Evans and later using rapper Charli Baltimore as a pawn in another love triangle with Kim—though many have attested that Baltimore was a true love of his. Biggie and Kim were dangerous in each other's presence.

"They could barely be around each other," dream hampton adds. "They were always fighting."

Meanwhile, Foxy was grappling with her own challenges on the road to fame, as rumors of a sexual relationship with Jay-Z when she was a teenager loomed overhead, coupled with Foxy herself having a very short fuse and often turning violent. In fact, a 1998 *VIBE* cover story led her to pull up on editor in chief Danyel Smith. "[Foxy] basically came up to the office and attacked Danyel," Gonzales remembers. "I don't know if she slapped Danyel in the face or some crazy shit like that, but she and Danyel got into it because [of the cover story]. I don't remember what the whole thing was about, but obviously Foxy didn't like it." *XXL* editor in chief Vanessa Satten echoed the sentiment of Foxy's behavioral patterns. "When you write a Foxy story, you kind of get enveloped into her world," Satten says. "Anything going on in her life at the time, you kind of become her confidant for the moment. In my experience, it turned into a point where we weren't on the same page. Sometimes she's calling me and she's threatening me, like she's going to come up to [the office] and do something. I don't think she ever outright said she would hurt me, but there were enough threats that we eventually got security at the back elevator because she started to wild out a little bit and we didn't know where it was going to go." Years later Foxy would attack a manicurist at a nail salon, leading to probation. She would violate that probation in 2007, after assaulting a woman with her cell phone due to an altercation stemming from the music blaring from her car stereo, landing her in jail for a year.

Foxy had a whole slew of beefs happening concurrently with her beef with Lil' Kim. In 1996, Foxy was involved in a baby beef with The Lady of Rage and New Jersey rapper Heather B. (of MTV's *The Real World* and Shade45's *Sway in the Morning* fame), but the latter's diss track to Foxy never saw a formal release. That same year, Queen Latifah dropped "Name Callin'" on the *Set It Off* soundtrack, with Foxy as the primary target. Latifah criticized her for her sexually charged music and set off some shots about Foxy's father. Foxy in turn claimed that Latifah had a thing for her. She was the first to attempt to "out" Latifah on record, so to speak, since Queen Latifah's sexuality was a clandestine point of speculation for years. Foxy used it to hit from the hip.

In fact, she continuously made Latifah's sexuality the focal point of her disses. Foxy's 1998 diss track "10% Dis" was no exception, throwing Brooklyn rapper Queen Pen into the mix. Pen had released the track "Girlfriend" with Meshell Ndegeocello the previous year, a song with lesbian undertones, a first for female rappers. Foxy challenged both Queens on the track:

> Ya'll confused ass chicks
> Now is you straight
> Or is you gay

Latifah in turn dropped "Name Callin' Part II" and Foxy barked back with "Talk To Me," continuing her homophobic lyrics. Eventually, however, Foxy and Queen Latifah made peace in 2000.

It would take two years from the start of Foxy and Kim's beef for the on-record disses to officially begin. In 1999, Foxy Brown released her follow-up album, *Chyna Doll,* led by the single "Hot Spot." On it, Foxy's voice is noticeably higher-pitched, a complete switch from her debut and arguably resembling Lil' Kim's tone. The first shot was fired when Puff Daddy jumped on Lil' Cease's song "Play Around" (off *The Wonderful World of Cease A Leo*) and accused Foxy of trying to sound like Kim. Kim, in turn, added in her own vaguely pointed lyrics on the track, presumably aimed toward Foxy (referring to her as a "bum" holding out her cup waiting for the Queen Bee to throw in some change). A year later, Kim's shots would become more direct on the title track off 2000's *The Notorious K.I.M.,* where Kim takes jabs at Foxy's mental health and her falling out of Def Jam's favor. Foxy came through in 2000 on the Capone-N-Noreaga (C-N-N) track "Bang Bang," off the Queens' duo's album *The Reunion,* in which she slams both Kim and Puff Daddy for sending subliminal messages in their songs. She even opens her verse with "Hot damn hoe here we go again"—Kim's opening line off Mobb Deep's "Quiet Storm Remix," as well as the opener to MC Lyte's "10% Diss."

The war wasn't stopping anytime soon—in fact, it was just getting fired up, four years after the tension started. The heat poured off the wax and onto the street in February 2001, when Lil' Kim and C-N-N were guests at New York's Hot 97 on the same day, and their entourages were involved in a scuffle in which one person was shot. Since C-N-N had had Foxy on "Bang Bang" and she had used that time to go off on Kim, Hot 97 became the scene of a confrontation. At one point, Foxy tried to call a truce, but her attempt was denied. The Hot 97 incident went to trial, as Kim later admitted to lying to the grand jury. She was sentenced to one year and one day in prison for perjury.

When Kim was released, the idea of *Thelma & Louise* returned to the table, now close to a decade later. "I legitimately sat in an office, ten years removed from the situation, and someone said, 'Ay, Clark, I'll give you a million dollars if you can make that happen,'" Clark Kent told me. The offer didn't even reach Kim or Foxy; it was shot down by their camps before they could even hear it.

The last close call came in 2013 at Hot 97's Summer Jam, when Brooklyn rapper Fabolous arranged to have Lil' Kim and Foxy Brown appear onstage together for the first time in close to twenty years. It never happened. Some say Kim wouldn't even entertain the idea; others say Foxy was simply late and didn't make it there on time. Foxy appeared on MTV shortly after to explain her side of the story. She said it didn't feel genuine. "If we can orchestrate a situation where it's real, then I'm with it," she told host Sway Calloway. "If it's not real, I'm not with it."

At face value, *Thelma & Louise* was the laziest title pick ever for a Foxy Brown and Lil' Kim collaboration. It's as if it were chosen from a random list of female pairs who happened to cause trouble. In hindsight, though, it's perfect. Here were two artists whose friendship was bound to die, either by their own hands or those of the people around them. The fame happened too intensely and too quickly, and the dialogue of "one or the other" came long before the concept of "both." Competition was inevitable, of course, but in a market where the two had to fight for their individual definitions of self-expression, it was only logical to feel that in the end, only one could exist at the top. They were both self-absorbed in their own success stories, overwrought that the other would somehow threaten their own happy ending.

In the end, they each drove away, killing *Thelma & Louise* once again.

Chapter Eleven

SOUTHERN HOSPITALITY

WHEN I POSED TOPLESS, THAT WAS *MY* IDEA."
I remember holding the promotional copy of Gangsta Boo's solo debut album, *Enquiring Minds,* in my hands right before its September release back in 1998. The album had a tiny hole drilled into the corner of the plastic casing, and a hole punched over the SKU, typical of promotional CDs sent to Sam Goody for in-store play.

On the inside cover, Gangsta Boo is palming her bare breasts, one in each hand. "I think it was because I saw Janet Jackson do it or something," she says, "and I knew if I was to do something like that, it would be iconic."

I blared that album through our store's speakers all throughout the week of the album's release, taking full credit for introducing "Where Dem Dollas At" to suburbia.

The rise of the First Lady in prominent rap crews was a common phenomenon by the mid- to late '90s. While New York City was still in the lead when it came to creating top-notch crews, other pockets across the country were assembling their own powerhouses, and finding a woman to join them became a necessity. This could be due to the success of Lil' Kim and Foxy Brown, since their positions were fixed and locked by 1997. This was especially true for Kim, who remained secure in her spot even after The Notorious B.I.G. passed away that March. In the summer of 1997, Puff Daddy began his reign with *No Way Out,* and with the August release of the single "It's All About the Benjamins," the proof was in the product that everyone still wanted to "bumble with the Bee," like Kim says on the song. Why wouldn't every solid rap team place a dominant, unapologetic woman at the helm? So that's exactly what they did.

"Honestly, real talk—Lil' Kim and Foxy Brown were definitely inspirations [for me] because for one, Foxy had brown skin like me, and I could relate," Gangsta Boo remembers. "For two, Lil' Kim was in Junior M.A.F.I.A., and I was in Three 6 Mafia then. They were always just around dudes. I respected shit like that."

Lola Mitchell, aka Gangsta Boo, released *Enquiring Minds* at nineteen years old, but by then she was already a local legend. At sixteen, she had joined Three 6 Mafia after meeting classmate DJ Paul at Hillcrest High School in Memphis, Tennessee. The group collectively secured a fan base, sliding through the regional mixtape circuit in the late '80s and early '90s, then grabbing more fans thanks to their 1995 debut album, *Mystic Stylez.* Their music was laden with dark symbolism (hence the "triple six" satanic reference in their name), though still accented with dreams of bigger ballin' and playfully poignant hymns of Southern living. They were classified as one of the torchbearers of rap's "horrorcore" subgenre, the hardcore-meets-horror sound, rap that is brutally honest about the dangers of the artist's surroundings to a criminally horrific level. Other horrorcore groups included RZA's Gravediggaz, Flat-linerz, and Geto Boys, though Three 6's biggest competition were Bone Thugs-n-Harmony, because of their similar style and rhyme patterns. Gangsta Boo was a necessary component of the Three 6 Mafia, then comprising Juicy J, DJ Paul, Lord Infamous, Crunchy Black, and Koopsta Knicca. Her mere presence broke up some of the bullish, monotonous male ego that often saturated their music. She was also one of the first female rappers to exist under the horrorcore title.

While Three 6 Mafia was a tight-knit crew, they were a business from the start, housed under the self-owned Hypnotize Minds label after the group parted from their original signers, Prophet Entertainment. The true success of their business acumen wouldn't fully come to fruition until much later. In 2005, they made their biggest impact with their eighth studio album, *Most Known Unknown,* yielding big-time crossover hits like "Stay Fly" (with fellow Tennessee natives Young Buck and 8Ball & MJG), "Poppin' My Collar," and "Side 2 Side" (with Project Pat and Bow Wow). In 2006, Three 6 Mafia made history at the Academy Awards for "It's Hard Out Here for a Pimp," their theme song to the Memphis street film *Hustle & Flow,* starring Terrence Howard and Taraji P. Henson (long before they would appear together on *Empire*). The single won an Oscar for Best Original Song, making Three 6 Mafia the first hip-hop group to ever win the award, and the second hip-hop act to ever take home an Oscar (Eminem was the first for his *8 Mile* song "Lose Yourself"). They performed the track onstage at the Academy Awards, another milestone for hip-hop.

Three 6's reach was highly limited at first, but they didn't even realize it back then, given their regional strength. "It's so weird, because we were already so big in our area. In Atlanta, Tennessee, just the whole Southeast region," Gangsta Boo recalls. "We had blown up when I was sixteen. I didn't even know that we wasn't even shit, really, to the rest of the world because we were in our own world."

On her solo debut, the track "Where Dem Dollas At" became a sleeper hit, nudging her album to a number fifteen peak position on the Billboard Top R&B/Hip-Hop charts (and number forty-six on the Billboard 200). Boo was known for her rhythmic cadence set to the backdrop of DJ Paul and Juicy J's moody production. In the video for "Where Dem Dollas At," she's clad in skintight dresses staging jewelry heists with metal briefcases before hitting the club later that night. All in a day's work. Gangsta Boo was the quintessential female figurehead for the dominating bouncy sound coming from the South—fiery, sexy, and full of unbridled sass. The spot as the only girl in the group was important, since every crew had that one standout female figure, but the Three 6 Mafia leaders had another plan in mind.

On the title track of their 1995 debut album, another female rapper named La Chat makes a cameo. Memphis local Chastity Daniels was a whole other breed of female rapper, leaning closer to gangster rap than anything else. Chat emitted a different kind of energy, one that brought an added dimension to the Hypnotize Minds roster. It was forward-thinking of the group to add a second female to their label (we wouldn't see it again until years later with Crime Mob), though initially it didn't sit right with Gangsta Boo. "I didn't like it. I wanted to be the only female," she admits. "It was other little things that happened, as well—way, way, way in the beginning. How she kind of came around, it was a little messy, that's all. And it was them that did that." "Them" is the guys running the ship, primarily Juicy J, who orchestrated La Chat's entry into the squad, as much calculated as it was needed.

"I don't talk about the materialistic things, I don't talk about sexualities, I don't talk about ass and titties. I always represent the struggle. I represent hustling mothers," La Chat says. "Because there's nothing out there for her, so I always represent them type of women." The early Memphis hip-hop scene was flooded with talent that would never penetrate the mainstream, though it still built the foundation for other acts to follow through. Chat made noise alongside fellow Memphis heatmaker Lil NoiD, hitting local shows and building their base. Juicy J came upon NoiD and supported him through his debut mixtape, *Paranoid Funk,* later making him a Three 6 affiliate. At one fateful talent show, Lil NoiD won first place and La Chat won second place. Chat gave NoiD her number, but someone else called instead.

"He was like, 'Wassup, wassup. Is this Chat? This Juicy,'" Chat remembers with throwback surprise. "I was like, 'Hi!' He was like, 'I hear you could rap. Spit something for us.' I was like, 'Uh . . . My momma's here!'" Chat was at most fifteen years old at the time. "Juicy was like, 'Oh, I don't mind. I thought you wanted to be a rapper. Aight, you don't want to do it.' So I was like, 'Damn, I'm missing my opportunity.'" Juicy J showed up to her house at midnight. No, actually, it was *Jordan* (Houston—Juicy's government name). "You've got Juicy. And you've got Jordan," he told Chat. "He was like, 'This is Jordan. Jordan is the businessman. Juicy is the artist,'" Chat remembers. That distinction would eventually teach both Gangsta Boo and La Chat a valuable lesson. On this particular night, La Chat took the opportunity to show "Jordan" what she was made of. "I went outside to rap for him, and he was like, 'Oh, yeah! You can rap.' About two days later, he came [over] and we were in my living room with the recorder."

Chat's participation wasn't immediate, even when she appeared on Three 6 Mafia's debut. "I was busy in the streets while they were doing the music stuff, and they signed their deal. I was managing, working a job," she says, "but I was still keeping my name out there. I was doing little shows everywhere." Juicy J circled back to Chat once they had their own label. "They came back to me and found me. They were like, 'We want to sign you.'"

By then, Gangsta Boo was heading into her second album, 2001's *Both Worlds *69*, which hit number eight on the Billboard Top R&B/Hip-Hop chart and reached number twenty-nine on the Billboard 200. The same year, La Chat was featured on "Chickenhead," Three 6 Mafia cofounder (and Juicy J's brother) Project Pat's single with Three 6, earning her a gold record. It was also the same year that she released her debut album, *Murder She Spoke*.

There was a balance struck with having both La Chat and Gangsta Boo on the label and in the crew, though it was a controlled one. Chat was known for her tomboy look and backtalk, while Boo was the sexier slick-talker. "That's one thing I commend Juicy and Paul and them on: they wanted to make sure I stayed Chat," La Chat adds. "I remember one time we went to [Atlanta's annual spring break party] Freaknik and we weren't even supposed to be rapping. I was thinking, we're just out. I was coming out in my little shorts. Juicy's like, 'Chat! Stop! You've got to be Chat!' I'm like, 'We ain't doing no show. We at the Freaknik.' He's like, 'No, no, no. You've got to stay Chat. We don't want dudes to see you like that. You better cover that ass up. You look good, though. But go back up there and change clothes.' So I had to go back, and we had only been there for an hour." Luckily, Chat saw all this as a plus. "That's a good thing—they had two women, and we were two different women," she says of herself and Gangsta Boo. "We had two images, and they made it work. If I started off wearing shorts and stuff, they would've went with it. But that's not how I came. I was always wearing the polo shirts, the baggy pants, the jogging suits, the hat. I love a hat. Kept a hat on. The jerseys. That's always been me. Because I'm the only girl in my family. I have four brothers, so I'm like a tomboy. But [also] I'm such a lady." Boo, on the other hand was regarded as "one of the guys" until puberty took over. "That's kind of when it started," she says of her sexy branding. "The 'Where Dem Dollas At?' and all that stuff. That's when I kind of started transforming, like, showing my shape more. Wearing more fitted clothes. Stuff like that. I wasn't dressing like a boy or nothing."

The fame of Three 6 Mafia as an entity grew, but so did the animosity between the ladies at the label. "Yeah, when they was mad at me, they hired her," Gangsta Boo explains. "We used to diss each other in songs because they used to tell her things, and then they'd tell me things and [then] put us on the same song, talking about each other. Real messy." Eventually Gangsta Boo parted ways with Three 6 Mafia, dropping the sequel to her debut, *Enquiring Minds II: The Soap Opera*, independently via R2 Entertainment. "Then Chat left, and that's when we became cool," Boo explains. "I reached out to her, because that was just like, 'Aight. Damn.' So we've kind of been cool ever since."

Comparing notes, they both had one important detail in common: inconsistent treatment in business. "As time went on, I started doing so many shows, and they was booking me like I was Three 6 Mafia," adds Chat. "I was doing so many shows, but I didn't see no checks coming in. So I started asking [Juicy J] about royalties and things like that. I don't know where the money got sewed up, but I just know it wasn't coming to me." Juicy J (or rather, Jordan, the businessman) advised her to get a lawyer. They never could pinpoint where her money was going, but it never reached her. "I just ended up having to go and do my own thing because I had a child, I had a son, bills, and things to do. When I was rapping with them, Paul and Juicy were like my manager and my record label. So they were in control of everything that I was doing." It was time for La Chat to go. "I had to do it because I'm a woman first," she says. "And I never had nobody have so much control over my life, my financial abilities and all that. I had to step on out."

Gangsta Boo had a similar story. "I was getting sad and depressed and stuff like that, because Paul was my manager, they were my producers, they were the executives. They were like everything. You know what I mean? It was like a conflict of interest," Boo says. "I didn't know nothing but them, and I just started to get over it. Like, 'Damn, I want to branch out.' We couldn't work with nobody else. It was all them."

In her early days, she went by Gangsta Boo, The Devil's Daughter, though after leaving the Satanic references in rap behind, she changed her name to Lady Boo. It was a necessary switch for her. Having been part of Three 6 Mafia from such a young age, she inherited a lot of their devil-dipped aesthetic, and once on her own, she was in search of something greater. "I wanted to do the church thing," she says. "I was like twenty-one years old. I was still young as fuck, trying to learn and shit. I was trying to do the religious thing. That didn't work for me. I was like, 'Okay, this is not working either. [Religious] motherfuckers [are] more crazy than Paul and [Juicy]. I need to figure out some more stuff.'"

Both Gangsta Boo and La Chat found their way out of the Hypnotize Minds fold, with their own sets of struggles, and their fortunes dwindled while Three 6 Mafia's grew. In 2013, Gangsta Boo rejoined the group under their new flag, Da Mafia 6ix, which also included original Three 6 Mafia members DJ Paul, Crunchy Black, Koopsta Knicca, and Lord Infamous. They released the album *6ix Commandments* that same year. Lord Infamous passed away in 2013, and Gangsta Boo left Da Mafia 6ix in 2014. La Chat returned to the fold for Da Mafia 6ix's 2015 project *Watch What U Wish* . . . Koopsta Knicca passed away that year. As for Gangsta Boo and La Chat, they finally collaborated on the 2014 project *Witch,* a testament to the fact that time heals all wounds. "I don't regret nothing that I went through or don't blame [Hypnotize Minds] for nothing that I went through neither, because if it weren't for them, I wouldn't be who I am today," La Chat says.

"It was easy to leave, but once I left, it was hard to watch them thrive," Gangsta Boo admits. "Not that I wanted them to fail, but I missed out on so many great moments. Like the Oscar, and that's when they really blew up. I don't regret it, I just missed out on it." Hindsight is always twenty-twenty. "I feel like now, twentysomething years later, I'm still living it. I am a part of the brand. I am Three 6 Mafia. I was the First Lady of Three 6 Mafia. I started out with them when I was fourteen years old. I was in the beginning. I don't care who the fuck came before me and all that shit. I was there in the beginning when we were recording and fucking broke as fuck, and we made our first money together. So I feel lucky to be a part of a brand that's still doing it right now."

Even deeper in the South, a different Mama was birthing a different sound.

In 1990, Percy Miller transformed himself into Master P and began his musical militia known as No Limit Records. His story has become the stuff of legend, starting out with moving tapes out of the trunk of his car in Richmond, California, to opening the No Limit record shop and then forming his own record label. In 1995, he returned to his hometown of New Orleans, Louisiana, to fill his army tank with a fresh batch of talent. At the time, Mia Young was working at Peaches Records, the oldest mom-and-pop record store in the country. In 1993, she released her regional hit EP *Da Payback* as Mia X. "I was doing shows every single weekend all over Louisiana, Mississippi, and Texas," Mia remembers. Master P's brother Corey "C-Murder" Miller, a frequent shopper at Peaches, was aware of the buzz Mia was building. "I knew absolutely nothing about No Limit and Master P," she says definitively. "In fact, aside from his immediate family, I don't think anybody in New Orleans knew about Master P. Like, at all."

During a visit back home, Master P and C-Murder went to Peaches Records to formally meet Mia X. "It was my off day," she adds. "My coworker sent him to my house. He came to my house, we had a conversation. He told me that he was going to work really hard to make the world's biggest record label. You could see in his eyes the drive. You could hear in his voice that he meant what he said. I believed it." Master P already had a female rapper on his roster, Sonya C, who was actually his then wife, Sonya Miller. But she had put down the mic to start a family with P, so the spot for First Lady was open. "Master P came to New Orleans for a visit, but was also looking for a lady rapper," Mia explains. She was already a star on her turf, so Master P was the one who had to earn his stripes. "I remember [Master P] came down to come to one of the shows, and we actually had recorded 'Bout It,' and I had to tell the crowd, 'Wait! Be easy with him. Be cool. Be nice. I'm going to rock with his label, y'all,' because the people didn't know him, and they wasn't really feeling him." She had to vouch for P on his own turf.

In 1994, Mia X officially signed to No Limit Records. "When I first got to No Limit, P didn't have any in-house producers," she says. "He had a few artists that were signed to him from California. The label was very much in its infantile stages. We didn't even have an office back then. It was like, really, really grassroots." But the label had a distribution deal with LA's Priority Records, known for acts like N.W.A and Ice-T. By 1995, when Master P officially moved back to New Orleans, it was game on. Master P and his two brothers C-Murder and Vyshonne Miller, better known as Silkk the Shocker, formed the trio TRU (The Real Untouchables). TRU cut their third album, *True*, in 1995, led by the single "I'm Bout It, Bout It" with Mia X. The song was produced by Louisiana production team Beats by the Pound (now known as The Medicine Men). It was still very rooted in West Coast flavor, with the same prominent pitchy synths mastered by Dr. Dre and his team years prior ("We call it the 'funky worm sound' out the Minimoog [synthesizer]," Chris "The Glove" Taylor tells me). In the midst of the cross-regional madness was Mia X's game-changing verse:

> *The bitch you love to hate, but yet ain't bold enough to face*
> *'Cause Mia X will finish first in this grand diva race*

Without having ever set foot on California soil, Mia X dominated TRU's cut with her New Orleans vibe, mixing it with the West Coast gangster rap edge. She released her debut album, *Good Girl Gone Bad,* that same year. "My core fans bought *Good Girl Gone Bad,*" Mia says. "In fact, *Good Girl Gone Bad* sold the same amount of records as *Da Payback.* I knew that that was my immediate fans." No Limit's success after major label distribution was a slow burn that provided a sizable push for the whole roster once distribution really kicked in. No Limit Records was an army, adding more and more soldiers with every album's cover art decorated in the glittery adornments of Houston graphic design firm Pen & Pixel. Mia X had garnered success from her "Bout It" verse, but her 1997 follow-up would make an even bigger splash.

"I think the world was ready for me."

Unlady Like arrived on June 24, 1997. It hit the number two mark on the Billboard Top R&B/Hip-Hop Albums chart and number twenty-one on the Billboard 200. Certified gold with no singles, the project made a statement, as Mia X collaborated with Foxy Brown on "The Party Don't Stop" (with Master P), along with "I'll Take Ya Man" with Salt-N-Pepa and Hurby "Luv Bug" Azor. While the world was still spiraling over the war between Foxy Brown and Lil' Kim, Mia X was happily collaborating with other female rappers. She would lose her status as the only female on the No Limit lineup once R&B singer Mercedes joined the army, but her status as the bona fide boss lady remained intact. "My friends had always called me Mama Mia," she says. "They said I act like an old lady and I thought I was their mom. But they always came to me for advice; they came to me to hold their secrets. So, at No Limit, it was me and a bunch of guys. It was a must that I maintain order. But that was easy because they were all respectful, nice young men. But me having the mother role, it was just second nature. It was just who I was. I didn't have to search really hard for an image." She would remain firm on her brand, all the way into Master P's posse cut-slash-anthem "Make Em Say Uhh!" as she reminds everyone who's the biggest Mama Mia on the certified platinum track:

> Forget the baby boys, it's the biggest mama Mia
> The Unlady Like diva, lyrical maneater

She essentially checked her male counterparts on their same track. With gumption like that, success was inevitable. Mia was always decked out in power suits, sometimes in bright colors, but looked like an executive ready to fuck up a board meeting with punchlines. It took consistency in her brand and refusing to stray for Mama Mia to get the success she wanted.

The third time was the charm, as 1998's *Mama Drama* became Mia X's most successful album, hitting number three on the Billboard Top R&B/Hip-Hop Albums chart and number nine on the Billboard 200, anchored by the hit single "What'cha Wanna Do." When Snoop Dogg joined No Limit Records that year, following his unceremonious departure from Death Row, Mia X's role on the team became less and less defined. "I didn't really get the same opportunities as a woman," Mia X explains. "I don't think P really knew what to do with me, or my look." Master P was juggling a label that through time carried over eighty art- ists. The few female No Limit Artists, like Mercedes, were pack- aged as ever-popular vixens. On the cover of Mercedes's debut album, *Rear End,* she's sprawled across the front of her namesake (a Mercedes-Benz) "rear end" up.

Mia had a following, but was never a priority. "So, [P] just kind of put the records out and let me do what I do. I'm just thankful to have a core fan base. I think I could've had more videos, just like some of the other ladies that was out during the time when I was. I think I could've had more promotion. But I was his first female artist, and I think he was just feeling his way through. But like I said, I didn't have the same opportunities. The boys got way more promotion, and I just think that he was just trying to figure things out with me." Luckily, she ended her run at No Limit Records on the highest note possible.

"Aside from not getting all of the money that I was supposed to get, my overall experience in hip-hop was good," she says. "Ev- erybody I met, no matter what coast I was on, I felt love. I did some great collaborations."

Two decades following her departure from No Limit, Mia X is still actively performing. She's fought uterine cancer and has even released a part cookbook, part memoir titled *Things My Grandma Told Me, Things My Grandma Showed Me.* The No Limit tank may have stopped rolling, but she certainly hasn't.

"I wish I would've gotten an opportunity to do more, but my overall experience? I can't complain," she says fondly of her time at No Limit. "I got love everywhere."

Missy Elliott and Da Brat would like to have a word about hip-hop's cookie-cutter depiction of women.

Chapter Twelve

MURDERS AND MISDEMEANORS

I'M SCANNING RANDOM VIDEOS OF INTERVIEWS WITH MISSY Elliott on YouTube, as my best friend Maryum looks on, over FaceTime. The videos are from 1997, on the set of Missy's mind-bending music video for her solo debut single, "The Rain (Supa Dupa Fly)." In one video, Missy's smiling rather coyly in her large vinyl jumpsuit that resembled a trash bag that she wore in the music video for "The Rain." In another she's seated, wearing a white T-shirt and platinum chain and that same smile, waxing philo-sophical about how her debut album will be delivered on her own terms, as she vaguely goes into a discussion of her record deal with Epic Records. Looking at this footage now, over twenty years later, I'm kind of fascinated by her confidence and seasoned approach to record delivery, since back in 1997, us laypeople regarded Missy as a "new" artist. She was anything but new. Back then, it was more a matter of looking on like, "There's a woman who knows what she wants!" And while that's true, it's also because she had a whole other music industry past of *fighting* for what she wanted, unbeknownst to us all. Looking at these old videos now, it's unbelievable to see her smiling and talking about her big debut. Twenty years ago, it was the facade of gleeful naïveté, but now—after knowing what went down—that's the smile of redemption.

I close my laptop. Panic sets in.

"How the hell do I write about Missy Elliott?" I say to my best friend rather frantically. "There's just so much to talk about." Maryum has a rudimentary understanding of hip-hop, but regards Missy Elliott like she's her aunt or some other not-so-distant relative. Like most of Missy's core fan base, Maryum is a hip-hop-adjacent music fan with an emotional attachment to Missy. I'm trying to figure out why. Not why is Missy so dope—I already know that. But why is Missy so captivating to a pop crowd who casually stumbles into hip-hop for happy hour but doesn't necessary reside there?

Maryum pauses. "Well, I remember when Missy did 'Get Ur Freak On' and made that *bhangra* beat for it." She starts bopping her head like the song is playing. It isn't. My BFF is Pakistani and plays the *dholki* drum, so she can tell you every artist who's ever cut a pop record that remotely leaned on South Asian production. "After that, we had the DJ play Missy Elliott at all of our weddings. No one made *bhangra* a part of hip-hop until she did it." Thinking back on it, Maryum is kind of right.

Long Island legends Eric B. & Rakim first introduced a Middle Eastern sound to their music back in 1987, when they sampled Israeli artist Ofra Haza's "Im Nin'alu" for the Coldcut remix of their classic "Paid in Full." Yes, there is a big difference between the Middle East and the South Asian Bollywood craze musically and geographically. Keep in mind, though, that when hip-hop is merely chopping up samples for beats, the result is more the brand-new product formed from those samples than the actual music of the country where those samples originated. It was Missy Elliott who brought that sound to a major hip-hop release with her 2001 track "Get Ur Freak On," a primarily sample-free beat that she co-produced with her lifelong creative partner, Timbaland. From the start, the two always sought to grab the attention of their audience in the most extraterrestrial of ways.

The year was 1989 when Portsmouth, Virginia, native Missy Elliott (then known as Melissa Elliott) first formed the group Fayze with her best girlfriends and brought her pal Timbaland—born Timothy Mosley—along for the ride to make beats. The daughter of a US Marine father and dispatcher mother, Missy was a choir kid who all along wanted to be a singer. So much so, that it distracted her from her high school studies so she opted to start a group. That's when Fayze happened. Timbaland at the time was known as DJ Timmy Tim and was forging his own path just a half hour away in Virginia Beach. Since their respective local music scenes weren't too far away, the two learned about each other and forged a friendship that led to Timbaland holding the duty of Fayze's producer.

The group cut a record in 1991 called "First Move," to little action. In 1993 they were renamed Sista, thanks to Jodeci mastermind DeVante Swing, who signed the group to Swing Mob, his imprint at Elektra Records. DeVante's Swing Mob doubled as a creative collective, later known as Da Bassment Crew, where he gathered a posse of musical talent in an effort to harness their creativity and create big projects under the guise of teamwork. Members included Missy, Timbaland, rapper Magoo, singer Tweet (as part of a group named Sugah), famed recording engineer/producer Jimmy Douglass, singer Ginuwine, trio Playa (which included the late Static Major), and others. They all lived together in a compound for two years, songwriting and producing around the clock. Their main project was Jodeci's third album, *The Show, The After Party, The Hotel,* released in 1995, though the bulk of the writing credits would land on DeVante's résumé. Missy has one credit on the project—a cowriter listing on the album cut "S-More," while Timbaland is noted as a cowriter on "Bring on Da' Funk" and "Time & Place." The team was basically a squad of smoking guns, churning out tracks aggressively on a daily basis.

"DeVante had everybody kind of in a competitive mode," Jimmy Douglass remembers of the Swing Mob experience. "He'd do a beat and say, 'Y'all write. Y'all write. Y'all write,' and he'd pick the one that he thought was the best." Sometimes the writers would get together in clusters, where DeVante would do intermittent critiques as the songs were being written, demanding edits in the middle of the writing process. "One thing about Missy that I always noticed she would do was say, 'I can't do that. I need to finish my song first, and you can say whatever you wanna say, but I can't finish it with you telling me what to do.' She would refuse to do it unless she could go off by herself in the room and sit there and write her vision out. She was vehement about that. She would have it no other way, or else she wouldn't work."

With an upbringing like Missy Elliott's, she had no room for weakness or flimsy commands from those around her. In her 2011 episode of VH1's *Behind the Music,* Missy reveals an early life filled with sexual abuse (she was eight years old when her sixteen-year-old cousin began molesting her, which went on for nearly a year), poverty to the point of having no running water, and domestic violence so extreme that she saw her father pull a gun on her mother. These were just a few of the experiences Missy Elliott endured as a child, though that survival instinct and unending resilience are what made her firm in her creative stances and unabashed in her artistic risk-taking. She never feared hitting rock bottom; she had spent her childhood there. Music was her constant, the thing she held closest to her. No one could sway her on her vision for it.

Eventually she would break free from the Swing Mob in the interest of her own creative pursuits, along with the trauma of working under the thumb of DeVante. The setup has been loosely compared to a prison, in some accounts, a grueling schedule of forced creativity and constant demands to deliver. In Timbaland's 2016 memoir, *The Emperor of Sound,* he revealed that DeVante would keep the team locked in the Rochester, New York, compound for days on end with no food, often verbally abusing them, making them do outlandish tasks, and also screwing them out of their earned royalties for songwriting and production (evident, once again, on the Jodeci project liner notes). It was a torture that Missy refused to experience again. "She was one of the first to say, 'I don't wanna do this,' and left," Douglass explains. The other members eventually followed suit, but Missy went first and kept pushing forward on her own, networking, meeting people, and making moves. "I remember I'm coming back from Rochester with [Ginuwine's] 'Pony' in my hands, with no deal, no nothing," Douglass recalls. "The whole [collective] had fallen apart." Missy was strategic, leveraging her previous Swing Mob status to secure relationships with the likes of Puff Daddy and others. Puffy gave her a chance, bringing her in on some of his side projects like the 1996 Bad Boy remix of MC Lyte's "Cold Rock The Party" (off Lyte's fifth studio album, *Bad As I Wanna B*), on which Missy harmonizes on the hook. That version was ultimately released as the album's single, becoming Lyte's second-highest charting single in the United States (reaching number eleven on Billboard's Hot 100). That same year, Puffy added Missy to a track by R&B singer Gina Thompson called "The Things That You Do," which Puffy coproduced with Rodney Jerkins, better known to the world as Darkchild. These were two impactful opportunities for an artist like Missy, who literally networked her way right into the fold. No Swing, no Mob.

"I'm in my car in New York City and on the radio on Hot 97 they're playing this record," Douglass recall. It was the Bad Boy remix of "The Things That You Do," where Missy introduces herself with her now legendary "Hee-Hee-Hee-Hee-How" ad lib before launching into her rap.

"The radio people went, 'Whoa! What? Who is that?!'" he recalls. They played the song three times over, asking listeners to call in and identify the mystery woman.

Jimmy smirks and says, "I'm goin' in my head, 'That's fuckin' Missy . . .'"

By the middle of 1997, hip-hop was in a state of chaos. Tupac had been murdered in September 1996, Biggie in March 1997. Bookended between those two deaths was the uprising of rap's twin sexual dynamos, Lil' Kim and Foxy Brown. Everyone was scared of what the cards might hold for the genre, as it was just beginning to show a profitable return. The sad reality was that the aftershocks of the back-to-back tragic deaths gave rap sales a giant boost. Biggie's first posthumous project, *Life After Death*, dropped two weeks after his passing, and in its first week moved close to 700,000 units. The jump in album sales was significant from just the year prior. Take Snoop Dogg's follow-up, 1996's *Tha Doggfather*, which sold 420,000 copies in its opening week. After Biggie passed, something changed. Maybe the mainstream was rabidly consuming rap music, assuming that all the big names were going to leave them soon. After all, Pac and Biggie leaving consecutively was crazy. Whatever the motive, sales boomed, hip-hop grew even bigger, and the question became, "What now?" It was a lesson in both greed and prejudice, since rap music was now synonymous with inner city violence, and for suburbia, that violence was just so naughty and tempting. That was a short-lived fetish, however, so something had to come to hip-hop's rescue. Or someone.

Puff Daddy would save the rap industry from itself during that summer by releasing *No Way Out,* turning the "shiny suit" into a lifestyle, not just his music video clothing choice. He made hip-hop fun and flashy, transforming Biggie's violent death into a celebratory homage to a friend, in which the late rapper's presence can be felt throughout. Puffy put the safety back on hip-hop's gun. Now was the time to do *anything* you possibly could to distract the mainstream from its perception of rappers and the music they created before they were inevitably shot [*insert eye roll*]. This time period gave Missy Elliott carte blanche to do her thing. Considering how much Puffy diluted hip-hop music, Missy had the opportunity to insert a whole new artistic angle and elevate hip-hop. Puffy's packaging hip-hop for the mainstream was a hip-hop purist's nightmare, though the alternative was killing the culture from within. Literally. So Missy found a way to love the music and still love the new way to introduce it. A mad scientist in the studio, her concepts behind the scenes became her trademark. She was rebuilding the career of the late Aaliyah, who rather abruptly left the shelter of her mentor R. Kelly's wing after it was revealed that Kelly and Aaliyah had married when she was just fifteen years old (he was twenty-seven). Aaliyah was a sublime talent and needed a team that would nurture her properly in the wake of the post–R. Kelly media frenzy. Timbaland and Missy were that team. Aaliyah's follow-up album, *One in a Million,* dropped in 1996, giving the artist a brand-new sound and style that would completely transform her art. Missy wrote the bulk of the project with Timbaland, while Timbaland also produced most of the project. Aaliyah's album was quietly giving the industry a glimpse of what Missy had in store with her own music, but they just didn't know it yet. Neither did Missy.

Missy and Timbaland created a unified force when it was advantageous to do so. With the hip-hop industry shifting gears and turning more toward the mainstream, someone had to shake things up and bring an abstract presence into the mix. Initially, however, Missy wasn't sure she'd be the one—at least not as a solo artist. Bad Boy tried to sign her, but she ended up with growing industry maven Sylvia Rhone over at Elektra, since Missy wanted to be more than just a cog in the label machine. Missy leveraged her own imprint, The Goldmind, in the deal, where she could cultivate her own talent. This was a massive move during that time, since a woman running her own mini ship under a conglomerate (also run by a woman) was a rarity. CEO Sylvia Rhone and senior vice president of A&R Merlin Bobb put their faith in Missy as her own executive based on her previous track record behind the scenes, though it soon became clear that she needed her own album. Sylvia Rhone pushed, but Missy was less enthused to bring her own work to the forefront. She had spent years in the background, the dark horse behind so many success stories, having worked with everyone from Busta Rhymes to Mariah Carey and R&B trios 702 and Sisters With Voices (SWV). Could she really write her own album, with herself as the leading lady? But the bigger a force Aaliyah became, the more Missy realized her talents could be used on her own work.

By the time Missy dropped her solo debut single, "The Rain (Supa Dupa Fly)" that spring, her reputation had already long been established as a quadruple threat: singer, songwriter, producer, and rapper. Sampling the Memphis soul of Ann Peebles's "I Can't Stand the Rain," Missy introduced a new standard of hip-hop that delved into the abstract, experimenting with rhyming patterns and sounds (that mainly came from Missy's own mouth, with a side of Timbaland). The Hype Williams–directed music video showed the world through a fisheye lens, with Missy donning everything from oversize overalls to a large trash bag–like inflated jumpsuit that would alter its shape with every dance move she made. The cameos in the video were a testament to the friendships Missy had made throughout her tenure in the industry, who now supported her solo artist status. This included Timbaland, of course (still her friend and co-conspirator, with his own growing track record), but also Bad Boy's Total, 702, Lil' Cease, Puff Daddy, and Taj from SWV. There was also a range of female rappers present in the video, including Lil' Kim, Da Brat, and Yo-Yo. Missy was a movement in herself, and the whole world took notice. The song catapulted onto the radio, peaking at number six on the Billboard Hot R&B/ Hip-Hop Songs chart, though it only reached number fifty-one on the Billboard Hot 100. The weak rating was due to the fact that in the summer of 1997, record labels ditched physical singles, so units were measured by the sale of an entire album. Billboard therefore couldn't tally those singles effectively. The rules would be rewritten in 1998, but this would perhaps be the last time Missy lost out to a glitch in the matrix. Still, the single set a tone for the kind of artist we were about to experience: hip-hop's Andy Warhol, who tweaked and twisted the norm and introduced us all to a bizarro world with a whole new audio/visual experience.

"You never got bored with what she did," Douglass remembers. "It was always cutting-edge, interesting, and fresh." It also cut through the middle of the current trend of prominent female rappers using sexuality to shock. Missy was equally shocking, though her aesthetic was dramatically different from theirs. Still beautiful, still art, but refreshingly individual. She and Lauryn Hill became the polite antithesis to their peers. "When Lauryn came out, I was like, 'You know, from my money, between you and Missy, you both have extraordinary talents right now that you're delivering to your audience, and you're both needed in your own unique ways,'" Douglass recalls. "'You're both running a dead heat to me.'"

Missy recorded her album in a week's time. "Missy could write four to five jams a day, easily," says Douglass. With a nickname like "Misdemeanor," she was stealing her own lane in hip-hop. Her platinum debut album, *Supa Dupa Fly*, landed at number one on the Billboard Top R&B/Hip-Hop Albums chart and number three on the Billboard 200, and was nominated for a Grammy for the Best Rap Album the following year. *Supa Dupa Fly* was full of throwbacks to the past, while simultaneously thrusting us into the future. Timbaland's production was heavily electronic, though it had this groove element to it that was reminiscent of decades past. This made the project timeless in its own right, and it was all thanks to Missy's creative direction. She did it all on her terms, even collaborating with her theoretical competition (Lil' Kim on "Hit 'Em Wit Da Hee" and Da Brat on "Sock It 2 Me"). Everyone loved Missy Elliott, and with good reason. Steve Huey of AllMusic said *Supa Dupa Fly* was "arguably the most influential album ever released by a female hip-hop artist," and "a boundary-shattering postmodern masterpiece" that "had a tremendous impact on hip-hop, and an even bigger one on R&B, as its futuristic, nearly experimental style became the de facto sound of urban radio at the close of the millennium." Most rappers were making music to ride around to in their expensive cars. Missy was traveling in a spaceship.

"The radio is stuck right now," she told MTV in 1997. "Everything sounds the same. As far as video-wise, everything looks the same. So, we feel like we're coming in, and we're gonna change the whole thing." That's exactly what she did.

Chapter Thirteen

SAVED BY THE BELL

THIS IS CRAZY, 'CAUSE THIS IS HIP-HOP MUSIC," LAURYN HILL said in amazement as she stood on stage at the 41st Grammy Awards in 1999, accepting the award for Album of the Year for *The Miseducation of Lauryn Hill*.

Lauryn knew all too well that she had just made history but still wanted to remind everyone who she was and what she represented. Before her solo debut opus, no hip-hop artist had ever taken home that honor. The whole project was a series of firsts.

In 1996, as The Fugees were wrapping up the summer leg of their tour for *The Score*, Lauryn Hill was disgruntled. This began to show toward the end of their tour, especially during the (what was once) playful battle between Lauryn and Wyclef onstage, where they would take light R&B songs and reword them into these jokey little wisecracks aimed toward each other. "There was a point in maybe the last two weeks where we discussed as a band: 'I don't think they're playing. I think they are serious right now,'" Questlove remembers. "It was tension. I only say that because it was one of the nights where the freestyle didn't hit the way that it normally does. I think we were in Houston and she did this whole thing over Faith Evans's 'Soon As I Get Home.'" The real song is this flirtatiously romantic track about getting a lover back, as the hook says, "Soon as I get home, I'll make it up to you / Baby, I'll do what I gotta do." Wyclef and Lauryn would reword it to say they'll write rhymes for each other. This night, that rhyme-writing sounded hostile. "'I'mma write some rhymes for you, 'cause that freestyle was wack . . .'" Questlove recites Lauryn's freestyle with a laugh. "I just had this feeling . . . it wasn't for show." Never mind the fact that her relationship with Wyclef had come to a dramatic close, he was also releasing a solo album before she was. In an interview with *Rolling Stone* in 2008, Hill's former manager Jayson Jackson recalls a phone call from Lauryn during that '96 tour.

"I can't believe these muthafuckers," she told him about her parent label, Columbia Records. "I've been talking about making my solo record for the longest and they're doing everybody's solo record but mine! I'm leaving the group, I've had it." Even when she managed to escape her romantic ties to Wyclef (she started dating Rohan Marley, the son of the late reggae legend Bob Marley, around this same time) creatively speaking, Clef was still getting the upper hand. Even Pras was readying *Ghetto Superstar,* so if Wyclef's Achilles' heel was the "girl going solo," why was Lauryn the last Fugee to do it? Within months, Lauryn would become pregnant with Rohan Marley's child and Wyclef would begin recording *The Carnival.* Lauryn appeared on five of the tracks on Wyclef's album, and soon after its June 1997 release, he was publicly discussing his part in Lauryn Hill's solo project. Now that he had successfully finished his album, he could move on to hers. Or so he thought. "I did bring up the fact that Wyclef was saying that he was going to produce her album," says Michael Gonzales, who penned the September 1998 cover story on Lauryn for *The Source*. "And she thought that was kind of funny and actually started laughing." Wyclef wouldn't touch this project.

"I don't wanna fuck with them, I just wanna get a whole new crew," was what Lauryn told Jackson when he suggested she contact Donnie Ienner, who was the chairman of Sony Music at the time, the bigger corporate umbrella over Columbia Records. That "new crew" would ultimately leave out Wyclef and Pras entirely. Lauryn assembled a team of young creatives, and she named it New Ark. The roster consisted of Vada Nobles, Rasheem Pugh, and twin brothers Johari Newton and Tejumold Newton. Other musicians entered the fold, like current Roots member James Poyser, who solidified his working relationship with Lauryn when he produced "Retrospect for Life" (with No I.D.) on Common's *One Day It'll All Make Sense* in 1997. Longtime affiliate Commissioner Gordon was brought on as an engineer, plus a young piano-playing UPenn student named John Stephens (later known as John Legend) and Che Vicious (then known as producer Che Guevara). "One of the things that she said to me was that she had the blueprint for *Miseducation* in her head for a long time," Gonzales says. "She knew exactly what she wanted to do." Lauryn had a goal in mind for a certain kind of vibe, where even her instruments would be tuned slightly off-key to add a different texture to the sound. Her aim was to make organically soulful pop music. It was all part of her plan for the Lauryn Hill solo launch.

"With Lauryn, there was immediate talk of a solo record once *The Score* sold twenty million albums," says author Thembisa Mshaka, who was senior advertising copywriter at Sony Music during the *Miseducation* era. "She had full label support to create an album. They supported her recording process from top to bottom."

Lauryn traveled to Miami, Jamaica, and New York City to piece the project together with her new team. She hit the world-renowned Tuff Gong Studios in Kingston, which birthed Bob Marley's most prolific work, as well as Chung King in New York City. "You can't just run off and do that, you need label support and you need label transparency," Mshaka explains. "The issue wasn't letting her do what she wanted to do," she adds. The label was very willing to let Lauryn rock, but the biggest question was, what would a Lauryn Hill record sound like without Wyclef? "They just didn't know what they were going to get." They knew Lauryn was a star, but there was still a buried distrust in her ability to flex on her own without her male counterpart. Oh, ye of little faith.

What they received was a cross-cultural work of art, an audio memoir of Hill's recent life. This time she strummed her own pain with her own fingers, discussing a then unidentified heartbreak (later learned to be Wyclef), the decision to have a child when everyone around her suggested otherwise, all the peaks and valleys of success, the highs and lows that come with being a Black woman in her early twenties experiencing life. It was soul music, it was hip-hop, it was authentic. But the label had an agenda for their female star that conflicted with Lauryn's vision. "When they got the album, the issue wasn't so much that it was a mixture of hip-hop and R&B," Mshaka adds. "It was that they wanted to lead with something like 'Killing Me Softly,' which had blown up for *The Score*." Having her own plan was a greater shock than it was a gift.

"The buzz on the album in the building wasn't as popular as you might think," Columbia Records A&R Rich Nice told Mshaka in a 2018 interview for *Okayplayer*. "And her being a Black woman added touchiness to it. There was a 'who does she think she is' in the building. The climate from some senior execs was that they were not in favor of the record." When she presented some spoiler tracks to the label bigwigs in a meeting, they pooh-poohed it. In their eyes, it was an "experimental" project, and they wanted nothing to do with that. They wanted an R&B album from their crowned R&B singer and pulled no punches in expressing that fact.

Lauryn left that meeting in tears.

For the label, Lauryn's skill-set was singer first, rapper second, yet in her heart it was the opposite. Hip-hop was Lauryn Hill's pedigree. She had spent years at that point as a lyricist, working to earn a spot on the top MC lists that most males dominated. Now, with her first solo album, she wanted to blend her ability to sing with her indomitable ability to rhyme. "But because she had so much pop success with the records where she was doing a lot of the vocal heavy lifting, Columbia wanted to continue in that vein to start off her album. They wanted to market and promote her the same way they would Mariah Carey. They wanted a pop star," Mshaka says. "There was that tension in the building between the A&R team and the record company. As a result of that, there were forces afoot to leak 'Lost Ones' and force the label's hand." Columbia didn't want Lauryn's introduction to the world as a solo artist to begin with rap, but she did. Someone from her camp (who prefers to remain nameless) leaked the audio file to DJs so that it reached the radio faster than the label could control, thereby making her post-Fugees return all about hip-hop.

And that's exactly what it did.

"Lost Ones" was leaked onto the streets, much to the chagrin of the label and in the face of their strategy. With that, it was clear that Lauryn Hill was not playing any games. The song is a diss track at its core, though it is also a womanifesto, and a declaration of independence for L-Boogie. The pieces of the puzzle of her recent life, and displays of anger, started falling into place: she was talking about Wyclef. By this point, still, it felt like she was describing creative differences. Money got in the way, as did Clef's desire to be the main attraction. The song was full of energy and anger. Lauryn was charged up. When "Lost Ones" hit radio, it was the kind of track that the DJ played three times in a row. The label had no choice but to acquiesce, making her official single "Doo Wop (That Thing)," another song that was rapped, yet with a sung hook.

Lauryn knew she had a hit album, even when the label had yet to realize it. "She was really excited about the album. I don't think she was that happy ever again," says Gonzales. "Even though she had all this success with The Fugees, this was something she was doing on her own." The most disheartening aspect of the pre-*Miseducation* rollout was the label's distrust in what Lauryn Hill could accomplish as a solo hip-hop artist. Was she underestimated because she was a woman? And more specifically, a Black woman? Probably, especially when their eyes were on the presumed bigger prize of rehashing the "Killing Me Softly" business model as if it were the only tool of her trade, especially when Hollywood was knocking on her door—at the time courting her for the lead role in *Dreamgirls*. There was so much more in store for Lauryn Hill, yet Columbia had no idea.

The Miseducation of Lauryn Hill arrived on August 25, 1998. It swiftly landed at the number one spot on the Billboard 200 and broke a record for the highest number of first-week sales for a female artist, with 422,624 units sold. Lauryn Hill became a pop music darling without having to compromise her mission to create an honest work that reflected all sides of her musical persona. By then Lauryn was pregnant with her second child with Rohan Marley. And recording part of the album at Marley's Tuff Gong Studio gave Lauryn an almost built-in legacy, an extension of the Marley clan.

Decorated with school themes, right down to the Ras Baraka–

assisted interludes and school desk/chalkboard album art, the whole project was a learning experience. "Lost Ones" already set the hip-hop tone, though the number one single "Doo Wop (That Thing)" showed just how far Lauryn could go when it came to blending various eras of music. "Everything Is Everything" was another giant (with John Legend on the keys), a track where Lauryn Hill managed to successfully show both her singing and rhyming chops. There were religious undertones scattered throughout, too, as songs like "To Zion," "Final Hour," "Forgive Them Father," and "Tell Him" are all heavily biblical. Her cover of Frankie Valli's "Can't Take My Eyes Off You" found its way onto the album, despite being originally recorded for the *Conspiracy Theory* soundtrack. It did provide added mainstream appeal to a wider audience who didn't come for the rhymes, though they stayed for them. The project has a beginning, a middle, and an end—Lauryn starts off on an angry note, but travels through a range of human emotions and lands on peaceful self-discovery.

"There's just something that women can do in music and stories that men just can't," Rapsody explains. "That's what Lauryn showed me."

The Miseducation of Lauryn Hill touched on subjects that were hardly part of the hip-hop vocabulary before the album's existence, yet flooded it after. Emotions, heartache, questioning self-identity. These were all concepts that a young Black woman was experiencing at twenty-three and inserting into her art. Remember, her peers were writing graphic rhymes about sex.

But Lauryn Hill experienced her own fair share of sexism and claims that her morals potentially didn't match her music. When it was revealed that she had previously been in a relationship with Wyclef, it was also correctly assumed that the relationship had taken place while he was still married to Marie Claudinette. Then she had two children with Rohan Marley, to whom she was presumably not married. She was taken to task for her November 1998 cover story with *Details* magazine, for which she appears on the cover painted in gold and wearing red hot pants and a tiny tank top. "But Hill, the rhapsodic Christian proselytizer, is not everybody's idea of a black female role model," writes Debra Dickerson in a critique of Lauryn Hill for *Salon* in 1999. "For one thing, she often dresses hoochie-style. Worse, she has two out-of-wedlock children with her live-in boyfriend, Rohan Marley (one of Bob's many children). Hill may embody the best of young black womanhood to some people, but to others she's just a hypocrite, or worse, a danger to the community's endangered morals with her hip-hop halo." Referring to her clothing choices as "hoochie-style" was a dramatic exaggeration, though despite being beloved, Lauryn Hill posed a threat to the stark lines that divided women in hip-hop. You couldn't exude sexuality if your goal was to deliver a message. Hill straddled a line when most chose sides, and while she was the first (and the last) to do it so effectively, she was not without her fair share of haters—both male and female, unfortunately—along the way.

Still, there was something different about her industry fairy tale that separated her from other hip-hop artists. Lauryn Hill wasn't just a hip-hop superstar—she was a global icon. Her fame touched territories rappers had never entered before. "That *TIME* magazine cover she got," Questlove says, "that made a difference." The moment had him cheering "the way Robert De Niro did in *Goodfellas* when Joe Pesci became a made man." One of real hip-hop's own had graduated to the proverbial next level. "[The Roots] benefitted from the domino effect of that *TIME* cover," Questlove adds. "All of a sudden, non-hip-hop people were like, 'I read that Lauryn Hill cover and now I'm into you guys.' I just think that for the greater good, she was such a key component to the movement really meaning something. Especially right on the cusp of the Internet."

As fast as *Miseducation* dropped, Hill was slapped with a lawsuit from the New Ark team she had assembled to help craft it. On November 19, 1998, Vada Nobles, Rasheem Pugh, Johari Newton, and Tejumold Newton filed a lawsuit against her, claiming that they had a heavy hand in the songwriting, production, and arrangement of the album, while the back of the album's packaging makes it a point to highlight that this was a one-woman operation. The plaintiffs in the lawsuit claimed that Lauryn only gave them an oral contract in the form of a prayer huddle, though once they saw just how great the project was, they wanted bigger recognition for their contributions.

"This is the thing that has always stuck in my craw: this idea that because the producers on this record sued her about *Miseducation,* it somehow diminished her level of being the creator and the conceiver of this idea of *Miseducation,*" Mshaka says. "She definitely had a very focused and specific idea of what she did and didn't want, and in her mind these people were being commissioned and hired . . . and *paid* to do that work. They did that all on a handshake or whatever, and none of that is Lauryn's fault." Lauryn had an established history as a producer, having coproduced every song off *The Score*. She also wrote/produced "A Rose Is Still a Rose" for Aretha Franklin, later composing/producing "All That I Can Say" for Mary J. Blige. Hill even directed the video for Common's "Retrospect for Life." The lawsuit denied her versatility completely. The biggest blow was the outrage that Lauryn Hill had a whole team behind her while she was the face, as if male stars haven't been doing the same thing for years.

"Michael Jackson had a team, Prince had a team," Questlove expresses. "People don't even know that Stevie Wonder probably only wrote thirty percent of his lyrics. Gary Byrd and [Stevie's] ex-wife Syreeta [Wright] wrote a majority of the lyrics. Stevie was music." There was a naïveté to Lauryn Hill's creative process that landed her in the hot water. "I think part of me just wishes that she knew how business was conducted," Questlove continues. "Yes, I agree that you should have a business arrangement with your team so that there's a complete understanding. Part of our elation with Prince's work is the fact that, 'Wow, he's a child prodigy! Arranged, conceived by Prince!' That's just a press angle. Prince had mad help. On paper it looks good; guy's a genius. He does everything himself. Had [Lauryn Hill] simply explained that and had arrangements, I'm sure that shit would have been smooth sailing."

Unfortunately, it wasn't smooth sailing. "If you're an up-and-coming production crew looking to get on with a twenty-million-selling recording artist who is now going solo, you should be protecting yourself," Mshaka says. "They got stars in their eyes, and they thought it was all love and incense and daps and peace and whatever. Then when the record blew up, they came back feeling like they had been wronged."

Lauryn Hill's response to New Ark was that they were looking to capitalize on her monumental success as if it were their own. "I don't consider what she did was as scandalous as the press or the world made it out to be or as maybe she made it out to be in her head," Questlove adds. "That's how music is made." By February 2001, the lawsuit had been settled out of court to the tune of $5 million. The album still lives on in infamy. Lauryn Hill broke a record for receiving the most Grammy nominations by a woman at the 41st Grammy Awards, with ten nominations. She set a record that same evening by taking home five awards, the highest number of Grammy wins by a single artist in one ceremony at the time. Those are just a few of the accolades, coupled with a world tour that consistently proved Lauryn Hill had earned her place as the household name she is today.

Yet there was no follow-up.

"It almost feels as though maybe there's a shame factor that prevents her from coming out," Questlove says.

Perhaps the greatest miseducation of Lauryn Hill is that she thinks the world still cares that a team helped her create her classic album, when really all the world wants is another one.

Lauryn Hill, singing our lives with her words.

ABSENTEE BALLADS

I knew that when writing this book, this part of my favorite artist's career would be the hardest subject to broach: the absence of Ms. Lauryn Hill.

It was the spring of 2001, and the *Essence* Awards were scheduled to air, featuring a surprise performance by Lauryn Hill, her first since vanishing in 1999 after sweeping the Grammy Awards and embarking on a lengthy world tour to promote *The Miseducation of Lauryn Hill*. It was a pleasant tidal wave of exposure for the New Jersey queen, especially in the eyes of someone like me, who hadn't been able to get enough of her ever since Rita Watson first ripped apart that playground cypher in *Sister Act 2*.

Lauryn Hill sat onstage at the *Essence* Awards looking broken. She was wearing a denim jacket and long skirt. Her head had been shaved. A Rastafarian friend of mine once told me that when you shave off your dreadlocks, you've either been through something extremely difficult or extremely great. I knew in my heart it was the former. I had been deep in the music industry for two years and had heard the rumors: Rohan was cheating with her personal assistant (who also happened to be a relative of Lauryn's). The whole family knew, except Lauryn. She exiled herself within the same house as everyone, sequestering herself in a back room. This could be (and probably is) all hearsay, though if you ask anyone tangentially close to the nucleus, this is what they will tell you, almost verbatim. She was blindsided. Allegedly Rohan was also married to someone else, unbeknownst to Lauryn. It was the Wyclef situation all over again. How could the two loves of her life damage her in succession? Whatever truly happened behind closed doors doesn't matter much. She sat on that stage, cradling an acoustic guitar and wailing her heart out.

I remember an old video from The Fugees' promotional package for *The Score* showing Lauryn sitting with a guitar, strumming those same couple of chords. Years later, that video became fodder for guitar enthusiasts, who would often mock her amateur strumming skills. In the promo video, she joked about how Wyclef was teaching her how to play the guitar, but he was the worst teacher. If he spotted fingernails on her hands, he would bite them off. I remember thinking that was a little creepy, but after learning that the two had a clandestine relationship, I guess it was something of a playful gesture. I guess. I often wondered if, during that post-Wyclef, Rohan-pain-causing era, she would play those chords and think of a happier time, possibly the last time she had been so happy. The story goes that during the recording of *The Score,* Wyclef broke up with Lauryn. A fight happened during the recording of "Ready or Not" and Lauryn burst into tears while singing the hook. I always knew it sounded a little too passionate, especially in a song where she uses the word *defecating*. Apparently Pras still can't even listen to that song because of the visual that's forever painted in his mind.

Once again, here she is, on that *Essence* Awards stage, covered in invisible bruises from back-to-back battles with love. She's singing the biblically infused "Adam Lives in Theory," a song rich in hidden meanings. Many extend the biblical metaphors to mean that Lauryn is Eve and Rohan is Adam. Or is Wyclef Adam? Is Rohan the apple? Are Rohan and Wyclef both Eve and their mistresses the apple? Who knows. There's a line where Lauryn sings:

> *Drifting from the way, she got turned down one day*
> *And now she thinks that she's bisexual*

Some might say Lauryn swore off men, but it could be perceived as this: If you're kissing the lips of a man who has kissed another woman, are you kissing that woman, too? This is a song that Genius.com has attempted to decode, but there will never be a successful breakdown until Lauryn herself gives us one. Following that awards show, Lauryn was scheduled to perform in Brooklyn at the African Arts Festival. I had to see it for myself.

July 5, 2001. Lauryn arrives onstage at the festival. She has a sheet of paper in her back pocket with lyrics scribbled on it. She told all of us in the crowd that the words hit her at random times (this I already knew from *Miseducation* interviews). Some of these lyrics came to her in the shower. She credits God as her true composer. She performed about six songs, and she cried. So did I. In hindsight, as a grown adult, I now realize something. Lauryn Hill was only twenty-six years old in that moment, baring her soul for an audience just wondering where the hell she's been for the last few years. She was only twenty-three when *The Miseducation of Lauryn Hill* debuted, which means she was only twenty when *The Score* came out (she turned twenty-one that May). As I write this book, her eldest children, Zion and Selah Marley, are almost the same age their mother was when she first entered the eye of the music industry hurricane. She was the age of many present-day SoundCloud rappers, who we collectively call confused little children with no real understanding of who they truly are, or of the industry and fan base that envelop them. But we canonized Lauryn Hill and made her our hero, only to desert her once she deflated our idyllic image of her.

> *They hail you, then they nail you, no matter who you are.*
> —"Superstar," *The Miseducation of Lauryn Hill*

I went backstage that day. I had heard a rumor that she was bound for Italy, so I brought her a map of Vatican City. Two years later, she would condemn the pope and all the priests within those Vatican walls, so the running joke is that I gave her the directions on how to get there. She was beyond pleasant, and the shape of her face only changed when Rohan approached her to escort her into a Range Rover. Then she was gone.

When her *MTV Unplugged* episode first aired, everyone was rattled. We were coming off 9/11, and due to the political undertones of her new music, MTV thought it would be disrespectful to immediately air the special (she recorded it around the same time as that Brooklyn performance). We all saw it. She wept, we wept (well, at least I did). Her voice was gone, sounding like it was stretched beyond its limits and ready to snap.

Almost ten years later, when I interviewed superproducer Salaam Remi for an unreleased Lauryn Hill cover story for *The Source,* I asked about that night. "The night before *Unplugged* was recorded, she went to soundcheck," he recalled. "She came by my studio in Manhattan; Nas was there with me. We were sitting out talking till pretty late, and she had a guitar and was playing and singing songs. Hence why she's hoarse on the *Unplugged* recording, because she was up in the studio the night before with Nas and me—playing her songs and singing and letting me hear what she'd been writing."

So, her voice wasn't gone in the sense that she'd lost her touch—which is what most assumed. She was just out of practice, not constantly using her instrument. Maybe it was slightly bruised. I remember learning that when a woman is pregnant, her voice changes. Lauryn recorded *The Miseducation of Lauryn* when she was pregnant with Zion. Described by vocal coaches as a contralto, Lauryn almost hit whistle tones during the *Miseducation* recording process (listen to the runs at the end of "To Zion"). The pregnancy hormones might've helped with that. Later on, she revealed in a video interview during the Tokyo leg of her Miseducation World Tour that she would keep a scarf around her neck, sip tea, and avoid talking in between performances to preserve her voice. If the hormones were gone, then maybe those notes were too, which could also explain why she went so hoarse, so fast during the *Unplugged* performance. In 2002, *Entertainment Weekly*'s David Browne reviewed the performance and referred to her vocals as "raspy and cracking with emotion." He further poses this dilemma, which fans were facing as they watched her sing in pain: "Hill puts her audience in an uncomfortable position: Are we supposed to feel we contributed to her crisis by buying so many copies of *Miseducation*?" It's like we all let her down.

Following the turn of the century, we lost Lauryn Hill. In her place we got Ms. Hill. Many would turn their noses up at that new formality, yet when white feminists refer to themselves as "Ms.," it's perfectly fine, even seen as an act of power. If there were any small example of just how unfairly Black women are scrutinized, placed under a microscope, it's this one. I remember referring to her as "Lauryn" in an interview with Rohan about his coffee company. He said to me, "You're brave. Even I call her Ms. Hill." I remember thinking, *I'm sure you do.*

I won't rehash the disorganized performances, that religious figure in her life named Brother Anthony (mainly because I still have no idea who he is), and even now the streak of tardiness that's left her a punchline of memes. I recall waiting two hours for male rappers to perform, and there isn't a meme to be found about them. Once again, Black women.

In 2004, The Fugees briefly reunited for *Dave Chappelle's Block Party,* which was released as a film a year later. The Fugees attempted to return with some music, releasing the sloppy "Take It Easy" track along with some rough cuts, including a song where Lauryn interpolates the hook to the Jackson 5's "I Wanna Be Where You Are." That latter cut was the closest to "Lauryn-sounding" that we had heard from her in years, but the chemistry was gone, and the project never released. In 2005, she collaborated with DJ J.Period on his mixtape tribute *Best of Lauryn Hill: Fire & Water,* and appeared on some deep cuts and remixes from artists like Nas and John Legend.

Lauryn unfortunately went to prison in 2013 for failure to pay taxes. She's since returned to the spotlight here and there, most recently for the twentieth anniversary of *The Miseducation of Lauryn Hill* tour dates.

Most will point to the now revealed relationship with Wyclef as the cause of Lauryn Hill's downward spiral, since it's the only piece of evidence they have to work with if they're not behind the scenes to hear the other gory details. Others will see the dramatic makeup, the baggy clothing, the excessively late set times as indications that she's unhinged, crazy even, with a level of narcissism that enables her to scoff at anyone for questioning her decisions. Fans who still show up for the performances are equally held responsible. It's not fan loyalty; it's enabling an artist that the industry has now decided should be neutralized. Why is it so much fun to attack and belittle a woman who at one point was held in the highest regard? Is it because the world loves to be proven right, that no woman can sit at the top and remain there without having some sort of breakdown? They hail you, then they nail you.

Sometimes I think about what music would have been like had she never left. Here was a woman who sat at the top of people's top five rappers lists. She was the most pleasantly confusing phenomenon. Artists like Drake—who combine singing with rapping—rarely namecheck Hill as one of the main reasons they have a career. Though when Drake sampled Lauryn Hill for his song "Nice For What," she reminded everyone in a freestyle over Drake's beat:

> He took the sample, my shit is classic
> Here's an example

When I interviewed Nicki Minaj in 2010 (for that same unreleased cover story), however, she credited Lauryn Hill as the godmother of her singing-slash-rapping style. "She was a big part of the reason why I started wanting to incorporate singing into my music," Nicki said of Lauryn. "I felt confident that if Lauryn could write her own material, rap and sing, and hold her own with the boys, then so could I. She's just a shining example that, as a woman, you can have your cake and eat it too. And she's beautiful at the same time. I mean, it just gave me confidence." In 2016, Nicki fell to her knees and bowed at Lauryn Hill's feet when she met her.

There isn't a lack of music, either. It's sitting in a vault somewhere; some of it lives on Salaam Remi's hard drive. Questlove has heard it. "There's an album's worth of amazing shit," he says. "I know she still has the goods."

Respect must be paid to female rappers like Queen Latifah who did the singing/rhyming on record first, but Lauryn Hill perfected that combination, and I'm sure even Latifah would agree. It's one of those situations where you have to ask yourself if lightning can strike twice when it's locked away in a bottle with the cap tightly shut. Who really knows. I asked Salaam Remi if he thought Lauryn Hill would return one day and bring us the new music we've wanted from her since she abruptly vanished in 2001.

He replied, "Only one person can answer that."

Chapter Fourteen

THE COME UP

DIGGA DIGGA!" THE WORDS BOUNCE OFF THE HALF-OPEN CAR window of a Ford Taurus as it whips right past Rah Digga and me while we're standing on the curb of a busy city street. The drive-by fan is referencing the opener to Rah Digga's verse on Flipmode Squad's posse cut "Cha Cha Cha," where Rashia Fisher introduces herself by her nom de plume: "Digga Digga! First name Rashia / Sweetest person, had no idea." Her reputation precedes itself. As a seasoned battle rapper from New Jersey who also appeared on The Fugees' *The Score*, Digga showed she had promise for the mainstream. That, and a resemblance to a familiar face.

"Sylvia Rhone signed me because she said I kind of looked like Lauryn," Rah Digga says with a laugh.

The desire for a crew's First Lady kept growing, and by '98 Rah Digga had drifted beyond Outsidaz and aligned with Busta Rhymes's Flipmode Squad.

But in 1997, Rah Digga was in panic mode. She and her Out-sidaz groupmate Young Zee had a baby on the way, so a substantial income was needed. Pronto. During one of Zee's studio sessions, Q-Tip was there assisting on a remix. A very pregnant Rah Digga was sitting in the nonsmoking section. "I just turned to Tip, and was like, 'Yo, I got like thirty days to get a record deal before I have this baby,'" she remembers. "And he's like, 'I'll sign you!'" She and Q-Tip had already forged a relationship, since Rah was working the Lyricist Lounge circuit, hosting showcases and performing. Eight months pregnant, Rah Digga was taken to Elektra, where she met with Rhone for all of five minutes before getting her deal. "Her exact words were, 'I was just telling Q-Tip that we need some fresh blood up here,'" Rah says of Rhone. "Because at the time, Yo-Yo and MC Lyte were the girls on the label." Her participation on *The Score* (Rhone referred to her as "The girl from the 'Cowboys' video") coupled with her favoring Lauryn physically was enough of a push to get the deal going faster than she had imagined. It might have been a much slower process had Rhone realized she was pregnant.

"I did find out that after the meeting, they were like, 'Oh, we didn't know she was pregnant,'" she remembers. "I didn't gain any weight my second trimester, and my third trimester, I was just getting belly, but like, curvy with a belly." The late-stage blossoming of her pregnancy proved to her advantage. "I think they felt better once they realized I was eight months. I think they were probably looking to put me right to work or maybe they weren't sure if a baby could possibly slow things down. I don't know."

The album-recording process went into motion, but in February 1998, a fire swept through Q-Tip's home studio and destroyed most of A Tribe Called Quest's catalog. He had a lot going on in there. "And here I go like, 'Hey, when is my album coming out?'" Rah says. It was one of a few problems they encountered. "I think we had creative differences as well, which is funny because I kind of consider myself a Native Tounge-r," Rah adds, a nod to the Native Tongues collective that included groups like A Tribe Called Quest and De La Soul, along with Monie Love and Queen Latifah. "Q-Tip was my favorite producer at the time, but I just couldn't . . . fit. Musically, we just couldn't click. There was no track that he was coming up with that I felt was runnin' enough for me," Rah recalls. Q-Tip had spoken with his longtime friend Busta Rhymes about Rah Digga. Busta was formerly a part of the group Leaders of the New School, who joined A Tribe Called Quest on their classic single "Scenario."

Q-Tip trusted Busta. "I just think eventually he had a conversation with Busta like, 'This girl is awesome. I have no idea what to do with her, and she drives me crazy,'" Rah says. Busta invited her to studio sessions, but she started getting antsy. Busta was also an Elektra artist with his own imprint, Flipmode Entertainment. "So now I'm breathing down his neck," she says, though all the hustling paid off. "He took a liking to me, so it worked out because I didn't have to lose my record deal."

Her debut as part of Flipmode Squad finally came with the release of 1998's *The Imperial*, as Busta Rhymes unveiled his new regime—Rah Digga, Rampage, Baby Sham, Lord Have Mercy, and Spliff Star. Rah Digga was the ideal First Lady for this crew: her energy matched Busta's, and she was trained in the battleground so her lyrical dexterity was second to none.

The hot pursuit for First Ladies was still happening from coast to coast. Missy Elliott was now both a seasoned artist and executive, and she started working on rolling out her own roster of artists, like she had wanted when she signed her deal with Sylvia Rhone. This was a chess move that never happened before, where a female rapper with mainstream cachet was cultivating the talent of other female rappers. One of Missy's projects was rapper Mocha, who scored her first big break on another Missy artist Nicole Wray's debut you single "Make It Hot." Mocha had all the makings of a potential star, as her collaborations with Missy proved her potential to stand out with a voice that set her apart from her peers. She had a raspy tone that was still sweet. She almost sounded like, well, mocha. Her lost chance, however, happened when she was in the studio with producer Bink working on a track that was supposed to become her official solo debut single. She was recording in a smaller booth at New York City's Baseline Studios, opposite where Jay-Z was recording his fifth studio album in a larger space. Jay was brought in to hear the beat and liked it for himself. Mocha was asked if she would offer it up to Hov (did she even have a choice?) and the song became "You, Me, Him and Her" on *The Dynasty: Roc La Familia,* the album that doubled as Jay-Z's unveiling of his own regime at Roc-A-Fella Records, which included his own First Lady of the Roc, Amil. As for Mocha, she never had the chance to shine after that.

In 1998, Jay-Z was on his third album, *Vol. 2 . . . Hard Knock Life,* and was looking to incorporate a new female rapper into his crew. It started with the single "Can I Get A . . ." Initially, the Irv Gotti/Lil Rob–produced single was intended for Irv's Murder Inc. artist Ja Rule, but one fateful day in the studio, Jay-Z heard the track and wanted it for himself. Irv gave it to him under the condition that Ja would be featured. Jay wanted to add a female component to the song, asking a female rapper from around the way named Liz Leite to come to the studio to lay down some vocals. She came with her friend Amil Whitehead. After a few attempts in the booth, Liz's rhymes just weren't hitting for the track he had in mind, but Amil wowed Jay and ended up on the track instead. Liz still found her way onto the album through the chorus to "It's Like That" and makes a cameo in the video for "Can I Get A . . ."

At the time, the girls were part of a group called Major Coins (along with another girl named Monique), though Amil proved to be the real dime. Amil had no real aspirations of being a soloist at that point, and she even felt a little guilty that Liz's shining moment had somehow become hers. When opportunity knocks, though, you answer the door—even when you're not really ready for it. Amil later signed with Roc-A-Fella Records and appeared on a number of Jay-Z's tracks, including "Nigga What, Nigga Who (Originator 99)" and "Do It Again (Put Ya Hands Up)," before releasing her debut album, *A.M.I.L.* (*All Money Is Legal*), in 2000. While Amil had a distinctive voice, her heart wasn't in it, and she wasn't prepared for sitting in the eye of the storm of the Roc-A-Fella Records rise. "I wasn't there mentally," she told *Billboard* in 2014. "I was in my own world. Was I prepared? No. Did I realize what was happening right before my eyes? No." She entered the fold on a whim, honestly, but during her greatest popularity, her son was suffering from serious asthma and her duties as a mother were her priority. "I started to rebel," she added. "I rebelled against the industry because it's not what I wanted. I hated traveling. I wasn't at after parties or the club." It wasn't an ideal ending with her label, especially when rumors surfaced that she had been in a relationship with Jay-Z and it had gone sour (she's dismissed them all), but Amil left her situation on the highest note possible by understanding that she wasn't designed to be there.

While Southern hip-hop had been its own powerful niche for over a decade, in the late 1990s South Florida was still a blip on the rap radar, an outlier at best. Maybe it was because of 2 Live Crew's lewd entry into rap music years prior or simply because "the South" and "Florida" are viewed more as country cousins than siblings, but the music happening in South Florida (particularly Miami) didn't get its wings until it was Trick'ed into it, so to speak. In 1998, rapper and entrepreneur Trick Daddy dropped his debut single "Nann Nigga," a punchy track of the times, where he struck a playful balance of the Miami-drenched booty bass music with an added Southern flair that gave the region the kick in the ass it needed. Bass-heavy and bouncy, that was Trick's sound. It could live in a strip club, on a beach, or in a car, and "Nann" was the first taste of that. He featured local rapper Katrina Taylor, known to the Miami circuit as Trina, on the track. "Everything happened so fast," Trina remembers of the "Nann Nigga" single. "It was insane after that. As soon as it hit radio, we got a deal for the record through Atlantic Records, and as much as I can remember, I just never stopped working."

In the music video for the tune, she's wearing a diamond-encrusted bra, and her sharply commanding cadence crystallized a style that would become her own personal space in a market now flooded with female rappers from coast to coast. "Nann Nigga" became Trick Daddy's first big hit, and he inked a deal with Atlantic Records, creating the Slip-N-Slide imprint. Trina joined the ranks as Slip-N-Slide's First Lady. She had the allure of the current regime of rap vixens, though being associated with Trick Daddy gave her a unique flair. Trina was the boss lady of a region that had yet to be fully conquered by hip-hop. It was open season for takeover, as rap's growing empire was getting more and more pronounced, both commercially and culturally.

Hip-hop was still growing, and women were showing their potential. Foxy and Kim were working on their second albums, Lauryn Hill was the belle of the ball, Missy was a force, and even Gangsta Boo and Mia X were still out there. There was success and staying power happening simultaneously, no longer mutually exclusive. With many of the First Ladies, though, they were still filling a quota at face value that simply added a balance to the all-male aesthetic everyone was still used to, despite so many women rising up the rap ranks. This First Lady time period predates any social media backlash for not being more inclusive of women.

No, having a woman present was merely because men felt like she should be there to be uniform with other rap crews that often doubled as their own record labels, so they saw the marketing potential of having her there, too. It was still not *completely* about the talent, but there was enough money pouring in to support a sole female rapper's career. Hip-hop was in its multi-platinum era and its presence was no longer a surprise. It was a come-up for everyone involved. Hip-hop was expanding and women were earning their labels back the money being invested in their careers. There was still more money to be made—until of course, there wasn't.

Lil' Kim and Lauryn Hill—two sides of the female hip-hop paradigm—at the 1999 Source Hip-Hop Music Awards.

Chapter Fifteen

THE TIPPING POINT

I KNOW SOME STRIPPER JAWNS THAT KNOW HOW TO RAP . . ."

That was all Questlove needed to hear for his eyes to roll. It was 1999, and The Roots were just on the brink of what would become their slide into stardom, beginning with their fourth studio album, *Things Fall Apart*. The album dropped the day before the Grammy ceremony where Lauryn Hill swept up the awards and the heart of America, so the timing was perfect. "The thing about *Things Fall Apart* is that we were on the edge of working with people who weren't signed yet but in less than six months would not only be signed but actually would eclipse us," Questlove remembers. "And Eve was one of those people."

Eve Jeffers's first real taste of the industry came when she caught the ear of Dr. Dre. A friend of Eve's, a drug dealer she called her "homeboy management," offered her the opportunity to meet with one of Dr. Dre's right hands, who was scoping out talent in Philadelphia, since it was an untapped resource for hip-hop talent. After an impromptu audition, Eve was on the first Los Angeles–bound plane smoking out of Philly. She went by the name Eve of Destruction, and at seventeen, she joined the budding Aftermath Entertainment. At five feet seven, Eve was taller than most of the girls before her. Lil' Kim didn't reach five feet, Foxy and Trina were only five feet two. She had cropped bleach-blond hair and a curvaceous frame. She would later describe herself on the song "What Ya Want" as "Five-seven, thick in thighs / every thug's dream wife, see the love in their eyes?" Even at seventeen, she walked in and made an entrance.

The man she auditioned for was Mike Lynn, who worked on artist development at Aftermath at that time. Lynn reached out to label producer Chris "The Glove" Taylor to work on grooming Eve. "She knew how to rap," Chris remembers. "She didn't know how to do songs." Within a short period of time, Eve sharpened her song-writing abilities and evolved into a full-fledged verbal threat. A self-proclaimed "pit bull in a skirt," she rhymed from this standpoint of no nonsense, where she knew she was beautiful, but also knew she could rhyme. Her debut came on the *Bulworth* soundtrack on the aptly titled "Eve of Destruction."

Eve was eighteen and living in LA, ready to take over. Then her time at Aftermath abruptly ended. The story of how it all went down is still unclear. "[Dre] dropped me in like eight months," she told DJ Whoo Kid in a 2011 interview. "He dropped me because I kept showing up to studio sessions I wasn't supposed to be at, trying to get on records. I was feisty; I was doing way too much. I'm glad he dropped me." Chris has a different take. "She left," he says with a laugh. "Everybody left. They got tired of waiting. I left Aftermath, too." Eve was later scooped up by Ruff Ryders, an Inter-scope imprint. "She walked out the room with Jimmy [Iovine] and walked in another room with Jimmy," Chris says.

Back on the East Coast, Eve was on the grind, doing double-duty as a dancer at the New York gentlemen's club Golden Lady in the South Bronx and a rapper in the Philly scene. The environment there was changing, too, as the street element of rap was overshadowing Philly's whole "City of Brotherly Love" vibe being promoted by groups like The Roots. Rappers like Beanie Sigel were putting the grittier side of Philly on the map, aligning his group State Property with Roc-A-Fella Records. The Roots were still figuring out how to hit the mainstream while remaining authentic. They were already hugely successful touring, but they hadn't yet hit their commercial pinnacle, though they sought to create a bigger scene in Philly with like-minded artists. "As a band, we decided to collectively have these jam sessions at my house," Questlove says. These sessions became mini breeding grounds for local talent and eventually grew into a concert series called Black Lily, expanding to venues like The Five Spot in Philadelphia and The Wetlands in New York City. The goal was to create a concert series that would live on its own, even when The Roots were touring. The jam sessions catered to highlighting female talent, as artists like soul singer Jill Scott, harmonious duo Jazzyfatnastees, Marsha Ambrosius's first group Floetry, and rising singer Jaguar Wright were just a few examples of the talent that would enter and leave through the Black Lily doors. "I'll say, in the beginning, it was granola-ish," Questlove jokes. "Whatever idea of what people had about what The Roots' psychograph was, the idea of coffee-shop chicks and part-time poets . . . it was organic." Artists like Mos Def and Talib Kweli, known collectively as Rawkus Records' Black Star, frequented these homegrown jam sessions under Questlove's roof, though a switch had begun to happen when Beanie Sigel's State Property started showing up. Beanie had gone to school with The Roots' Black Thought, but it was former Roots member Malik who brought him into the fold. This changed the element of the parties. What was once a haven for artistic expression was now a party with a bunch of street dudes bullying to get on the mic. "I'm just like, wait, the vibe's starting to get lost," Questlove adds. Young artists were there, too, just trying to be musical, as singers like Bilal and Jazmine Sullivan were a part of the jam sessions eons before they hit the R&B world. "Bilal's underage, Jazmine Sullivan is ten years old. I'm like, all these underage kids are here, people are opening the windows, my neighbors are complaining. Malik's thug-ass muthafuckin' friends are putting out their blunt ashes on my carpet, and now we got stripper jawns taking over the microphone, but the Jazzyfatnastees are over in the corner getting mad 'cause they can't get the mic time." ("Jawns," of course, being the versatile Philly slang often used to describe a woman.) "It was starting to get weird." He calls it the "Alpina Element."

"The Alpina glasses are like what the mushroom [haircut] is for Salt-N-Pepa or the dookie earring," Questlove explains. "Alpina glasses are like some Philly drug dealer look." The glasses feature big aviator-shaped lenses with a long gold bar that runs over the top, for that added "I'm wealthy, but is my money legal?" flair. "Once that element started entering the house, it was just like, *okay*. Everyone will famously cite that that's when I started calling the cops on my own self. Like, 'There's a disturbance at 2309 Saint Albans Place.' They'll be like, 'Sir, we're looking at the listing, this is 2309 Saint Albans Place.' 'Uh, yeah, there's a disturbance.' 'Sir, are you saying there is a disturbance in your house right now?' So, it was like that sort of thing."

Eve reportedly entered into Questlove's orbit through the Alpina Element, impressing people with her mic skills, though Questlove had no idea and tuned out her selling points even though his comrades praised her highly. "I didn't have any personal interaction with her because by that point, I was a little miffed that my house was becoming a completely trashed zone every Friday night," he jokes. In addition, Malik's drug use had become a full-fledged addiction, just in time to finish recording and mixing *Things Fall Apart*. "[Malik] had gotten ejected from Sigma Sound Studios, so as a result, we were kicked out of that studio." Questlove had to smooth things over in order to finish the project. "I kinda pleaded a case to the studio owner that I really wanted the same consistent sonic element to be on the album, and for me to go to a whole other studio and record there would really just ruin the vision," he says. "[The owner] knew that it was just Malik. It wasn't me. He had always taken a liking to me. So basically, the compromise was we would find a studio for the vocals to be recorded and I could maintain tracking the music at Sigma, our home base. Me, Scott [Storch], Kamal [Gray], and Hub [Leonard Hubbard] would track at Sigma, and then Malik and Tariq [Black Thought] would track at a place called The Studio in Northern Liberties, Philadelphia."

Once the other half of the group was out of sight, the music took on a new life, so by the time Questlove heard it, new voices were added to the mix. One of them was Eve. "We weren't too communicative when it came to the product," Questlove admits. "So as a result, my first introduction to her voice was backgrounds on 'Ain't Sayin' Nothin' New.'" The track was initially not even a contender for the album, though in the middle of tracking, there it was, complete with Eve on the ad-libs. Questlove heard it for the first time in the middle of an interview for *The Source* with Kim Osorio, where he was showing her how The Roots' music is made. In the middle of the interview, Questlove asks an engineer, "Who is this?" They reply, "That jawn Eve."

"I'm like, 'Who's Eve?'"

Her voice was more pronounced on the Roots' soon-to-be-hit single "You Got Me," originally featuring Jill Scott. At the behest of The Roots' label MCA Records, Jill Scott was swapped out for Erykah Badu for added commercial appeal. Eve managed to stay on the track, though she wasn't listed as a guest feature. "I had no idea about 'Eve of Destruction,' so as far as credits were concerned, I did them how I normally do credits: I just list them movie-style," Questlove says. "It was MCA's idea for 'The Roots featuring Erykah Badu—You Got Me' or whatever. That was just it. I didn't want to think like, 'Oh, I'm leaving Eve out of history.' I knew that MCA did it because they wanted Erykah Badu's name to be familiar to radio programmers when they started bringing the song to them."

"You Got Me" only reached number thirty-nine on the Billboard Hot 100, though it became the centerpiece of The Roots' success story. In 2000, the song won a Grammy for Best Rap Performance by a Duo or Group, which was monumental, given the fact that a return to the streets was happening in hip-hop as seen through Alpina shades. It's a look that Eve needed at the time. This could have been the track to break *her,* too, yet she was buried in the liner notes.

So in essence, Eve *was* left out of history, while helping to make it for another musician.

"I know that Scott Storch begged Eve to introduce him to Dr. Dre," Questlove says. "I know that through that whole 'You Got Me' thing, that Scott was just like, 'Please, please, please, pretty please introduce me to Dr. Dre.'" Storch would later produce "Still D.R.E." off Dr. Dre's *2001* comeback project, marking the producer's departure from The Roots to heavily commercialized rap music. So, Eve proved useful in another way, too.

Eve's exclusion became a sore spot, especially since she was denied the Grammy for "You Got Me" due to her only being listed in the credits and not as a featured performer. She was also left out of the music video.

"I apologized for not being more thoughtful about the whole

process. It's been a major issue," Questlove explains. He regrets not crediting her properly, especially after realizing what a special artist she is. "What I want to make adamantly clear is that it really wasn't ill-intentioned," he says. "Not at all. It was just a lot of miscommunication. I probably would've figured out a way to make it work, but back then I wasn't as thoughtful."

A decade later, Questlove attempted to do right by Eve when she appeared on *Late Night with Jimmy Fallon,* but the whole event turned into a disaster. "I was going to give her my Grammy, but the Grammy broke, so it's in two pieces," Questlove says with a laugh. "We tried to create a moment and I was like, 'All right, I'll give her my Grammy.' That was a very bad idea. I gave her the Grammy, she's like, 'It's all broken, I don't want this.' That was Jimmy's first year [as host], so Jimmy didn't understand awkward Black girl lingo." Eve was still as straightforward and sharp as ever, now a star. Picture the awkward-by-nature Jimmy Fallon attempting to hand her a broken Grammy. Questlove sighs and then laughs. "That didn't go over too well."

Eve triumphed anyway, releasing her debut album *Let There Be Eve . . . Ruff Ryders' First Lady,* which broadcast to the world that she was now, as stated, the leading lady of the house that Swizz Beatz built and DMX popularized. Eve had a handful of solid singles on the double-platinum project, including the intense "Love Is Blind," featuring Faith Evans on the radio version. The album made history, as Eve became the third female artist to hit number one on the Billboard 200. The first had been Lauryn Hill a year earlier, with *Miseducation.* Foxy Brown was the second, when she dropped *Chyna Doll,* her 1999 follow-up to *Ill Na Na.*

While Eve was settling into her fame, artists like Foxy Brown were tasked with reminding everyone of theirs. After all, the growing number of women was great and all, though hip-hop's attention span was waning, and waiting for new projects from artists made fans more and more impatient. Foxy Brown's albums were released three years apart, which might as well have been a decade.

After solidifying her status as a high-ranking rapper with her debut, Foxy wanted to be more hands-on with her next project. She enlisted a star-studded cast of producers for the album, including a young Kanye West, Swizz Beatz, Deric "D-Dot" Angelettie, and Irv Gotti. The latter produced the *Chyna Doll* introductory single "Hot Spot" (with Lil' Rob). On the single, Foxy rhymes in a higher pitch, sparking the aforementioned jabs from Puffy that she was imitating Lil' Kim. Foxy showed her support for other rappers on the female posse cut "B.W.A." by including Mia X and Gangsta Boo. It was a move that spoke volumes. Here she was, arguably rhyming like Lil' Kim before Lil' Kim got a chance to return (her second album, *The Notorious K.I.M.*, came out a year after Foxy's follow-up), showing support for other women. Their feud was still lingering, and these were all subtle jabs.

Lil' Kim meanwhile was just dipping her toe back into the collaborative pond when she appeared on two tracks off Missy Elliott's second album, *Da Real World*. Fearful of the sophomore curse, Missy made it a star-studded affair, bringing in a number of big names like Kim, Eminem, Aaliyah, Da Brat, and Beyoncé. While the album didn't chart as high as planned (debuting at number ten on the Billboard 200), the quality of the work showed how Missy was still evolving as an artist, bringing in stronger rap elements. The album's biggest hit was the remix to "Hot Boyz," which featured Nas, Q-Tip, and—guess who?—Eve.

In August, Charli Baltimore, another Philly native, finally dropped her debut album, *Cold as Ice*, via Untertainment Records. Charli met the Notorious B.I.G. in 1995 through mutual friends. She said in an interview with BET that she and her friend hacked the voicemail to B.I.G.'s cell phone, and for months would listen to the voicemails left by various women. "So I came up with this whole concept for his Christmas gift that I was gonna write this rap," she reveals in the interview. "And all the girls and all their names were in this rap." After delivering the rhyme in front of B.I.G. as his gift, the wheels turned in his mind to groom his next star. Lean with light skin, Charli's body didn't match her mouth, where her rhymes flew out like venom. "Big liked that I looked a certain way, but when I spit, I spit hard," she adds. While Charli was another protégé turned paramour of The Notorious B.I.G. in 1996 (up until he died in 1997), she exhibited a stronger street vibe to her music, aligning with some of the hardest girls around for the "Thorough Bitches" track, featuring The Lady of Rage, Gangsta Boo, Queen Pen, Da Brat, and buzzing newbie Scarlet.

During that summer of 1999, something other than hip-hop was under fire, for once: the age-old business model of the music industry. A pair of college students sent the music industry into a tailspin with an invention called Napster.

The RIAA reported that in the decade following the advent of Napster (from 1999 to 2009), the recording industry took a hit estimating $55 billion. It all started on June 1, 1999, when Shawn Fanning launched the beta file-sharing program Napster on his college campus, Northeastern University, with friend Sean Parker. While music piracy was always a quiet killer to the music industry in the form of bootlegging, this new technology took that practice to the next level. Record labels went into panic mode, questioning where these perceived cataclysmic changes would take them.

Music piracy immediately became the industry's worst enemy, as fans no longer felt the need to roll up to a big box store and purchase a CD—not when they could easily download a song for free. On one hand, this capacity exposed the greater hip-hop audience to all different talent, both signed and unsigned. On the other, it threatened to dismantle the very system that was put in place to keep the money flowing, and once that happened, budgets had to be cut, belts had to be tightened, and assets (read: artists) had to be sacrificed.

Who were simultaneously the greatest assets and greatest casualties in hip-hop? Women.

IV

So Much for the Afterglow

Chapter Sixteen

SEX (STILL) SELLS

"THEM SEX KITTENS GET ALL THE BREAKS! THEY HAVE *ALL* THE luck!"

That's Rah Digga after I remind her that she lost out to Lil' Kim on the remix to Mobb Deep's hit single "Quiet Storm." The remix dropped in October 1999 and featured Lil' Kim. She hadn't made much noise since The Notorious B.I.G. passed away in 1997, popping up here and there on a few tracks. This one proved to be the money shot.

It was about a year before Prodigy would pass away, and he and I were in the rec room of his Williamsburg apartment building with my friend Jon, conceptualizing my podcast. Prodigy demanded he be the first guest, my pilot episode, if you will. My friendship with Prodigy came when I interviewed him right after he was released from prison in 2011. Five years later, we wrote a book together called *Commissary Kitchen: My Infamous Prison*

Cookbook, which detailed meals Prodigy made while in prison as he battled sickle cell anemia. The prison system is known for feeding inmates the most toxic, nutrient-deficient food, so P (as I affectionately called him) would create his own meals with what little he could purchase from the commissary. Having a friend who is a hip-hop legend left me open to receiving so many cool stories, and there we were, talking about them in his apartment building. Talk about blessed.

We got into the subject of writing rhymes and I brought up the controversy surrounding Lil' Kim, since Biggie's *Hard Core* reference tracks were still being leaked, now twenty years after his passing. "I was in the studio when Kim wrote her verse," Prodigy confirmed. "I was right there when she wrote it and when she said it." That verse would have a ripple effect that he never imagined.

"Aight, so, when we was working on 'Quiet Storm,' we were in a studio called Soundtrack in the city on Twenty-First Street," P explained. "While we were working on that song, that was the heights of heights of heights for Mobb Deep's popularity. Everybody was on their Mobb Deep shit. We just did *Hell on Earth,* about to drop this *Murda Muzik* album." Their hype was bigger than it ever had been. "So, everybody would come to that studio and sit outside our doors just to listen to what we were making," he said. "Kanye used to do that. I saw Eve out there a bunch of times. I saw a lot of different rappers. It was all love. We would come out and show love to them. They were just really interested; they wanted to hear what the fuck we was making. A lot of rappers started booking sessions next to us, just so they could be in the same studio and they could hear. If they had the same vibe they'd be like, 'Hey, put me next to Mobb Deep. I heard Mobb Deep's in Studio A. Put me in Studio B.'"

Rah Digga was in the studio next to them when she learned that Lil' Kim had been chosen for "Quiet Storm," after Rah had been recording her album *Dirty Harriet* next to them for over a year. "Yo, she came into the studio pissed!" Prodigy said of Digga. "She was so mad. She was like wanting-to-fight pissed. She was like, 'What the fuck, yo?' I'm here every day! You ain't put me on the muthafuckin' song? Fuck y'all.'" It wasn't pretty.

"Oh, I was mad about it! I was mad about it," Rah Digga tells me. "I still am a really huge fan of Mobb Deep. I'm one of their cult followers. I literally worshiped the ground they walk on, but I was playing it cool because they were right next door [in the studio]. They couldn't see that [I was mad], but I still let it be known." She found out in the middle of the "Quiet Storm" process. "I think I was even there when they were still writing to the beat. I'd been bugging them, 'We've got to do a song!' And when I found out that Kim got on it, a part of me was angry . . . not *angry* angry, but that was the song that could've like . . . did it for me." She was also hip to the rumors that Kim didn't write her own rhymes. "Word on the street was that Kim wasn't writing her own stuff," she says. "I couldn't stress it enough to the world that I write my own rhymes." That "Quiet Storm" verse-writing moment changed Kim's reputation. "When she did ['Quiet Storm'], it almost made all of that go away," Digga says. Rumor had it that Foxy Brown, among other rappers, was also miffed about the missed opportunity. With good reason—the single became one of the biggest in Mobb Deep's history, and gave Lil' Kim the post-Biggie push she needed to move forward with confidence.

And so, even at the turn of the century, the rift amongst the Sex Kittens and the Nubian Goddesses was still apparent, though the latter were becoming gradually extinct on a commercial level. The only move, it seemed, was to join the former, since record labels were now cutting their budgets and paring down their artists' releases by what could guarantee a sale. Sex still sold.

On March 21, 2000, Miami maven Trina debuted *Da Baddest*

Bitch, her first entry into hip-hop as a solo artist. The project was part sexually charged, part storytelling, as Trina was both empowering women and making songs that could live on the radio and in a club. On the hit title track, she raps:

The bigger the bank, the bigger the Benz
The better the chance to get close to his rich friends

"I just feel like people are entitled to their own forms of expression, and I feel like you should be able to say whatever you want to say," Trina explains of her brazen style. "I think you have to be comfortable enough within yourself and your own skin and your own identity to be able to be sensual or provocative or unapologetic or whatever. If you're not, you're always the one that has something to say. You just need to be comfortable in your own skin to celebrate a woman doing whatever she feels she could do for whatever that reason is. And that's just how I always felt. It's such a cliché thing to say that men can do it and women can't. Women could do any- and everything they want to do with dignity and respect and morals, as well as a man. You just have to be able to handle yourself with respect and do what makes sense for you."

Trina was fresh off touring with label head Trick Daddy when the album hit the pavement. It would become a nonstop ride for her for years. "Before you knew it, I was on to my project, and before you knew it, I was on another tour," Trina says, "and then I was on to another record. Then I was on the road. It was like a nonstop roller coaster. It just didn't stop." Her popularity was building, and while her debut didn't enter incredibly high, it stayed on the Billboard charts for close to a year.

Rah Digga's *Dirty Harriet* was released in April 2000, led by the single "Tight." Previously known for her tomboyish aesthetic, Rah arguably ventured closer into that forbidden Sex Kitten territory now. She knew who she was as an artist, right down to her signature rugged vocals ("Voice alone scare your ass to death like *Stigmata*," she raps on the "Tight" remix), but the label was dabbling with changing up her image in the hopes of making her sexier, since that was presumably the only way to sell more records. "Initially, my very first photoshoot with *Trace* magazine was the first time I was introduced to hair weave, and I just remember crying," Rah Digga says. "I was sobbing uncontrollably because as they were coming to me with this track [of hair], there was glue on it. I just burst out in tears like, 'You can't put that in my hair!' They had to stop the shoot. I had to be consoled. I was the little kid in the corner scared like, 'No, what is that thing? Get that thing away from me!' I never experienced hair weave. I didn't know the process. So, I calmed down, I let them put it in, they did my whole hair, and after they did it, I'm looking in the mirror like, 'Pretty!' So, every photoshoot thereafter, I was like, 'Can you do that thing with the glue?'"

While Rah argues that the label didn't force a sexy switch upon her, hip-hop at large took notice of the change and began to criticize her for it. "It had absolutely nothing to do with the visuals. It had everything to do with the director. Nzingha Stewart directed it. I had these meetings with Lil X, Hype [Williams]. I studied all types of different treatments. Then I had the meeting with her, and I'll be honest, I didn't like her treatment the best. [But] I gravitated to her and her story. This was a female director. This is her first major video that she's attempting to shoot. She's coming under the helm of Hype Williams." After spending time with Stewart and hearing her story of trying to break through in the film world, Rah Digga made her decision. "I just turned to everybody, and I said, 'And that's who's going to do my video!'" she adds. "That's why the 'Tight' video is what it is." In the video, Rah Digga looks futuristically sexy, a strange balance of street and sci-fi. "It was supposed to be like a female Spider-Man," Rah Digga explains. "People took so many connotations from it. They were like, 'What is this dominatrix?' They really didn't understand the visuals, and for me, honestly, I didn't think about it like, 'This is setting the tone for my branding for the rest of my career.' I didn't think about any of that stuff. I just thought about, 'This is a female director trying to get her shot, and I'm going to give it to her.'"

It was a move that backfired. Digga's label was pandering to the sex-demanding audience, though that wasn't necessarily Rah Digga's fan base. So instead of allowing for her to experiment, fans barked back. There were still *some* hip-hop fans who didn't need their favorite female stars in tight clothes and fake hair, though not enough to make record labels feel like those artists could sustain their success without a glammed-up makeover.

Even Da Brat released her third studio album, *Unrestricted*, a week after Rah Digga (on April 11, 2000) with a highly noticeable switch in her look as well. She was hitting the gym and had even signed a modeling contract with Wilhelmina. The cover art for the project shows Brat made up with her hair relaxed, her previously tight twists gone, wearing an airbrushed bodysuit that was a collage of herself in various sexy poses—including one in a bikini. The music changed, too, built for mainstream endurance with a crystal-clear desire to cater to a new (broader) audience. The rhymes were still there and so were Da Brat's fans; the album swiftly jumped to the number one spot on the Billboard Top R&B/Hip-Hop Albums chart. While Brat was ditching her harder side on record, she maintained it in the streets. A month before her album released, Brat was in Atlanta's Buckhead neighborhood at the Chili Pepper nightclub when she beat a woman for entering the VIP area uninvited. Some reports say she pistol whipped the clubgoer; other reports say she hit her with a bottle of rum. Regardless of the weapon, the woman left with gashes on her head that required three stitches. A year later, Da Brat pled guilty and the charges were reduced from aggravated assault to reckless conduct. She paid a $1,000 fine and was sentenced to eighty hours of community service plus a year's probation. This would not be her last altercation in a club—later in 2007 she was arrested for attacking a waitress with a rum bottle at Studio 72 in Atlanta. For this she was sentenced to three years in prison for aggravated assault, plus seven years of probation and two hundred hours of community service. She snuck an album in between court cases—2003's *Limelite, Luv & Niteclubz*.

By the summer of 2000, Lil' Kim was back in form. Her follow-up album, *The Notorious K.I.M.*, was a reintroduction of sorts to the Queen Bee. It was a title she earned, even before Beyoncé, though Kim had to reestablish herself as rap royalty, and with good reason. For one, it was the first solo project Kim had released since her 1996 debut. It was also her first release on her own imprint through Atlantic Records, Queen Bee Entertainment. Kim was rather forcibly removed from Biggie's shadow following his murder and given center stage to showcase just how much power and commercial viability she had when she was standing alone. Her tracks struck a balance between sex and pop, with singles like "No Matter What They Say" and "How Many Licks?" with Sisqó. *The Notorious K.I.M.* sold the most records for a female rapper that year, signifying that while Lil' Kim may have taken a hiatus from recording albums, she hadn't lost her touch, and was back with a vengeance.

New talent and old beefs were still boiling. While Foxy Brown squashed her war with Queen Latifah this year, she was in the midst of a new one with Eve. Foxy was allegedly having an affair with Ruff Ryders' leader DMX. Foxy was the First Lady of The

Firm, supposedly sleeping with the leader of Eve's crew. It was like fraternizing with the enemy.

Foxy was already beefing with Left Eye over rumors that Foxy was with Left Eye's man, Andre Rison. Meanwhile, MC Lyte came for Lil' Kim and Foxy Brown on the Rah Digga track "Where U at Mama?" because Foxy had titled a diss track "10% Dis" and Lil' Kim had opened her "Quiet Storm Remix" verse with Lyte's "Hot damn hoe here we go again." Here we go again, indeed. More fighting ensued among women. Maybe they were just venting and taking it out on each other, since record labels were having a financial crisis and spots were limited for women to grow. Still, more women kept coming up.

In 2000, a young rapper from the Castle Hill projects in the Bronx was starting to make noise. Her name was Reminisce Smith, rapping under the name Remy Martin. Remy lived in the same neighborhood as rapper Big Pun, who was building a name for himself as part of the Terror Squad with fellow rapper Fat Joe. Pun's debut album, *Capital Punishment*, made history in 1998 as the first platinum hip-hop album to come from a Latino. Remy was looking for a way to connect with Pun, and found it through a mutual friend who brought her to his house. She rapped an audition for him, with that very verse later appearing on Pun's posthumous album *Yeeeah Baby* on a song aptly titled "Ms. Martin." Pun died of a heart attack and respiratory failure in February 2000, though prior to that, he and Remy forged a friendship and a solid working relationship, clocking hours on end in the studio and honing Remy's skills. Remy had two songs on *Yeeeah Baby*: her aforementioned show-out cut "Ms. Martin" and "You Was Wrong" with Fat Joe and Ruff Ryders member Drag-On. Later that year, Remy paid homage to her mentor on the remix to the Brownsville, Brooklyn, duo M.O.P.'s breakout single "Ante Up (Robbing-Hoodz Theory)," with the line, "Wish I could bring Pun back." That remix would secure Remy's place in hip-hop. Her verse was tough, laden with lines about unapologetically robbing anyone:

> *So keep acting like you don't know where the funds at*
> *And I'mma show y'all motherfuckers where the guns at*

Remy lived at the intersection of grimy and sexy. She didn't rhyme about having sex like her predecessors, though she rocked fur coats like they did. Instead, Remy was spitting bars about guns and loot. She was signed to SRC Records under Universal Music Group through Fat Joe's Terror Squad imprint. "I'll never forget the day Remy called and [New York DJ] Steph Lova said, 'Come on! Let's go meet up with Remy!'" remembers Hot 97's *Ebro in the Morning* cohost Laura Stylez. Steph Lova was Stylez's mentor at the time, and a close friend of Remy's. The two showed up to meet the rapper outside her soon-to-be record label. "We were outside of the building, and Remy had just signed her deal," Stylez recalls. "It was such a special moment to see someone's dreams come true. I was kind of just a fly on the wall witnessing all of it. We happened to have bumped into Raekwon right outside of the building, and he was showing her mad love. Real personal moments, that as a hip-hop fangirl, I was like, 'I can't believe I'm witnessing this.'" The Terror Squad had their first female artist.

The First Lady narrative was still alive and well.

In Chicago, a rapper named Shawnna scored her first mainstream look when she appeared on Ludacris's "What's Your Fantasy" off his 1999 debut album *Incognegro*. The track was remixed to add Trina and Foxy Brown, appearing on Ludacris's major label debut *Back for the First Time* a year later. Shawnna was previously part of a duo named Infamous Syndicate, though Shawnna would blast beyond the Chi-Town borders when she became the first female artist signed to Def Jam South through Ludacris's Disturbing tha Peace imprint. More women were entering the race.

Straight out of Englewood, New Jersey (previously the home of Sugar Hill Records), came Lady Luck, who was featured in Jay-Z's tour documentary *Backstage* in September of 2000. The year before, Luck had been featured in *The New Yorker* as the subject of a piece called "Hip-Hop High." The article detailed her signing with Def Jam while she was just a junior in high school. In the piece, Def Jam's then president Kevin Liles breaks down the female rap constituency for *New Yorker* writer David Samuels. "When you think about Eve, if Eve's man was in a gunfight and he got shot, she would pick up his gun and start shooting at the other guy," Liles said. "Lil' Kim would fuck that other man. Rah Digga would stab that other man." Then came Lady Luck. "Luck would have a great time with that man, and then hit him in the head with a bat. So, all of them have their own special qualities."

Those "special qualities" were more like marketing strategies that women consistently had to adhere to. Rah Digga could only stab a man, she couldn't fuck him. Lil' Kim could fuck a man, but didn't have the gall to stab him. Luck, theoretically, could do both, but apparently wouldn't stab a man, opting for a bat instead. All that really translates to, "You can be the sexy female rapper, you can be the violent female rapper, or you can be the rapper that likes to have fun but won't take no lip." Can you be all three? God, no. How could a label market you if they didn't know how to box you?

Lady Luck caught her break after a series of freestyles on New York's Hot 97 led her to Def Jam's door. "We were doing a lot of songs" before her deal, Luck remembers. "Nobody signed me. Different people had different criticisms of me, even though on my seventeenth birthday, I was at Lil' Kim's house with all the MCs and them. She was working on [*The Notorious K.I.M.*] at the time, and I had rapped for her on the phone." Luck was supposed to work on some material for Kim, but that never materialized. Then came the serendipitous freestyle battles on Hot 97. Every morning for a week, Ed Lover hosted a segment where artists would come and battle. Luck was lining her opponents up and knocking them down one after another, impressing Ed Lover. "So, I went to Hot 97, after winning on the radio for like a week," she remembers. "After the third day, I knew they were going to let me win because every day, they were like, 'It's a girl.' No matter what I said, it was going to be lit." While she was at Hot 97, "the secret little bat lines started ringing, and it was Def Jam." A couple of different labels had called, inquiring about this badass battler who was gaining support on the radio airwaves, roping in listeners with her intricately aggressive delivery. During her week of freestyles, a number of labels wanted in. "I had meetings with everybody. I went to Bad Boy, and then Lyor Cohen called my house when I was in school," she remembers. "I come out of school and they got this car service for my little young ass. They turned me out. Little bitch was on welfare, and they sending jackets and fresh fruits! I don't even know if we washed the fruits, we were so low-class back then! I was loving it, enjoying free lobster. Let me tell you. I knew I was going to sign with certain people, but I just wanted a nice dinner. It was amazing." Lady Luck locked into a five-album deal with Def Jam, reportedly worth somewhere between $500,000 and a million dollars.

Her appearance on the remix of multisyllabic Queens rapper Pharoahe Monch's "Simon Says" (with Redman, Method Man, Busta Rhymes, and Shabaam Sahdeeq) was monumental. Monch was a part of critically acclaimed duo Organized Konfusion, and his solo single "Simon Says" became his biggest commercial hit. The remix was prime real estate for an artist like Lady Luck, since

Monch's core audience was underground rap fans, though the song was gaining mainstream traction—it was the best of both worlds for her big appearance. Her luck with Def Jam, however, ran out rather quickly. "Kevin Liles made a lot of promises," Luck says. "Kevin looked me in my eyes and promised me this one, that one, this one, that one." From big money to big exposure, big guest features, anything under the sun. "And I love their roster," she adds. "Def Jam was so iconic, and it just seemed like it was right at the time, as a child. It got messy, but Def Jam just seemed like the move at the time. They were very aggressive."

Luck was devastated during a meeting with Liles in front of writer Aliya S. King, who was shadowing Luck for a year for a feature in *The Source*. King asked Liles when they expected to release Luck's debut album. His response: "Luck's album will drop when she's going to change the face of women in hip-hop." That reply brought Lady Luck to tears. How do you swallow that pill, when you were told that there was room for your style, only to then be informed that what you brought to the table was not enough? "I was young, and I've always been a tomboy," she tells me. While her current style is far more seductive and sexy, back then she was dipped in baggy T-shirts and jeans, with a fitted baseball cap and a chain around her neck. "I come from the era of Da Brat. I come from the era of MC Lyte. So, I think I'm just dressing hip-hop. I'm a girl from New Jersey. I think I'm embodying what I represent. At the time, it was Kim and Foxy, but not everybody was selling sex, sex, sex. [Def Jam] made it seem like there was room." Apparently not, at least at Def Jam, and Lady Luck's album never saw the light of day.

"I was in LA with Kevin and we met up with Foxy," she told Aliya S. King in 2016. "He put a baseball cap on me before we took a picture and that was it. I was supposed to always rock a baseball cap. I never wore hats like that. But when the president of Def Jam slaps a baseball cap on your head, you wear it." What was that about?

"My mom has her opinion, and this is not my own," Luck says. "My mom has an opinion that Def Jam signed me to keep me out of Foxy's way, and her theory was that another label might've did things differently." If only.

Missy Elliott, grabbing all the light in the room as always.

Chapter Seventeen

CHASING PAVEMENTS

WE CAN EITHER THANK Y2K OR BLAME Y2K FOR WHAT HAP-pened to hip-hop once the year 2000 closed out. Nearly two years removed from the Napster craze, the RIAA scare of looking to annihilate anyone pirating music was inching toward mass hysteria. The sales numbers were dropping, but the industry didn't yet understand the magnitude of just how low they would go. For hip-hop in general, the plan remained, "Drop some hot shit or miss out on the pot of gold." And by "hot," the labels meant commercially viable enough to compensate for the difference they were feeling based upon the historical bottom line. A turning point was on its way.

By 2001, Jay-Z and Nas grew tired of talking around each other and made their beef more direct. The two had been circling for years with subtle jabs that all really spoke to the overarching competition for who could be crowned the King of New York. While that was a big enough reason to start a battle, fuel was added to the fire when Nas threw Jay-Z headfirst into a feud on Nas's track "Stillmatic," by taking a line off Jay-Z's commercial hit "Izzo (H.O.V.A.)" and changing it to "Is he H to the Izzo M to the Izzo?" (meaning *homo*). Jay-Z took his response to the stage of Hot 97's Summer Jam in 2001, unveiling his song "Takeover," off his prolific sixth studio album, *The Blueprint,* which arrived on September 11. On the track he calls out Nas by name: "Ask Nas, he don't want it with Hov. No!" Nas had to recover from the disappointing sales of 1999's *Nastradamus* and returned Jay-Z's favor with guns blazin' on "Ether," off his fifth studio album, 2001's *Stillmatic.* This was a record label goldmine waiting to happen. Male rappers were causing controversy (that stayed on wax) yet making alternative-radio-ready hits. Those cost the labels nothing yet gave them everything. Labels could breathe a sigh of relief that their male rappers were no longer turning their battles into violence, so what was a little showmanship that just happened to attack another artist's sexuality, financial status, and ability to get girls? "Take my money," was the label's response to all that.

For women, it was a little trickier. That Nubian Goddess/Sex Kitten debate was practically dead, as almost every female artist on the scene was styled and branded as some variation of a Sex Kitten, with extravagant clothing, elaborate makeup, and hair extensions. Record labels started placing a cap on the number of female rappers they signed, due to the expense of their upkeep—hair, makeup, wardrobe, etc. "This happened at magazines too, when it came to the budgets for cover stories," echoes *XXL*'s Vanessa Satten. The catch-22 was that while labels theoretically could no longer afford the expensive upkeep of their female rap artists, they only wanted to sign them if they maintained that glam aesthetic. This issue came into play with touring as well.

"There's so many tours that I've been called out to do where they send this big list of women," Trina recalls. "You have all of these names and then all of a sudden, the tour doesn't happen." The reason? "'Well, you guys are so expensive. It's going to cost this much to move this girl, and this girl to this hair, and this girl to this makeup,'" she continues. It's still bars over beauty. "Of course, you want to look beautiful and amazing, and you want to look your best, but I think you're going to do that anyway. That's who you are. So, there are ways to make it work. I just feel like, as a woman, that's why you have to constantly keep your foot down on their neck and keep going hard. Because you always have to fight for that extra power that you deserve."

The quality of the performances were forcibly top-notch for women back then, too, while the men were allowed to be a little more rugged. "When it comes to different platforms for concerts and things, guys . . . I see them get a lot more leverage and a lot more of a platform," Trina continues. "But I don't feel like their shows are as put together or as organized or as thoughtful. [With women] there's dancers, there's costumes, there's all of this stuff that's going on to make it exciting. But if a man is just rocking on the stage with their jeans sagging and they start rocking the mic, it's like a pimped-out show. You're paying top dollar."

It's like the labels were saying to women, "Here we are. Entertain us. Wear your sexy outfits and dance. Talk about sex, shake your ass. That's what the audience wants. They don't want to know about how lyrically skilled you are; not without looking good. Only we can't afford to make you look good, unless your record is selling. But by the way, we've cut the budget to market your record." Vicious cycle.

A rift began to appear at this point, where only proven money-makers were getting their due shine. Fortunately, there were many. Eve dropped her platinum second album, *Scorpion,* in 2001 and returned to her roots (pun intended), as the lead single "Let Me

Blow Ya Mind" (with Gwen Stefani) was produced by both Dr. Dre and Scott Storch. The single was a personal milestone for Eve, as a peak position at number two on the Billboard Hot 100 made it her highest-charting single. Add to that a Grammy Award for the then newly minted Best Rap/Sung Collaboration category. She kept the heat going a year later with *Eve-Olution,* and her track "Gangsta Lovin'" with Alicia Keys also checked in at number two on the Billboard Hot 100. She spun off into film at this point, with roles in both *Barbershop* and *Barbershop 2,* among others. Then, things stalled. Her only hit for years was the moderately successful "Tambourine," which only appeared on the *Wild Child* soundtrack and other television shows like *Gossip Girl* and *Girls.* Much like Eve herself, even her song only showed up for Hollywood. Eve learned all too well that money was drying up in rap. She took her talents to the silver screen (and to the daytime talk show *The Talk*) and never looked back, only briefly popping back up in 2013 with her *Lip Lock* album, which sold only 8,600 copies in its first week.

After a film role in *She's All That* in 1999, Lil' Kim embraced the soundtrack world, too, when she joined Christina Aguilera, Pink, and Mýa for the remake of the classic "Lady Marmalade" in 2001 off the *Moulin Rouge!* soundtrack. The single hit number one in both the US and the UK, showing the world that Lil' Kim was just as much a pop icon as she was hip-hop royalty. It was in this same year that she officially departed from Junior M.A.F.I.A. and took a long absence from her business relationship and friendship with Puffy. She changed up her peers on 2003's *La Bella Mafia,* working with producers like Mobb Deep's Havoc, Scott Storch, and Kanye West. She showed her own production capabilities on album cut "This Is a Warning" with R. Kelly and landed a hit with the Timbaland-produced "The Jump Off," a single later remade by Nicki Minaj in 2007, predating her beef with Lil' Kim.

Her unexpected win also came from 2003's "Magic Stick" with

50 Cent, which boosted its way to the number two spot on the Billboard Hot 100. It was clear that Lil' Kim was on a hot streak and planned to stay there, though mainstream media couldn't quite grasp the understanding of the world Lil' Kim had made for herself thanks to consistent heat and a strong fan base. "Her lil' feet could never fill Biggie's shoes, of course, but on *La Bella Mafia,* Kim slips into the latest Manolos instead," said a review of the album in *SPIN* magazine, "spitting sass all over the hottest tracks big money can buy." Kim was simply hitching a ride on the mainstream wagon like so many of her male peers, yet the credibility of her work was reduced to a description more fitting of an episode of *Sex and the City.* Hip-hop understood her direction, as *The Source* gave her 4.5 mics. "This is the project that showed the world that Lil' Kim's rap career could survive without Biggie," says *The Source*'s then editor in chief Kim Osorio. "Though she had maintained her celebrity throughout, she put her focus back into music, owned her own skill, and proved the naysayers wrong." *La Bella Mafia* debuted at number five on the Billboard 200 and earned Kim a double platinum plaque. That kind of success is a double-edged sword, as critics are saying she's no Biggie, but why would Biggie even be brought up six years after his passing? Clearly Kim wasn't trying to be B.I.G., nor was he able to write her rhymes.

Lil' Kim continued to push forward, even when her prison term began two years later.

She dropped her fourth studio album, *The Naked Truth,* on September 27, 2005, the same day she started her sentence for perjury and conspiracy stemming from the 2001 shooting outside Hot 97. *The Naked Truth* garnered critical acclaim, right down to the simplified cover art, revealing only Lil' Kim's face. *The Naked Truth* was the first and only album by a female rapper to ever achieve the coveted five-mic rating in *The Source,* and gave us the singles "Lighters Up" and "Whoa."

Foxy Brown ditched her high-pitched Kim soundalike vocals and returned to form on 2001's *Broken Silence,* bringing her signature ruggedness back on what was to become a Grammy-nominated project, as well as reintroducing her Caribbean roots. Cameos include dancehall artists like Spragga Benz on the lead single "Oh Yeah," along with Baby Cham, and Wayne Wonder. Foxy also concocted some sonically different hits for the mainstream, like her third single "Candy," with singer Kelis, who was already on the come-up with her single "Caught Out There." After this project, Foxy Brown hit a hard road, starting in 2003, when she parted ways with Def Jam rather suddenly. She was interviewed by MTV in February of that year and gushed about the sequel to *Ill Na Na,* titled *Ill Na Na 2: The Fever.* The album was slated for a May 2003 release and was geared to make the same impact as her 1996 introduction. Foxy was prepared to create an album that was completely transparent, since now so much of her reputation was for her outlandish behavior, not her music. She was even supposed to collaborate with Lauryn Hill on a song called "Everyday People," where the two would provide a side-by-side breakdown comparison of themselves and their perceived rap images, highlighting how they're different yet really the same. This particular track would have been mutually beneficial to both Foxy and Lauryn, especially since Lauryn was still in partial hiding. Then the album was deaded and Foxy was mysteriously gone from the label.

When Jay-Z assumed the position of president of Def Jam in 2004, Foxy returned to Def Jam. In the middle of the recording process for her next album, *Black Roses,* Foxy began losing her hearing. Within months she was completely deaf, due to a sudden sensorineural hearing loss, and announced in December 2005 that she would be undergoing an intricate surgery to remedy the issue. Though *Black Roses* had been canceled, as Foxy was not able to deliver a project while deaf, her hearing was restored by the following June.

Her mental health then became a focal point in criticisms, as well as her prison sentence in 2007. "We used to write each other letters," Prodigy told me, since he too was serving a term during that time. It was as if Foxy Brown hadn't made her mark significantly enough, and was wiped away by rumors and speculations, including one in 2013 where she was accused of claiming that she and Jay-Z had an affair. She showed up on *RapFix Live* for that interview, flanked by Sway Calloway and Big Daddy Kane, with tears welling in her eyes as she discussed the decade-long undercurrent of negativity that would follow her. "You know me, I'm far from weak," she said to Sway. "Like *XXL* said: 'The last real bitch alive.' You already know me: I'm as strong as they get, but after a while it becomes like, 'Let her live.'"

For Missy Elliott, 2001 was the kick-off of a string of consistent releases back to back up until 2005. It started with *Miss E... So Addictive* in May 2001, which featured songs like "One Minute Man" with Ludacris and Trina, plus "Get Ur Freak On" (later remixed with Nelly Furtado), and "4 My People." She lost Aaliyah in a plane crash in August of that year, though she managed to keep going through her grief. The following year she was *Under Construction*, and her single "Work It" became another massive it. *This Is Not A Test!* came in 2003, and *The Cookbook* in 2005, where she was noticeably thinner. While many assumed her dramatic weight loss came due to vanity, she was actually battling Graves' disease, an autoimmune disorder that results in an overactive thyroid, causing significant drops in weight and bulging eyes. Missy showed both symptoms.

Her releases hit a pause, though her reign never stopped, as Missy would consistently be reintroduced to the pop audience for over a decade. It was a testament to the strength of her hits, proving she truly was the queen of her craft. Missy performed "Get Ur Freak On" at the 2015 Super Bowl during Katy Perry's set, and then "Work It" popped up in 2018 as part of a viral video where a woman named Mary Halsey performed the song at an outdoor karaoke party. Missy eclipsed hip-hop.

After already wowing with verses on Lil' Kim's "Ladies Night" remix and N.O.R.E.'s "Oh No" remix, Hot 97's Voice of New York Angie Martinez dropped two back-to-back albums: 2001's *Up Close and Personal* and 2002's *Animal House*. Angie signed with Elektra under Sylvia Rhone after deals were offered up following her appearance on "Ladies Night." She waited awhile before accepting. "I still didn't know if I wanted to do an album, but I took the meetings to understand the opportunity being offered," she told Rashaun Hall in an interview with *Billboard* in 2001. "It wasn't until a year or two later that I realized I wanted to do this. So, I went back to Sylvia [Rhone], and luckily she was still into it." Martinez was one of a select few female disc jockeys in New York City and arguably a gatekeeper to radio success. Male and female rappers revered her, so her entering their platform and still being welcomed was massive. For the first time, a woman who commanded respect in media was showed the same respect as a musician.

While her songs didn't chart incredibly high, she did score a platinum hit with "If I Could Go" featuring Lil' Mo and Sacario (off *Animal House*). She discusses the balancing act of being both a radio jock and an MC in her 2016 memoir, *My Voice*. Angie brought an entirely new energy as a rapper, considering her day job was spent interviewing them. As a radio star, she managed to insert that same level of personality into her rhymes, a rarity for men and women on the mic. Her time as an artist, though, was short-lived, since the double life took a toll on her mind and her body. "But the real question that I started to have was whether I had the same hunger to be famous that I saw in others who were," she wrote in her memoir. "The truth is that deep down I had this small fear of being too famous."

By the time 2002 rolled around, more changes were afoot. Aaliyah had passed away in August 2001 in a plane crash, and a month later the country was stunned by the devastating events of 9/11. In April 2002, Left Eye died tragically in a car accident in Honduras. Loss was everywhere, and every corner of America was feeling it in different ways. In hip-hop, the lines between commercial and underground became increasingly apparent as the mainstream sound continued to evolve into a poppier direction. Artists like Midwest rapper Nelly were hot on the scene, dropping big singles like "Hot in Herre" that became immediate crossover hits. Eminem was on his fourth album, *The Eminem Show,* which sold 7.6 million albums, the most for any genre that year. The independent rap scene was also once again growing, since major labels were reticent in signing new acts and indie labels had started forming to counter that deficit. For every super-mainstream artist, there was an independent artist to match. There were also independent crews like the Anomolies, whose primary members were Big Tara, Invincible, Kuttin Kandi, Pri the Honey Dark, and Helixx.

Brooklyn rapper Jean Grae released her debut, *Attack of the Attacking Things,* via indie label Third Earth Music. The album garnered critical acclaim due to Jean's visionary style of writing and punchily smooth delivery. On what felt like the opposite end of the earth from Jean Grae, Trina released her follow-up, *Diamond Princess.* While her first project had been more controlled by the hands of her label, this one had a stronger Trina touch. She enlisted Missy Elliott to handle the production duties this time around, changing things up for the Miami rap queen, as Missy was now groomed for making pop hits and brought that energy to

Trina's project. Trina collaborated with many different female rap voices, too, including Missy, of course, on "Rewind That Back," and "Ladies 1st" with Eve. Trina's label Slip-N-Slide had previously signed another female artist named Brianna Perry, who also appeared on Trina's album on a song called "Kandi" (then using the name Lil Brianna). Trina made it a point to maintain camaraderie among her female peers. "For me, I just kind of was in my own lane, and I wasn't really amongst all of [the beefs]," Trina says. "Most of the women, I had already met, and it was all love, so I was happy to work with these women. Whether it was a feature or a collaboration or a performance or to do another record, I was just inspired by it, so I was like, 'Let's work,' as opposed to anything else."

There was only one steady beef that circled Trina's orbit: Khia. The Southern female rapper first arrived in 2002 with her explicit single "My Neck, My Back" off her debut album *Thug Misses*. In 2004, she collaborated with Trina's mentor Trick Daddy on a song called "J.O.D.D.," off Trick Daddy's album *Thug Matrimony: Married to the Streets*. Her momentum continued, and she even collaborated with Janet Jackson in 2006 on the song "So Excited." All this success came on the strength of her first single, as Khia continued releasing albums every few years, even taking time in 2008 to join VH1's reality competition series *Ego Trip's Miss Rap Supreme*, though she was booted by the second episode. There was always tension between Khia and Trina (perhaps from Khia's early collaboration with Trick Daddy) though it all came to a head when Khia suggested that she wrote Trina's biggest hit "The Baddest Bitch." That rumor was never proven to be true, and Trina's outlook on the so-called beef even today is a calm state of *unbothered*. "Here's my thing: people don't love it; they're entertained by it," she says. "They're only excited by it for the moment that it's happening. As soon as it dies down, they're back to their regular schedule. They don't really care who wins the beef or not. They're around as a bystander to watch this whole circus happen. Beef to me is when somebody has done something physically to you. You put your hands on me, you crashed my car, you done something way out of line that's disrespectful. That's beef. Beef is not when someone is saying something crazy."

She also doesn't beef with strangers. "First of all, beef is never going to be with me if we don't know each other," Trina says. "I'm not beefing with somebody I don't know. I find that silly. For me, that takes a lot of energy. I am working so hard, trying to do and build and live and be happy and take care of my family. We only got twenty-four hours in a day. In that twenty-four hours, I'm not going to waste five hours of that to dedicate to imaginary beef with some person that I don't even know, that I've never had a conversation with. That I've never said anything foul about. I'm not going to waste my time. I don't care what you say about me, because I don't know you. You're talking to the air." Case closed.

"That's how I deal with that."

By 2004, Remy Martin finally returned, only now she went as Remy Ma. Producer/artist Dre of the production duo Cool & Dre has a clear memory of first meeting her during studio time with Fat Joe: "I could remember being in the studio and Remy would get there, after going through some wild shit in the hood. [Fat] Joe would always tell her, 'Rem, you've gotta stay out the projects. You've gotta chill,'" Dre recounts.

"But Remy was about that action."

Remy Ma's Castle Hill projects pedigree gave her an edge that many of her peers were still lacking. "Remy was talking that real-life shit," Dre adds, "and she was living it." Her upbringing was less than stellar; drug abuse was all around her, and she'd had to take on a maternal role with her siblings. "You could tell that Remy has been through a very tough life and has been through so many challenges," Laura Stylez says. While she was always rhyming (early on in the form of poetry), Remy was caught up in street life when she got her big break. "People were actually scared of Remy," Stylez continues. "Certain people didn't know how to handle her energy, but Remy talked that talk and she walked that walk. Plus, she was just so fucking talented. Raw talent like that? To see that at that time was just so empowering." Remy was an aggressive rapper as much as she was a fearless one. "She could chew out some of the best," Stylez adds. "She wasn't scared of out-rapping anybody, male or female. She wanted all the smoke."

While 2004's guest appearance on Terror Squad's hit single "Lean Back" gave her leverage for her big debut, she wouldn't release hers until 2006. *There's Something About Remy: Based on a True Story* arrived on February 7 (on the anniversary of Big Pun's passing), though her album's lead single, "Whuteva," came in August 2005, followed by "Conceited" that December. "With 'Conceited,' I just did the record because I felt like everybody needed to feel like there's something special about everybody," Remy told me of the track in 2017. "You may not be the prettiest girl in the world, but you have nice hair, maybe you have nice skin, maybe you have nice handwriting. Everybody has something about them that's desirable by someone else. I just feel like we lack that so much."

The lag in releasing Remy Ma's album was mainly due to her label's negligence of the project. SRC wasn't really moving the needle with their album releases, and Remy was left to her own devices when it came to marketing the album since they barely did. Her self-promotion involved a lot of unnecessary legwork, especially for an artist signed to a major label. Her third single, "Feel So Good" with Ne-Yo, came in April 2006, though by the next year she had left SRC and inked a deal with Capitol Records. Remy Ma had all the makings of a star: her rhymes were hard, her style glamorous. "She's just lyrically gifted," Dre says. "On another level, she is one of those chicks that . . . if she's in a [rap] cypher with you, you better be on your A-game because she's trying to murder you. She's a beast." Her battle/beef with Lady Luck was heavily publicized, as well as an extensive war with Foxy Brown. Her fight with Foxy started in 2004 during an interview with AllHipHop where she loosely jokes about wanting to be the only female rapper. "How do I feel about them? Stay wherever they at, don't drop a song, don't do nothing, let me be the only one. I'm having so much fun. I hope they never come out," she says with a laugh. "Nah, I wish everyone the best of luck. Just don't drop when I drop. That's all I got to say. Matter of fact, just don't drop at all. It'll even be better."

Remy and Foxy took their fight offline and had a few physical altercations. It was Remy's fighting spirit that led her to a lengthy absence from music. In July 2007, Remy was involved in an incident with her friend Makeda Barnes-Joseph, which left Makeda shot twice in the abdomen after Remy accused Makeda of stealing $2,000 from her. Remy was arrested for attempted murder and released on $250,000 bail. The following year, Remy was sentenced to eight years in prison on two counts of assault. It could be chalked up to when keeping it real goes wrong, though Remy was a different person back then, she admits.

"People know more about me now," she told me in 2017. "I was more guarded before. We grow up in an environment that teaches you to show no emotion. You've got to be hard. You've got to be a certain way, and people didn't know me. They thought they knew me, they thought they knew what I was about, but nobody really knew me. But now, some people could say they know me. I'm happier now than I was then."

REMY'S SHOT AT LUCK

They have a saying in my church," begins Lady Luck. "'I can't be perfect. But I can be perfectly honest.' So I will be perfectly honest with you. The devil caught hold of me for a couple of years back then, and at that time, I was out on bail for some crazy shit. I went to jail. I was really out of control."

Given the timeline, Lady Luck had a rough start to her career. While being signed to Def Jam at just seventeen, she fell victim to the label rinse cycle that attempted to market her individuality while abiding by the traditional standards for their female rap artists who could deliver a healthy profit margin. It was all beyond her control, though she still had her bars beside her. Everyone knew that Luck was a beast on the mic, with or without an album. The only problem was where to put that energy. She found a place, though.

The year was 2004, and Remy Ma was up at Hot 97 with Lady Luck, Amil, and a few other rappers. "So, we went to the radio station, and me and Remy was going head to head," Luck recalls, "and you can suppose it got the best of me because it's always been like a little competition, at least in my fucking head. I always wanted to be the best." Luck also wanted Remy to do a collaborative mixtape with her and Philly rapper/Timbaland mentee Ms. Jade, but "Remy wasn't responding to me the way that I felt she should." Meanwhile, Luck was rapping, but she was also trapping, street hustling against the law. "At the time, I am also living a double life as a criminal. So, I am in Massachusetts doing criminal things, and my cousin calls me and tells me that Remy is down here talking shit about me. Now, this was not true. This was not true at all, but my cousin threw me in the fire."

New York's Fight Klub hosted a battle between Lady Luck and Remy

Ma where the winner would take home $20,000. That's a lot of money, but for Luck it was a shot to defeat Remy. The battle lasted for several rounds, as Remy challenged Luck for not being successful. She went on to target Luck's sexuality, her money, and her cars. Of course, Remy also brought up the elusive collaboration that Luck wanted. Luck returned with her own batch of threats against Remy, including a line about snatching Remy's chain and a few about taking her man. The battle hit its breaking point near the end when Remy was clearly getting the upper hand. "I started that battle," Luck admits, "and then after I started that battle, they told me I lost." That wasn't good enough for Lady Luck; she had to take it a step further. "I called Hot 97, and I was like, 'Yo, they said this bitch beat me,'" she now remorsefully recounts. "I singlehandedly blew up the Fight Klub, and I singlehandedly blew up that battle. It would've died that night if I didn't call the radio. I did all of this. I made this whole fucking mess." This battle made Remy Ma one of the leaders of the new guard of female rappers. Within a few months, Fat Joe released "Lean Back," which made Remy even bigger. After that, she got to work on her solo debut album, *There's Something About Remy: Based on a True Story*. Luck did not experience the same fate.

Their war would continue for over a decade, before Remy's time in prison and after it. It all came to a head in 2018. "At one point, Remy was on the radio, and I'd been throwing shots at her," Luck says. "Every interview, somebody was bringing her up, and I was throwing her under the bus, the train. And she did a freestyle down in DC, and she had mentioned my name." Luck's fans egged her on with that, visiting her social media pages trying to prompt a response to the mention. It was about to happen, too. "I wrote a couple of verses," she says, "but when I watched the video for real, I realized that I don't think she meant to say my name. I think it was an old verse." The "Lady Luck" reference came by accident, at least in Luck's opinion. "And I had enough. I had enough of putting out that energy. It felt forced. I didn't have that energy in me anymore."

There's no easy way to play victim in this blood sport, though Lady Luck is easily a victim. Signed as a teenager and told to "just be herself," actions proved louder than words, as Def Jam ultimately sidestepped Luck for not being who they wanted her to be, something they couldn't even accurately pinpoint at the time. So there she was, left to her own devices, finding alternate ways to make money while still attempting to penetrate hip-hop. Her beef with Remy may have never happened had she not been so mistreated by her label and had she been given the chance to really shine. She might still be in the bitter barn, but she's matured since then and managed to sustain a career in both music and television, appearing on VH1's *Love & Hip Hop: New York* with then fiancée Somaya Reece.

In 2018, Luck released the track "Homage," discussing her distaste for female rappers beefing, herself and Remy Ma, even Lil' Kim and Foxy Brown. Remy heard the track and reached out to Luck. At long last, the war was over, and Luck was relieved that that chapter in her life was now closed.

"We settled it from there."

Chapter Eighteen

WHERE MY GIRLS AT?

DON'T GET TOO COMFORTABLE."

That's what an artist manager of a moderately famous rapper said to me as I sat in my broken office chair at my record label publicity job. I thought, *How could I ever be comfortable? My fucking chair is broken.*

His remark was layered because the year was 2005, basically the turning point where most hip-hop purists will admit that they stopped listening to hip-hop altogether until about 2011, when West Coast rapper Kendrick Lamar released *Section.80*. A weird scramble was happening, a shift, if you will. The South was about to reiterate that they were the new hub for hip-hop, and everyone was about to believe them. It was a time for hip-hop's expansion, though is there such a thing as *too* much?

The artist manager who unintentionally commented on my office chair ergonomics managed a Southern rap group. Biting on a toothpick, he scoped out the office and looked the walls up and down, nodding like he was an architect about to blast the building and reconstruct the whole thing. A year later he had his own imprint at the label and a corner office. A few years after that, he was fired and his artists were promptly dropped from the imprint, which has since folded. That was the turnover rate of the early 2000s in hip-hop.

Hopefully he didn't get too comfortable.

You're probably at the part of the book where you're thinking, *How much longer before we get to Nicki Minaj?* because Nicki arrived from what the mainstream perceived as a massive drought when it came to female artists. Despite history proving that there could be so many successful women in hip-hop, the notion of *the one* was still embedded in everyone's brains. The "HIT MAKER," the LAURYN HILL, the LIL' KIM who could have a war with the FOXY BROWN, so one of the two could be knocked out of the race, leaving us with, yes . . .

THE ONE.

But there wasn't just one. Not for close to ten years.

Numbers two, three, four, five, six, and so on passed in and out through hip-hop's doors. While labels were still looking for that special lady, they were reestablishing their faith in their male artists. Plus, the fellas were forming their own little cartels, and labels wanted in on that bag. In 2006, Rick Ross dropped his single "Hustlin'" right off the dock of the *Port of Miami*. Ross quickly became a fixture in rap, despite a dent in his street cred when it was discovered that he had a past working as a corrections officer. Still, his homegrown label Maybach Music Group would arrive three years later, timed with the release of Ross's third studio album, *Deeper Than Rap*. It was deeper than rap; it was back to rapping about drug money and now the Black Mafia Family and all of the things that the '90s had advised rappers to leave behind, only this time the money was much greater, the clothing more designer, and the cars more luxury. Years back, rappers were thrilled to talk about their Lexus, but now Ross was dropping singles called "Maybach Music."

Albums weren't selling like crazy (the aforementioned *Deeper Than Rap* still hasn't gone gold), but it became a singles-driven world, as websites and blogs would premiere a song to be widely consumed and purchased in single form. This all predated streaming music, so the route for many rappers turned entrepreneurs turned kingpins was to release some songs and sign a bunch of dudes and hope one of their songs broke, too. *Dudes* being the operative word.

In 2017, Rick Ross explained to Power 105.1's *The Breakfast Club* why he never signed a female rapper to Maybach Music Group. Early rumblings suggested he was about to sign DMV artist Audra the Rapper in 2010 after meeting her a year prior. It never actually crystallized. "You know, I never did it because I always thought, like, I would end up fucking a female rapper and fucking the business up," Ross told the hosts frankly. "I'm so focused on my business. I gotta be honest with you. You know, she looking good. I'm spending so much money on her photo shoots. I gotta fuck a couple times." That's comforting.

As for Audra, she moved on to bigger things, with a spot on Oxygen network's *Sisterhood of Hip Hop* and her songs placed on hit series like HBO's *Insecure*. Maybach Music Group was (and still is) a boys club, the only female presence being that faint moaning voice of the woman who declares it's "Maybach Music!" at the start of any one of the roster's songs.

Opportunities for women were sealing up in hip-hop, as lingering budgetary constraints at labels felt more like excuses to not sign more female artists. Even the sexy First Lady status seemed threatened with extinction, at least until Nicki Minaj appeared on the scene. Then we had Grand Hustle bringing out Iggy Azalea, Taylor Gang had LoLa Monroe . . . so maybe there was still some room for the right kind of lady rappers?

Options were out there, though somehow limited at the same time. In 2005, there were still some legends around. Lil' Kim dropped *The Naked Truth* and Missy Elliott dropped *The Cookbook,* and those would be the last of their major label releases for a very long time.

Don't get too comfortable.

That same year, a jolt of eccentricity happened when a Sri Lankan singer/rapper named Maya Arulpragasam, known by the acronym M.I.A., released her debut *Arular,* a project that leaned heavily on multi-culti samples. Producer Diplo was just earning his wings as the go-to producer for shape-shifting a new electronic, urban-skewed production widely consumed by hipsters and devoured by the press. By 2007's release of M.I.A.'s *Kala,* Diplo was full speed ahead on the beats, working with production partner Switch. The producing duo came to be known as Major Lazer, and together they worked on M.I.A.'s single "Paper Planes," which would cross over to the other side of hip-hop into T.I.'s hands, sampled for the hit "Swagger Like Us," featuring Jay-Z, Kanye West, and Lil Wayne. M.I.A. was making everyone's head spin. Hip-hop had already been introduced to *bhangra*-inspired vibes by Missy and Timbaland, and here was someone from that part of the planet making the music and keeping it gully at the same time. The daughter of a Tamil Tiger, she was attacking the political infrastructures of everywhere while rhyming in off-key patterns to off-tempo beats. In the nicest way, it was a mindfuck.

The United States was still under the thumb of George W. Bush (we wouldn't get Barack Obama for another three years), so distrust for the nation itself was rampant and somehow that filtered into the music. It allowed for a new British Invasion of sorts, as Amy Winehouse and Lily Allen were a growing presence, thanks to Mark Ronson. Adele came a few years later to set a new pop standard, but artists like Lily and Amy, coming from London's gritty Rinse FM scene, were bringing an edgier vibe. While this lively, thriving, hip-hop-adjacent scene was happening, the heart of mainstream hip-hop was meeting its new leaders like the afore-mentioned Rick Ross and Dr. Dre protégé The Game, who released his debut album *The Documentary* in 2005. Queens shit-talker 50 Cent was on his second album, *The Massacre,* and developing his G-Unit Records imprint (the same imprint that would sign and then go to war with The Game).

Suffice it to say, hip-hop was split up, distracted by its own suc-cess, so outliers were able to slide in and add their own touch. This would in turn lead to the heavy dance influence that would infiltrate hip-hop and remain there for years to come. Think Pitbull, think Flo Rida, though before their invasion, it would present itself as a far more indie-leaning sound, owned by artists who genuinely just loved to make music for tiny nightclubs and dive bars. This genesis was warmly received by some and vehemently rejected by others. One of the wide receivers was the already established and super-artsy Kanye West, who met Canadian producer A-Trak and hired him as his DJ for a spell. A-Trak co-owned his own record label, Fool's Gold Records, and was dating a girl named Melisa Young from Chicago. She liked to rap, using the name Kid Sister, and A-Trak would release her singles on his label. In 2007, she became the Windy City's first prominent female rapper. "I remember thinking, 'Wouldn't it be cool if Kanye got on one of my songs? That would be cool, with the whole Chicago thing," Kid Sister says, as West is an-other Chicago native. "I didn't ask, I didn't make a big deal about it."

Kid Sister had a handful of songs and guest appearances, as her style was colorful and her rhymes harnessed an unorthodox combi-nation of rapping with Chicago's heavily rhythmic juke house music beats. She released a song called "Pro Nails," a playful tune about manicure and pedicure maintenance in the interest of staying fly. The song began buzzing over the newly minted social media arena.

"It was just timing," Kid Sister says. "The Internet was starting to get bigger, everyone had computers, and social media was starting." Myspace pages became a haven for self-promotion, as artists were finding each other online and growing their fan bases together (SoundCloud would later take this formula over). "The season before me was backpack rap," Kid Sister says, alluding to the underground hip-hop community known for its artists wearing bulky backpacks. Their promotional vehicle was also built from the Internet (in the form of message boards), though they rarely hit the surface. The only way to get out of the indie underbelly was to create something more widely embraced. "So, while 'Pro-Nails' was a rappity-rap song, it's still pop," she says. "It's a dance-pop rap song. That's why I think [it became popular]. It was accessible and danceable."

Kanye West in turn heard "Pro Nails" and loved it. He jumped on the song out of his own volition. "It's true! Nobody asked him to do that," says Kid Sister. On the opener to the song, he confirms that he joined his fellow Chicago native simply because he wanted to. She learned about the remix after the fact. It was a complete surprise.

"I was at a movie theater in Evanston, Illinois, when I found out," Kid Sister recalls. "I fell down on my knees and started screaming. It was pretty cool." The Kanye West feature gave Kid Sister leverage her female rap peers of the time didn't have, and she dropped her solo debut album, *Ultraviolet,* in 2009 (via Fool's Gold/Downtown/Universal Republic), collaborating with CeeLo Green on "Daydreaming," which became the album's fifth single. "I will always be grateful to Kanye for getting on ['Pro Nails'] and what it meant for me," she adds.

Before that moment, Kid Sister was already building her buzz overseas, part of the growing electronic movement that was swishing between continents and collecting each other's influences along the way. The UK's garage movement was offering artists like singer/songwriter/rapper Ms. Dynamite the opportunity to rap more over broken beats, which reflected a sound artists in the States were going for. Artists like Philly singer/rapper Amanda Blank were also entering into this new scene. As for Kid Sister, she was across the pond.

"I was touring preliminarily in Europe, and that was the artist I was on track to be: the girl who goes to Europe, who's like, cool," she says. "Perhaps that's part of the reason why [Kanye worked with me]." His fascination with the avant-garde was already evident at this point, as he'd ditched the street vibe that had earned him his Roc-A-Fella chain and was aiming more for Euro high fashion.

With the kind of quick success that Kid Sister experienced comes pressure, and her label began demanding pop-leaning tracks to launch her further into the mainstream stratosphere. As the only female to emerge from Fool's Gold Records at the time, it was harder getting her voice to be heard. "I think in hindsight I also relied on them a little too much," she says of the men around her, "and that ultimately led to what ended up happening, which was me going out on my own." Her failed relationship with A-Trak played another role. "It was helpful in the beginning and then it was very, very unhelpful later," Kid Sister adds with a laugh. "Advice to the ladies out there: Don't date your producer/label owner. Bad news."

Eventually, however, the convergence of hip-hop and dance reached a crossroads. The harbingers of that dance-y, rappity sound were inching closer toward the mainstream and ultimately changing the dynamic of the underground movement from which it came. "I had this inkling like, 'Hmmm, this doesn't feel right anymore,'" Kid Sister says. "'I'm rapping and rapping. This doesn't feel good anymore.' My gut instinct was to stop." That was her motivation to stop on a personal level, but a bigger movement was happening that ultimately curbed her enthusiasm for the music. "The reason I didn't feel excited anymore was because the music was going to this very white, very male, very aggressive place," she admits. "I'm just like, 'I liked dance music when it was brown and gay. I don't even know what this is.' The whole reason why I was excited about it in the first place was because there were no bros." But the bros had invaded, and taken over. Now if you owned a laptop and made a cultural reference, you were golden. Sponsored tours, big gigs. It was all happening. The most successful product of this formula was (and still is) Diplo. "We're artists. If you wanna be the business person, get the fuck out of art. You have no place here," Kid Sister says emphatically, though her remarks aren't aimed at anyone in particular. "That's not what this is about, and the part that's dangerous is that these guys *think* they're artists."

Female rappers were popping up in droves, though attempting to remain ambiguous. See, they would *rap,* but their beat selections were still somewhat dance and pop, so in the event that they could snag a crossover hit, they could ditch the rap tag altogether. White female rapper Kreayshawn would attempt this in 2011 with her track "Gucci Gucci," as part of her cheeky Bay Area collective White Girl Mob (cosigned by Bay Area viral rap cult leader Lil B, the BasedGod), though her success would fizzle and she would be replaced by another white woman, Australian glamazon Iggy Azalea, whose mentor was none other than Atlanta's Grand Hustle Records chart-topper T.I.

The narrative had begun to change all around, depending upon who was telling it, and labels had started searching for stories to sell in addition to music. Harlem native Azealia Banks knows that angle all too well. Banks's story within hip-hop could be told through a lengthy Twitter thread, as that's where so much of her controversy has lived. Super-talented, bold, and yet a product of the major label rinse cycle, Azealia saw firsthand what happens when hip-hop falls in and out of love with its female artists.

"I was trying to be an actress, I wanted to be a Disney kid so badly," Banks recalls with a laugh. As a child, she would go on casting calls and auditions with her mom, looking to break into theater.

"I think that my mind got really apt for art and finding solutions because of childhood trauma," she explains. "I had a really emotionally traumatic childhood with my mother. We weren't poor, we weren't starving, we weren't on welfare. We had things, but there was a lot of generational debris. My mother was the first of a new generation, in a sense. She was winging it as best she could." Azealia spent a lot of time in her room, keeping herself company while managing depressive episodes. "As a child, your brain is more malleable," she reflects, "so you're able to bounce back faster." She compares her childhood emotions to a ball, always bouncing. "As you get older, that ball can get deflated, but when you're young it's just that bouncing, that kind of got my wild creativity all over the place."

Disney didn't happen for young Azealia, though she would later keep a Disney theme in her work, heavily inserting a *Little Mermaid* thread with her *Fantasea* mixtapes and performing at the Mermaid Ball. She would drop random songs over social media to keep her creativity going, without a worry or care that they would land anywhere, though they did.

In 2008, at the age of seventeen, Banks signed to UK label XL Recordings after being discovered through her Myspace page. In 2011, she dropped the single "212," which became a viral hit. "I didn't know what the fuck was going on," she says. "I'm an AOL kid. I'm a Myspace kid. I actually had a manager say, 'We're gonna put your video on YouTube.' I was just like, 'Whatever. Who cares.' I didn't start rapping to do business. I just wanted to rap over these cool little beats and be that weird Black girl that I am." Then the majors came calling, and Banks quickly signed with Interscope. "You have Jimmy Iovine to thank for Azealia Banks," she says. "He's the one who unleashed me on all you muthafuckers." She remembers her signing day vividly. "Jimmy Iovine took me on this huge shopping spree. He took me to Harvey Nichols and let me go wild. He spent like forty thousand dollars that day. He actually bought me my first pair of

Louboutins. I remember thinking, 'I'm a bad bitch now.'"

Azealia garnered sizable critical acclaim in record time, first with her *1991* EP and *Fantasea* mixtape in 2012, then later with her debut album, *Broke with Expensive Taste,* in 2014. Known for cheeky raps and witticisms that can live on both high-speed instrumentals or smooth house beats, Banks was full of versatility, though she was never as widely promoted as other acts on the label. Interscope had released Lady Gaga's *The Fame* the same year Banks was signed. It was hard to shine on a label with such big names, including rappers like Eminem, who was readying his 2009 release *Relapse.* There was no room to nurture Banks, though she was able to flex creatively, a move she credits to Iovine seeing the potential in what she describes as her "complex brain." Her skill was evident even from "212": heavy drums, fast rhymes, a manufactured British accent rapping about hitting on women. Was it all too much? Was hip-hop not ready for the kitchen sink to be thrown at it the way Banks was planning to do? Maybe, though Banks says her plans were derailed because she refused to sign away all her rights to the label.

"Had I had a three-sixty deal? Oh please, you would've seen me everywhere," she says. "I wouldn't allow them to exploit my product." If she wasn't selling her soul, they weren't going to push her to make a profit, especially when their cut wouldn't be as significant. "I'm a Harlem bitch, I'm a hustler. I wouldn't let them hustle me. Thinking back on it, there were lots of deals that I thought we should've taken. There was lots of money left on the table, but I was young." It also came to a screeching halt in 2014 when Jimmy Iovine left Interscope. "That's when it all fell apart," she says.

Bank's story as an aspiring female rapper from Harlem transformed into a case study on her social media behavior and outlandish comments about other artists, particularly other female rappers. Her catalog remained consistent, dropping songs in the midst of controversy. The music kept fans coming back. And of course the drama continued, as beefs with everyone from Nicki Minaj to Lil' Kim, Iggy Azalea, and Remy Ma rose and fell over social media. The list goes on, though it's particularly centered on Iggy Azalea, as the two were embroiled in a back-and-forth that had onlookers debating who to side with. Do you defend the manufactured white female rapper who may one day destroy everything that hip-hop stands for, or do you side with the slightly unhinged but talented Black girl from Harlem, which would only motivate her to keep responding? While Banks's rap skills were still sharp, they were overshadowed by her online behavior—she would tweet remarks at people like everyone else does, but was labeled as an Internet troll whose traumatic childhood had left her a bully. "It's a narrative everyone wanted to assume: that I was broke and poor, came from the hood," she says. "It's trauma porn, and with Azealia Banks, everybody loves my trauma porn. They're just like, 'So how did it feel when you got shit on? Do you feel shitty? Awww. It must be so hard to be a woman.' I'm done with the trauma porn. Ask me what my favorite color is and what I like to eat in the morning."

Banks laughs about this whole dilemma in retrospect, and while she admits she still adds fuel to the fire online, she's more concerned about why people care so much about her opinions.

"I don't understand why people keep torturing themselves by subjecting themselves to me," Azealia says with a laugh. "I'm not coming around you, you're coming around me to complain about me. That doesn't make sense. Just go away. Heal yourself. It's not my fault you're addicted to my horrible opinions. I'm tired of people blaming me for their own stupidity and bullshit. Stop listening to me, look the other way. Turn your phone off. Unfollow me. There are so many ways you can rid your life of Azealia Banks, yet you choose to just stay here. And complain that you're here."

In January 2019, the *Guardian* published an article titled "Azealia Banks: Fearless Truthteller or Relentless Troll?" questioning whether

Banks's belief system is something to be celebrated (the way many do with an artist like Kanye West) or neutralized to prevent further damage. The article stemmed from an incident where Banks was escorted off an Aer Lingus flight and referred to the staff as "ugly Irish women." She's been involved in a series of violent incidents, like biting a female security guard on the breast in New York City. She's also used the term *faggot* loosely (though still has a largely thriving gay following) and made a few slurs about other celebrities, including former One Direction frontman Zayn Malik, whom she called a "curry-scented bitch." Banks has also been quite vocal about defending her stance on bleaching her skin, supporting many conservative views, and other things that in present-day society are deemed destructive, particularly toward the advancement of People of Color.

It's a long rap sheet, though to Azealia Banks's point, the question remains, why do people care so much what she thinks and what she does? There's a long list of men who exhibit the same behavior, though they're not as readily challenged for it. Perhaps the best solution would be to offer her a greater platform to release her music, since when that was in full view, none of this behavior seemed to matter.

It's the kind of scrutiny that doesn't happen to men as frequently, though Azealia Banks's brash commentary became her handshake.

"That's what makes life as a woman that much more interesting," she says. "Fuck guys."

Buried beneath Banks's outlandish commentary, however, is her music. As an artist, she's what many might refer to as *slept-on*. That's the term thrown predominantly toward women who are talented in their craft but never given the full open road to ride. It's a backhanded compliment, really. Many female rappers thrive without a major label push, but if they're not oversaturating the market, they're "slept-on," almost determining the fate of their careers by dismissing any track record of previous success and inadvertently cursing them, preventing any successful moves going forward. It's similar to *femcee,* the age-old descriptor of female rappers used to distinguish women from men in hip-hop. There are many *slept-on femcees* out there.

"I feel like it's always crazy that people to this day hit me on some, 'You're good for a girl,'" says rapper Snow Tha Product. "Women should be seen as talent, not gender-based. At the end of the day, I guess I get it. There are bigger issues in the world as it is right now, so that's not something that I super dwell on. What I don't like is when people write me off because I'm a female rapper. That offends me more." Snow started in hip-hop as a teen in San Diego, but moved to Texas to hone her craft. In 2013, she signed to Atlantic Records, but after little movement with the label, she departed in 2018. With a name like "Snow" and skin just as pale, the Mexican American MC struggled with her identity from the beginning.

"It sucks because I kind of get it from all angles. I'm not Mexican enough, I'm not dark enough to be Hispanic—to be brown. I'm not a white rapper, so I don't get the little clout that you get from being a white rapper, so I don't fit in certain scenes. I do try my best to represent my people, but sometimes that kind of alienates certain fans." Her pride turns to prejudice in the eyes of some. "They feel like I'm dividing them when at the same time I'm just repping, but then if I don't rep, it's like, 'Are you ashamed? Are you pretending to be white?'" In her near decade of rapping, Snow has managed to create a cult following by celebrating the loyalty of her fan base. "There's so many years, so much work, so much content, so many songs and shows, free meet-'n'-greets, shirts and merch, and then all the struggles people have seen me go through, like literally every time I've been snubbed or gone through stuff in front of fans," she expresses. "I think it grows that love so much more because they're like, 'Yo, she actually deserves it.' That's really all it is."

While Snow is a prime example of the term *slept-on* being used, her career, in hindsight, was something she wasn't prepared to handle. "I realize now that I'm older and that my son's growing up, I wasn't ready," she says of her time in the music industry. She even reached out to young rising Florida rapper Bhad Bhabie to show her love. Had Snow remained on Atlantic Records, the two would be labelmates. "I actually talked to Bhad Bhabie about this; I sent her a message," she says. "I said, 'Yo congrats that you got signed.'" Bhad Bhabie was signed at fifteen years old after she appeared on the *Dr. Phil* show and a clip of her backtalking an audience member and threatening to jump her outdoors went viral, birthing her meme-worthy remark, "Cash me ousside. Howbow dah?" Bhad Bhabie, born Danielle Bregoli, caught flak for being signed to Atlantic Records as a rapper when she was only known for one bratty snap. She has since proven the naysayers wrong, sustaining a whole career and making history in 2017 as the youngest female rapper to ever land on the Billboard Hot 100, thanks to her introductory single, "These Heaux." Snow is certain she wouldn't have survived that early awkward phase of her career, had she been in Bhad Bhabie's shoes.

"I don't think people give someone like her enough credit for being fifteen when she was signed and going through so much hate and turning that into a career," Snow adds. "Being able to survive that? Fifteen-year-old me? First of all, I was suicidal at a young age. I would've done something stupid. So when people hear me rapping about other female rappers, they think I'm shitting on them, and it's like, no. Everyone has their own journey and I know I wasn't strong enough to be able to ever have blown up all of a sudden." In the end, Snow's slow-brewed success kept her afloat as an artist, even when her label wasn't supportive.

"I always try to make sure my raps or my skills or my work ethic are the first things people say about me," she says. "So right now, one of the biggest reasons why I'm very happy as a person is because I do feel most conversations are about me either being underrated or how well I rap or how much I work. That's the best that can happen to me."

"I'm not sure what to make of the fact that my listeners call me underrated, to be honest," says Dessa, a Minnesota rapper and former CEO of Minnesota indie record label Doomtree. "On one hand, it's flattering. On the other, I bet most fans of independent music consider their favorite artist to be underrated, so I try not to let it go to my head." Dessa started releasing music in the early 2000s, and by 2010 had gained momentum. Her participation in hip-hop's indie scene brought her to the attention of critics, but she also faced challenges as one of the only female rappers to come out of Minnesota, a region only known for independent record labels like Doomtree and Rhymesayers, led by duo Atmosphere.

Today, as a published author and less-active recording artist, Dessa's lens is perhaps sharper now that she's no longer in the thick of it and can see where her opportunities and roadblocks existed more clearly.

"I've often benefited from being a woman in hip-hop," Dessa says. "The relative novelty can attract attention—and attention is a currency in and of itself in the arts."

The environment was vast, growing with new female artists who still seemed to lack proper exposure and respect. It was almost as if the lane to become that chosen one was wide-open, though a series of issues like money, social media behavior, branding, and lyrics (both talented and not talented) were all dumped into that lane as women bobbed and weaved to keep going. And they did.

"Sometimes I've been disrespected or dismissed as a woman," Dessa continues. "People have questioned my gender online, implying that a muscular, assertive woman isn't really a woman at all. I've been touched inappropriately by showgoers and promoters before, during, and after shows. If the question is, 'Does being a woman help or hurt you in professional settings?' the answer is *yes*."

Rapsody wowing fans with her unbridled lyricism.

Chapter Nineteen

INSIDE, OUT

IN 2014, I PLAYED MYSELF ON OXYGEN'S REALITY TV SERIES *Sisterhood of Hip Hop*. My close friend and fellow journalist Sowmya Krishnamurthy referred me for the job. On the episode in which I appear, I play a pushy journalist (accurate) who asks rapper Nyemiah Supreme a little too much about her personal life while her manager, Alex Rago, looks on in horror. Nyemiah was working with Timbaland at that point in time, and she was urged by the show's production staff to be cagey in her answers to my aggressive line of questioning, to further develop her character as the show's "difficult" female artist. That interview style is not my thing in real life, but hey, it was for the cameras. Nyemiah was also really sweet and really talented, so I felt kind of bad that was the "character" they had developed for her. These weren't the Real Housewives of wherever or some Middle Americans wanting to eat a pile of worms on a reality competition series. These were artists who really wanted to make their art into careers. Instead, they became the focal points of creative nonfiction. The series ran for two years, following a handful of female rappers around as they all clamored for a top spot in hip-hop. It was late to the reality television game, since Reality TV 6.0 had already happened.

If the first season of MTV's *The Real World* (set in New York City in 1992) marked the theoretical start of reality television, *Survivor* was the 2.0, where the initial setup was a cast that reflected a microcosm of society, dumped into a fishbowl and required to jump hurdles and do crazy things so they wouldn't die, or whatever. The 3.0 involved becoming purposefully crazy to be the zaniest cast member on any of the long list of shows that eventually rolled out (think "Dylan, Dylan, Dylan" from *Making the Band*). The 4.0 was *American Idol,* where if you had some musical talent, the world could watch you grow and then reenter society with a recording contract. The 5.0 was *Laguna Beach* and *The Hills,* dubbed "scripted reality," which is basically saying, "This isn't real life at all, but everyone uses their government names (except for Justin Bobby)."

The 6.0 was *Keeping Up with the Kardashians* in 2007 (jumping over the lavishness of *The Real Housewives of Orange County* in 2006 and completely taking it over), and nothing has been the same since. Of course, Reverend Run and his family did this familial setup first with *Run's House* in 2005, but the Kardashians made it an empire with some very forced character "development" to keep the momentum going. That, and they all went from looking like everyday people to glamazons as the series progressed. Once hip-hop got ahold of that business model, it was game over. This paradigm dictated the next ten years of hip-hop, especially for women.

In a flash, Viacom was taking over the whole shebang with a bunch of franchises. VH1's *Ego Trip's The (White) Rapper Show* was one of the more prominent ones in 2007, with MC Serch in hot pursuit for the most animated white guy who happened to rap. *Miss Rap Supreme* came next, along with MTV's *From G's to Gents*, which gave us the gift of RiFF RaFF. The irony here is that women were wedged in the mix as unruly "characters," never artists. "Let's throw the girls in a TV lineup with goofy white guys who try to use the N-word and a bunch of dudes who don't tuck their shirts in. That makes the most sense, right?" (Wrong).

This is how you set up perfectly talented female rappers for failure. You place them in a lineup like they're all leaned toward the mirror in a nightclub bathroom attempting to put on lipstick—some are elbowing each other, others are complimenting one another's shoes. Making new friends and new enemies. We all have our quirks, and what reality TV did to women in hip-hop was put them all in plain view in the spotlight, using hip-hop as the backdrop. We can't call it the worst formula, since it gave us Cardi B. But for some artists, reality TV became the greatest dice roll.

In 2014, after serving six years in prison, Remy Ma was finally free. That freedom ain't free for women, though. While Remy had served one of the longest terms of any rapper, male or female, she wasn't given the ceremonious homecoming many male rappers received upon their release, complete with a parade and abundant opportunities to record their comeback project, like Lil Wayne or T.I. or most recently Birmingham's Gucci Mane, whose prison term resulted in new music and a *New York Times*–bestselling memoir.

"When I came home, people were afraid of me," Remy told me in 2017. "People were acting weird. They didn't know what to expect of me, what I was going to do. I had this horrible reputation. It was just really bad. I just cried, and I said to my husband [rapper Papoose], like, 'Yo, this is crazy. What's going on?'"

On the day of her release, August 1, 2014, Remy left prison at 4:30 P.M. and by 8:30 that night, she was in the studio with DJ Khaled recording a remix of "They Don't Love You No More" with

French Montana, her first single since her sentencing. Her concern was focused on reversing the damage of her prison term.

In 2011, VH1 premiered the series *Love & Hip Hop*. Produced by entrepreneur Mona Scott-Young, the show centered around a rotating ensemble cast of both active and retired hip-hop artists and their love interests. With the late Chris Lighty, Scott-Young was cofounder of the massive hip-hop management company Violator, so not only was her Rolodex thick, but she understood the market. It started in New York with rapper Jim Jones and his fiancée, Chrissy Lampkin, though it moved on to artists like rapper and radio personality Joe Budden and expanded into multiple cities, including Miami, Atlanta, and Hollywood. The franchise galvanized viewers by the millions, quickly becoming the highest-rated series in several years for VH1.

For years the *Love & Hip Hop* franchise had been looking to add Remy Ma and Papoose, but it was never an idea Remy entertained, until she saw her post-prison reputation. "I told my husband, 'Yo, if we do this right, it's a possibility that I could humanize myself,'" she says. "People will see me as a wife, as a mother, as an artist, as someone who made a mistake and they're coming back, and they just want another chance at life. It just started with me wanting people to take me seriously and know that I'm not this horrible person that it appears to be if you just Google my name." So Remy Ma and Papoose joined the cast. Her mission was accomplished. "We went for it, and it worked," she says "I can't say without a hitch, but . . ."

In 2016, Remy returned hard as ever on the track "All the Way Up," with Fat Joe, French Montana, and Infrared, which appeared on Joe and Remy's collaborative return, 2017's *Plata O Plomo*. It was the double-platinum single that changed Remy's trajectory, from rising MC to prison inmate to reality star to rap legend, wife, and mother. "She was just in a way-better space, breathing easier," says Dre (of Cool & Dre) of Remy's "All the Way Up" process. "Just wiser, is what I'd say. She used that 'All the Way Up' record to cement opportunities for her that would go beyond just making music. Whether it's opening up a store in the Carolinas or doing a TV show with her husband. She's moving like a businesswoman. That's the big difference we've seen in her. She's really just moving like a businesswoman. We're really proud of her."

Remy had another hurdle to overcome, one she had no idea existed until she read an offhand Instagram comment. We're sitting on a sofa at her label, Columbia Records, conducting the interview. She's scrolling through Instagram and tells me about the shock she felt upon reading a comment under one of her pictures. "What did she say exactly?" She squints and tries to remember. "'I think she'd be prettier if she wasn't so dark-skinned.' And then it started this whole chain of things. You know how people comment and everybody just feeds off of it? People was like, 'Oh, yeah. She's a gorilla. She's black.' It was just crazy." It spiraled off into a greater conversation between Remy and her girlfriends. "I was talking to my friend about it, and she was like, 'Yeah, girl. You didn't know about the silent war between the light-skinned girls and dark-skinned girls?'" she says. "I was like, 'Um . . . no.' Then they were saying how girls in the strip clubs are a big thing. The bartenders and the dancers that are darker-skinned don't really get any type of shine at all. If a big artist comes in the building, they'll send [out] all of the light-skinned girls, and the girls that supposedly look quote-unquote 'exotic.' It's this whole big thing."

Colorism has always been present in the Black community, though it became more prevalent in hip-hop as the skin bleaching craze took off, with Azealia Banks being a proponent. It was something that North Carolina rapper Rapsody felt compelled to address once her platform grew. In 2007, Rapsody, born Marlanna Evans, debuted on famed producer 9th Wonder's follow-up album,

The Dream Merchant Vol. 2. After already solidifying her skills as part of the Raleigh, North Carolina, rap outfit Kooley High, the MC was ready to take her message to the masses. "As an artist, for me, there wasn't a space necessarily that I felt was represented as far as just being the girl next door, or just being yourself," Rapsody recalls. "Being yourself isn't enough to the world."

Her 2012 album *The Idea of Beautiful* marked a turning point in her career, as Rapsody challenged the European-inspired beauty standards that had flooded back into the market during the height of reality television and the Kardashian craze. "This was at the beginning of butt injections. I remember everybody was wearing waist trainers," she says. "You know, I grew up when you used to walk around with a bare face and just put on a little mascara and lipstick, and you were cool. But now you've got to have perfect eyebrows, you've got to have fake lashes. Nothing seemed real to me when it came to these women. Everything was fake from head to toe. Not necessarily saying that there's something wrong with that, but the fact that women felt like they had to do that to be seen or be appreciated, it just never sat with me well. What is this idea of beautiful?" Female rappers had previously delved into surgery, though more often after their careers had taken off, and then it wasn't celebrated. Many looked at an artist like Lil' Kim with sympathetic eyes for wanting to augment her body. Here it was par for the course in order to win.

For Rapsody, rocking a hoodie and a pretty face wasn't enough for the public. "We would get comments like, 'Oh, why is 9th dressing you that way?'" Rapsody recalls. "I wasn't sexual, I was clothed from head to toe, I don't wear weaves. Nothing wrong with that, but . . ." Despite being compared to the likes of lyrical legends like Lauryn Hill, Rapsody's whole style was attacked, right down to her music. "I didn't rap about being sexual. My beat selections, they were still soulful, and they were still boom bap, which people associated with just being old school," she says. "Like it didn't have a place to grow, to expand, to still be relevant. I'm too 'wordy.'"

The complexity of her rhymes was used against her as a reason for her lack of mainstream appeal. "'I don't understand what she's talking about because it's too complicated,'" she says, mimicking her critics. "Everything's just so very simple and straightforward and just handed to you on a plate. Nobody understands how to break down lyrics anymore. Like you can't even give a simple metaphor analogy . . . it just completely goes over people's heads. It was a challenge, I felt like, on every front imaginable."

Rapsody persevered, and in 2017 she made her debut with Jay-Z's Roc Nation with her sophomore album, *Laila's Wisdom*. The project escalated her critical acclaim, complete with two Grammy nominations for Best Rap Album and Best Rap Song (for "Sassy"). She was also the only woman nominated for Best Rap Album in 2018. Still, the subject of her looks became the topic of conversation. Like Missy Elliott, Rapsody was diagnosed with Graves' disease, which affected her perception of herself even more. "I was never an arrogant or conceited person, but I always knew I was cute," she recalls. "I was never like, 'Damn, I'm the most beautiful thing in the world,' but to go from that and then having Graves' disease and gaining weight and having my eyes bulge out . . . I was not happy with the reflection I saw a lot of days, for years, when I woke up in the morning. I guess you could say I had low confidence because of it. I would walk around sometimes squinting my eyes just to make them not look big. I probably looked crazy." Commenters called her ugly, a subject she addressed on her *Laila's Wisdom* track "Black & Ugly," though her real inspiration to keep going was her niece. "She's a young girl, dark complexion, and I pray she never has to go through this," Rapsody says. "But in order for her to know and to be confident, I can't let this get the best of me. I have to be the representation."

Rapsody's sexuality was also called into question simply because of how she dressed and rhymed. "One hundred percent, the way I dress and in videos, the way my rap hands would make a nigga think, 'Oh, she definitely likes women. She don't like us,'" she says. (Rap hands, or gesturing while rhyming, are mainly considered an attribute of male artists.) "Because if you rap like I rap, people don't think women are supposed to rap like that. 'Oh, why she rappin' like a man?' Like, what? Men don't fucking own hip-hop, for one. Rapping is rapping. It's an act. It's not something that's a man thing. It's the action. Anybody can do it."

For decades, however, the female sexuality debate has persisted in hip-hop.

"Sis, I didn't say, 'Hey, I'm gay,' until like last year!" Lady Luck says.

In her early rap days, Lady Luck had a fitted cap permanently affixed to her head. It was a noticeable fashion decision made by Def Jam to distinguish her from Foxy Brown, though it became an inadvertent signal of her sexuality. "You could see what the fuck I was," Luck says. "I just wasn't announcing it and putting it on the front street."

Female rappers were selling a fantasy to their male audience, whether they wanted to or not. It was the very concept Biggie introduced to Lil' Kim when he basically told her that her bullish bars had no place in rap and a deep throat was more marketable than a deep lyric. If your sexuality came into suspicion, where would that leave your success? There's a list of female rappers rumored to be gay, though for these artists, like Queen Latifah, their art has nothing to do with their personal lives. For her, that public admission didn't even matter. It still doesn't.

In a 2010 interview with *Rolling Stone,* Nicki Minaj cleared up a self-inflicted rumor that she was bisexual. "I think girls are sexy," she remarked. "But I'm not going to lie and say that I date girls."

Her early rhymes were dedicated to sexual fluidity, and very early on in her stardom story, she embraced the attention-grabbing title of "bisexual rapper." By 2010, that narrative was deaded. Whether she is or isn't bisexual is no longer up for debate, since at this point, her identity has eclipsed any gender preference and moved on to simply "star," yet still remains fluid in her rhymes. For those artists who openly identify as gay, however, embracing their identity is not something to hint at in their rhymes in the hopes of creating some hot fantasy for male listeners. This is just legitimately who they are.

"My family at the time was Orthodox Christian," Luck says. "So, I was in the closet myself. At the time, Ellen [DeGeneres] was like a hero for so many people, especially me, because I was super young when [she came out]. But to come out in the world, the way that it was . . . Nowadays, I appreciate how free everybody is." While Luck entered the reality TV realm on *First Family of Hip Hop,* she openly discussed her life with her former fiancée, *Love & Hip Hop* alum Somaya Reece. There was no more hiding, and she admits she was much happier once that happened.

An artist like Young M.A didn't really have a choice. Remaining true to herself was nonnegotiable, and the alternative made her not want to pursue music—her story almost didn't happen. Early on, she worked loosely with a manager who tried to style her in dresses and heels for events and performances. "I was younger then," she admits. "I knew I always wanted to do music, but at that point in my life, I knew I wasn't really ready for the industry." The (male) manager's suggestions were disheartening, so Young M.A put her dreams on pause, imagining a world where she couldn't be herself. "I didn't even express myself on being gay yet," she says. "I didn't even tell my mother yet. It was so much." Eventually, the music kept popping back up, and she saw the need to proceed. "I realized how much it mattered to people that I did music," she says. "I realized like, 'Yo, c'mon, this is your love,' and once I started to express myself on me just being gay and liking women, it became a little easier. It was like, 'Ok, I've got that weight off my shoulders. Now it's time to just go.' I just start going full steam ahead." Young M.A's whole aesthetic is pretty clear, right down to her name (the "M.A" stands for "Me Always"), and when her debut single was released in 2016, the secret was out: the fiery track, "OOOUUU," alluded to sex with women. From that point on, the Brooklyn-bred artist was praised for her street lyricism and uncompromising bars, and her 2017 EP *Herstory* further proved that.

Both male and female rap artists identifying as gay endured the threat of being publicly outed. In 1998, Wendy Williams (then a jock at Hot 97), told her listeners that one high-profile male rapper was indeed gay. This started a witch hunt for the "gay rapper," as if it were some shamefully shocking revelation. Williams was fired from the station for a number of reasons, but that comment was a major factor. However, the sensationalism surrounding Williams's remark drove many gay rappers, especially women, back into the closet. An anonymous source revealed to me that a legendary female rapper declined my book interview out of her team's concern that I would discuss her sexuality in print for the first time. (Just FYI: it was never going to be mentioned.)

While sexual identity in hip-hop is still such a clandestine subject for many established acts, newer artists who come out as members of the LGBTQ community from the start have no big reveal—in fact, it is never even pondered. There's no press statement, no team needed to do damage control, and no questions about what they're wearing and what it might suggest about who they're going home with. It's all out in the open, so their music speaks for itself. That's no shot to the LGBTQ artists who came before them who had to keep their lives under wraps to protect themselves, their record deals, and even their families, and often still do. But maybe some just don't care to put their business out there, though when they conceal it, it unfortunately becomes a bigger point for scrutiny. The new class is slowly growing hip to those tricks. Their generation, the tail end of the millennials and Generation Z, have no care for gay or straight. They live in the middle and operate as they please. We can thank groups like Yo! Majesty for paving the way.

Young M.A; Big Freedia, an artist embraced by both the trans and drag communities and known for her elaborate stage presence, bold wigs, and makeup; singer Kehlani (who identifies as queer); Detroit rapper Invincible (now known as Ill Weaver), who identifies with the nonbinary gender pronoun of *they*; and bisexual rapper Taylor Bennett, younger brother of famed artist Chance The Rapper—these are just a few of the artists who have made their own place in music while freely revealing this part of their lives to their fan base. Regardless of gender, hip-hop artists have always struggled with sexual identity and how it would affect their success. Now, however, selling a fantasy is nothing compared to the wins of selling reality.

"I didn't care what people thought," Young M.A says. "It was like, 'Yo, man, if they're going to accept me, they're going to accept me. If they don't, they don't, but you can never say I didn't try. That was my whole motto: If I never try, how will I know? So that's what I did."

Nicki Minaj in 2009, right before the glow up.

Chapter Twenty

FROM BARBIE TO BARDI

IT ALL STARTED IN A STAIRWELL.

The year was 2007, and as far as mainstream hip-hop was concerned, female rappers had run their course. The stars were the stars, so any next moves they made were expected. There was no fresh blood, no breath of life to suggest that once they moved on to other ventures, there would be a new guard waiting behind them to grab that baton.

And then there she was. Flanked by the man they call Big Fendi, Nicki Minaj sat on a step in a dank stairwell waving money and talking threats. You were waiting for the one woman to come through and overturn the industry? Well, here she was in the flesh, in bamboo earrings and blunt bangs, a little rough around the edges yet full of promise. She was being filmed for the street DVD series *The Come Up*, and had already been dabbling in the rap game. The Trinidad-born, Queens-raised artist had worked with hip-hop legends Full Force before taking her talents to Myspace, under the name "Nicki Maraj." Big Fendi found Nicki online and reached out to her, signing her to his street label Dirty Money. Born Onika Maraj, she changed up her name to Nicki Minaj at his suggestion, and dropped her solo debut mixtape, *Playtime Is Over,* in 2007. She followed up a year later with her mixtape *Sucka Free.* By 2009, Nicki was working with Debra Antney, CEO of Mizay Entertainment, who began grooming Nicki for bigger things. That year she released her third mixtape, *Beam Me Up Scotty,* which hit the jackpot thanks to songs like "I Get Crazy" with Lil Wayne and "Itty Bitty Piggy." Wayne spotted Nicki on that stairwell in *The Come Up* and signed her to Young Money. It was fast, it was furious. Nicki Minaj's success was moving at the speed of light, though no one knew just how fast it was traveling. But Nicki was full of homage to her predecessors, at least in the beginning.

The cover for her *Sucka Free* mixtape showed her squatting and licking a lollipop, a loose dedication to Lil' Kim's infamous *Hard Core* pose. She had also enjoyed the mentorship of Monie Love. By this point, Monie Love was working as a DJ at Philly's Power 99, and helmed her own Sirius XM show, *Ladies First.* Her boyfriend was an artist working with a producer named Andrew "Pop" Wansel (of Pop & Oak, who later produced Nicki's "Your Love"), who was also working with Nicki Minaj. After learning that Pop knew Monie, Nicki asked for her number. "I get a text out of the blue one day from some girl that says her name is Nicki Minaj," Monie recalls. "I was like, 'Yeah, right.' She was like, 'No, seriously.' We began a rapport. It was a very good one." Monie tried adding Nicki's remix of Beyoncé's "Sweet Dreams" (titled "Beautiful Nightmare") to Power 99, but "They would not touch it with a ten-foot pole." She added it to her *Ladies First* playlist since she could program her own music at Sirius. "She started getting booked to do shows in Philly because of that remix that I leaked," Monie says. "So, she became a fixture in Philly as one of her first markets that she conquered." Monie also gave Nicki her first interview on-air at Power 99.

"During that time, she had conversations with me," Monie says. "She told me how she did 'Ladies First' in some talent show at school or something. She was like, 'I loved Kim . . .' She seemed every bit appreciative. This girl was going to be next." Monie sent out the bat signal to other female rap legends, advising them of a new talent who was about to continue their legacy. Some were hesitant to believe Monie. Others had never even heard of Nicki Minaj. "I knew she was going to blow up, I knew she was going to," Monie says. "I was like, 'You are going to carry on your shoulders the heart and blessings of all the greats in hip-hop that came before you, because you are about to do so much damage right now. You are really about to make men get back into their books and start re-creating stuff. You're that dope!'" It was in the cards for Nicki to blow up, and Monie Love herself predicted it.

". . . and then she got on top and started crackin' on women, and I shrunk to the size of Thumbelina."

Nicki Minaj's success was swift and steady, and pushback from Lil' Kim was almost immediate. Nicki's constructed brand became an obvious nod to Kim, though without the credit. She referred to herself as the "Harajuku Barbie" (Kim called herself "Black Barbie"), donned colorful wigs, and even replicated more iconic Kim photos (later including her "Chun-Li" single cover in 2018, which features another pose similar to *Hard Core*). The look weighed heavily on Lil' Kim, who in the summer of 2010 ripped off her wig during a performance of "Crush On You" and snarled, "That bitch can have it."

The momentum didn't stop. Nicki's solo debut album, *Pink Friday*, was released on November 22, 2010, and sold 375,000 copies in the first week, with a debut at the number two position on the *Billboard* 200 (later hitting number one). She also penetrated the international market with "Super Bass" and snuck in a Lil' Kim diss on "Roman's Revenge" with Eminem. Nicki Minaj then did the inconceivable: she created an album tailored to the pop audience but full of both sharp and sexually charged lyrics for hip-hop fans, complete with a larger-than-life aesthetic that immediately separated her from the bunch and her rabid fan base in tow. It was Barbie Season, and it wasn't ending anytime soon.

Nicki Minaj came as a shock to most, since the hot pursuit for "the one" felt never ending, and here she was in the flesh (and a wig). She was like the hip-hop Voltron, a culmination of everyone from female rap's past: the Sex Kitten aesthetic, Nubian Goddess lyricism, and even the braggy quick-witted behavior from the '70s and '80s. What a perfect way to begin the 2010s.

The same day Nicki released *Pink Friday,* Kanye West dropped his fifth studio album, *My Beautiful Dark Twisted Fantasy,* featuring Nicki on the single "Monster" alongside Rick Ross, Jay-Z, and Bon Iver. Her verse became regarded as the best one among a group of adept male performers. Over time, Nicki began using street tracks and guest appearances to flex her skills, reserving her albums for the pop cuts that made the sales. She was maintaining her bars while making bank, a brilliant formula few have ever accomplished. It was the survival tactic of a born survivor.

As a kid growing up in Queens, Nicki endured abusive patterns from her crack-addicted father. She explained in an interview with Wendy Williams in 2010 that he burned down their house when Nicki was five years old after fighting with her mother. It's a topic she addressed in song, though the trauma arguably formed a shell around her that became the rough exterior she presented, even when decorated with bright colors. By 2012 she was a full-fledged pop star, and released *Pink Friday: Roman*

Reloaded on April 2. It didn't reap the same level of acclaim as her first album, though with the track "Starships," Nicki earned the honor of having one of the world's bestselling singles of all time. Hip-hop was becoming stratospheric in terms of sales, and Nicki Minaj was at the helm. She breathed life back into rap album sales by crossing her audience over into pop. It became a perfect storm. Everyone was jumping into hip-hop. Her Young Money copilot Drake was already coasting into uncharted territories with *Thank Me Later* and *Take Care*. Hell, even Beyoncé started rapping. Though Nicki's success posed a threat to the controlled environment of what happens when one of rap's own "blows up." In the summer of 2012, Nicki was scheduled to perform at Hot 97's annual Summer Jam concert. That is, until Lil Wayne pulled her from the lineup the day of her performance. Nicki was scheduled to perform on the main stage that day. On the festival's smaller outdoor stage, *Ebro in the Morning* cohost Peter Rosenberg dismissed "Starships," saying, "Fuck that bullshit" and opting to play some "real hip-hop shit." Nicki and her team caught wind of that insult and exited the Summer Jam lineup.

Nicki kept moving forward, venturing into acting with a small role in the film *The Other Woman* opposite Cameron Diaz in 2014. The year before, she became a judge on *American Idol*'s twelfth season, as well as releasing her fragrance "Minajesty" and a Kmart clothing line, the Nicki Minaj Collection. By 2014, she was worth close to $53 million. She was reaching Madonna levels of fame; cut to her 2012 Grammy performance, in which she performed an exorcism on her alter-ego "Roman." For once, a boisterous personality and strong musical foundation were allowed to coexist, and Nicki Minaj just kept getting bigger and bigger. Forget hip-hop— she was hanging out with Ellen DeGeneres. Like she once rapped, "Nicki ain't a rapper. Nicki is a brander."

Her third studio album, *The Pinkprint,* released on December 12, 2014, debuting at number two on the Billboard 200. Her breakup with long-time boyfriend Safaree Samuels became a public attraction, though not as much as Safaree's accusations that he wrote Nicki's lyrics for her. Full Force dismissed that rumor in a 2017 interview with DJ Vlad, as they recounted a story where A&R executive Jean Nelson suggested Nicki get a ghostwriter and Nicki vehemently refused. Jean was working with Lil' Kim at the time.

Meanwhile, the beef between Lil' Kim and Nicki Minaj continued to intensify. In 2011, Kim dropped her mixtape *Black Friday,* full of shots aimed at Nicki. Nicki's and Kim's fan bases began a war with one another as well, as social media trickled into the equation. Half of the online jury suggested Lil' Kim was sour over a younger artist's fame, and the other half accused Nicki of having no girl power. As Nicki became more and more inaccessible and unreachable due to her star status, it was Kim who was questioned about their feud. She reached her limit in 2018 during an interview with LA's REAL 92.3, where she asked the host, "If you fuck with me, why isn't this [interview] about Kim?" after being questioned again about Minaj. "If we're gonna mention one female, we need to mention them all. God bless her. What she did, she did. I wish her the best, I'm past that. I'm over it."

Once Remy Ma left prison in 2014, she went for Nicki, too. Their animosity first started in 2007 when Nicki released *Playtime Is Over* and wove through some loosely veiled jabs about Remy as "the chick with the crown" over a Terror Squad beat ("Yeah Yeah Yeah"). Before her prison sentence, Remy Ma was being groomed for the exact spot Nicki occupied for the seven winters and six summers that she was away. By the time Remy came out, she was ready to reclaim that top spot and bump Nicki out by doing what she does best: throwing down the rhymes. In 2017, Remy dropped "shETHER," a venomous track over Nas's beef-inducing "Ether" beat where Remy runs down a list of Nicki stealing lines and getting plastic surgery, and accusing Nicki of having sex with Gucci Mane. This spiraled into a Roxanne Wars Redux. Nicki charged at Remy on two guest spots—one on Gucci Mane's "Make Love" and the other on Jason Derulo's "Swalla." Foxy Brown even checked back in to diss Remy Ma like she had in years past, releasing "Breaks Over," on which she went after Remy Ma—going so far as to remark on Remy's tragic miscarriage, though Remy brought her own heat when she called Foxy a "deaf bitch." Even Roxanne Shanté's original sparring partner Sparky Dee came to play with "Open Casket," though she said her contribution was all in fun. "They're not making any sense," Sparky said of the battle. "They're going back and forth for no apparent reason, and they're not saying anything, honestly. They're just saying who got the biggest titties, who has the biggest butt." The beef culminated in Remy Ma's Hot 97 Summer Jam performance in 2017, when she brought out Lil' Kim, Young M.A, and a then unknown Cardi B, along with Queen Latifah, MC Lyte, Rah Digga, Monie Love, and The Lady of Rage, to collectively perform Latifah's classic "U.N.I.T.Y." "That moment for me alone was like, 'Wow, this is fucking Queen Latifah, man.'" Young M.A remembers of the event. "'I'm seeing her right here, right now.' Just to get that love and embrace all this love with all of these queens that's on the stage next to you is like . . . you can't explain it. It's just something you've just been working for." In a move of great symbolism, Nicki Minaj was not invited to join those queens, though infamously, her face did appear on the Summer Jam screen when Remy performed "shETHER."

As other women in rap unified, Nicki's connection became more distant. In 2010, I asked Nicki Minaj if she felt there should only be one woman at a time in hip-hop.

"Not if they're all bringing it," was her reply. "I think the issue with females in hip-hop is that they lack consistency. You have to be diligent. You could be the hottest person on the planet, but if you don't put out a record every year, people will lose that momentum for you. And people will lose interest. Fans are very, very fickle. So, it's not about hip-hop. Yeah, hip-hop does have maybe a short attention span, but I think that a lot of that blame falls on the artist to continue to be relevant. Not everybody can do that. So in the meantime, all of the girls out there right now, just step your game up. That's all."

One artist was up for the challenge.

In 2015, Bronx native Belcalis Almánzar entered the sixth season of VH1's *Love & Hip Hop: New York* as a social media star remaining loyal to her incarcerated fiancé. "What intrigued me about Cardi B was, from the moment I saw her, I couldn't stop watching," explains Kim Osorio, then a writer for the *Love & Hip Hop* reunion episodes. Cardi grew a fan base over Instagram based upon mini testimonials and clips that doubled as confessionals and venting sessions about whatever crossed her mind. Nicknamed "Bacardi" by her parents, she had the full Caribbean spectrum with both Dominican and Trinidadian heritage. She eventually turned to stripping to earn money. "I was poor as hell," she told DJ Vlad in 2016. "I had a boyfriend that was beating my ass. I had to drop out of school. I was living with his mama and two pit bulls in a bedroom. It was crazy." She was introduced to *Love & Hip Hop* through New York's DJ Self, and quickly became known on the series as the unapologetically outspoken cast member, quick to shut down castmate Peter Gunz and throw a shoe at Asia Davies. "I had mixed feelings about her initially," Osorio admits. "I was like, 'How much more ignorant are we gonna get?' Mixed feelings aside, I was so guilty of being entertained. I saw her, and I kept watching her clips, I kept going to her page."

At the end of 2016, Cardi left the franchise after two seasons to launch her career in music. While she first appeared as a guest feature on the Shaggy song "Boom Boom" in 2015, Cardi was in the hot pursuit of building her presence in the streets now that TV land already knew her. In 2016 she released her first mixtape, *Gangsta Bitch Music, Vol. 1,* followed quickly by *Gangsta Bitch Music, Vol. 2* the following year. All the while, Cardi was building her personality along with her mic skills. In February 2017, Cardi opened for Yonkers rap legends The Lox on their Filthy America . . . It's Beautiful tour, joining Lil' Kim and Remy Ma. "She was better than what I thought she would be," The Lox's Styles P told me following the tour. "When you're an opening act and it's not as crowded, people don't give all of their energy. She was giving all of her energy and had the crowd and gave the energy [back]. She's going to be one of the biggest tour acts in the world."

Within a few months, that would become a very realistic possibility. Her first single as an Atlantic Records signee, "Bodak Yellow," released on June 16, 2017. The menacing beat hugged Cardi's threatening vocals as she charged her competition near and far. She wasn't coming for other female rappers she was coming for *everyone.* The song quickly became a milestone for Cardi, as the single stayed at number one on the Billboard Hot 100 for three weeks straight. Cardi was only the second solo female rapper to ever reach number one—the first was Lauryn Hill with "Doo Wop (That Thing)"—and the fifth female rapper to ever have a number one single on the chart. She then received a Grammy nomination and quickly morphed from stripper into America's Sweetheart. Cardi was honest and genuine, and despite having a rough life, she still appeared so naive. It made her lovable.

Conversations turned toward whether Nicki Minaj would welcome another female rap star to the top of the heap, considering she had occupied it solo for so many years. In September 2017, Nicki congratulated Cardi over Instagram for hitting her Billboard milestone.

Cardi B was now taking over hip-hop, and fast. In the beginning of 2018, she collaborated with megastar Bruno Mars on the remix to his hit single "Finesse." In April she would crystallize her status as superstar with the release of her debut album *Invasion of Privacy*. The album skyrocketed to number one on the Billboard 200, moving 255,000 units. The accolades continued to roll in, as Cardi then became the first female rapper to have multiple singles ("Bodak Yellow" and "I Like It") reach the number one spot on the Billboard Hot 100. As the streaming music world began to be counted in the Billboard tallies, Cardi set more records with every album cut released. Further, she made history again as the first female artist to ever have every song on her album certified as at least gold by the RIAA. Add to that several additional Grammy nominations, and Cardi B was on a roll.

She was also inviting the world into her life with unfiltered honesty. Cardi had no secrets. The birth of her daughter, Kulture, in July 2018 (with chart-topping Georgia rap trio Migos's Offset) became a worldwide event, bringing her fan base along on the journey through social media. Cardi B marked a new breed of female rapper, one who didn't factor her success into her decision to have a baby and embraced both motherhood and sexuality in real time. That, and she remained brutally honest. "She's authentically hip-hop," Osorio says. "I think Cardi was so real that she's the type of person who if someone writes her rhymes, she's gonna be like, 'Someone wrote my rhymes.'" She also openly admits to having breast implants, fake hair, and everything in between. "She isn't the first female artist that's been put together in this way," Osorio adds, further proving how hip-hop Cardi is. "We come from that whole true school of keeping it real and owning what you do," Styles P says, echoing Osorio's sentiment. "I think she's very honest and real with her feelings," he says. "She's definitely ghetto, but she says super-intelligent shit. I think her character and her personality and her realness are just real epic." Cardi eventually won her first Grammy in 2019 for Best Rap Album for *Invasion of Privacy*. A female rapper once again grabbing the gramophone for Best Rap Album. Her stiletto is still firmly in hip-hop, though she's a part of the pop world now, collaborating with Maroon 5, Jennifer Lopez, and newcomer Latin powerhouses Ozuna and J Balvin.

Nicki Minaj continued her own reign of hits in August 2018, when she released her fourth studio album, *Queen*. The project arguably reiterated Nicki's stance that she was the top female rapper. She later made history in November 2018 as the first woman with one hundred appearances on the Billboard 100, all within the same decade. Her collaborations with artists like Ariana Grande, Beyoncé, Madonna, and Zayn Malik prove that she too can venture into whatever domain she damn well pleases. Both Cardi B and Nicki Minaj lived at the top, when most said it couldn't be done.

For Nicki, the "Regina George" complex haunts her—the same one fellow Queens native Roxanne Shanté was accused of thirty years prior. This is the creep of animosity toward anyone who follows you after you've enjoyed uncharted success. "We can say Nicki is coming off as a mean girl or she's making these weird moves, and then we can say stuff about Foxy and Kim, but I also wanna know—now and twenty years ago—what the fuck is it like to be a female rapper?" asks Vanessa Satten.

Really, though, what is it like to be a female rapper? To be told you're not pretty enough or sexy enough, then too sexy to the point of slutty? If your lyrics are too hard, you're trying to be a man (and maybe you're even gay), which depletes your selling power in a market that wants femininity. If your looks are too light, then you're pandering to the mainstream and out to kill the last pure drops of hip-hop left. Do you band together and love each other, or do you disband and wage a war?

The rise to the top for female rappers is over, yet somehow it's still far from over.

"It's funny to me that everybody's crying about female unity," Rah Digga says with a laugh. "It's like, okay, where was this female unity energy when y'all was calling everybody old and washed up, and 'out with the old and in with the new' and 'it's time to change the guard'? Where was that energy then? Now y'all care about all of us getting along?" Did women ever really *all* get along? We know now that they definitely didn't.

"Yeah, newsflash: We didn't even get along in our era," Rah says. "The difference is, we understood that it wasn't about us as individuals. It was about the empowerment of females in hip-hop and pushing the culture forward. You think we were all kumbaya on our off days? Absolutely not. Females couldn't stand each other. Kick each other's backs in. I mean, granted, it wasn't as transparent as it is now because of social media, but when it was time to rise to the occasion, we banded together."

That's not as necessary now, since women no longer have to collectively fight just for a seat at the table. Now they're fighting for a spot at the head. And as Nicki Minaj and Cardi B have each made history in their own ways, they may never unify, and that's fine. But it's like Cardi B said in 2015, in what became her most infamous line on *Love & Hip Hop: New York:*

"If a girl has beef with me, she's gonna have beef with me . . . forever."

Megan Thee Stallion proves that every season is a Hot Girl Summer.

GIDDY UP

Lauryn Hill is onstage on Martha's Vineyard, over fifteen years after *The Miseducation of Lauryn Hill* debuted, and she's performing her ass off like the album just dropped yesterday. It's the 2014 Summer Madness Music Conference & Festival, and the theme is "Ladies First." Hip-hop spanning every era is in attendance: MC Lyte is there, Monie Love is there, even BET award show Black Girls Rock founder DJ Beverly Bond is there. Lauryn Hill is closing out the festival with a Sunday evening performance. Debbie D is in the audience with Sha-Rock, watching Lauryn Hill do her thing. In the middle of Lauryn's set, the two turn to each other and high-five.

Debbie proudly smiles and says to Sha, "We created this."

It's the dawn of a new day, a day that never would have happened had the pioneers not ventured outside for a jam. But that feels so far away compared to now. Now there are streaming services instead of sound systems connected to light posts. Pioneers never really released singles; now thanks to Spotify and Apple Music, an entire project is released as nothing *but* singles. Things have changed dramatically. Beyoncé raps now, Cardi B is the main attraction at the Met Gala. Hell, hip-hop surpassed rock as the most dominant genre, so basically all popular music is hip-hop music. It makes sense, since all music can essentially be traced back to Black music at its root.

Women are everywhere now in hip-hop, yet the argument of who can rise above the rest still remains. Yes, *the one.*

First of all, I'm from Houston
Picky bitch, I'm choosy
Feel like it, I'mma do it
New-new with the new shit

Her name is Megan Pete, though due to her five-feet-ten, athletically thick frame, she was christened Megan Thee Stallion. Megan is the first child of a female rapper to become a female rapper. Her late mother, Holly Thomas, rapped in Houston under the name Holly-Wood, and Megan grew up inside of a recording studio. As a young child, she carefully watched her mother write rhymes and deliver them during recording sessions, because her mother opted not to put her in day care.

"Just growing up watching everything my mother was doing from so young, I'm just thinking, that's how it's supposed to go," Megan tells me of witnessing her mom's musical process. "My mama practiced a lot, and I saw her in her bed writing all the time. She didn't know that I was watching her do that. So I'm growing up and seeing that's the norm." She applies that ethos to her own art. "I'm just always practicing. I always want to be sure," she adds. "That's just what it is in hip-hop: you never know when somebody's gonna ask you to rap. You never know when the opportunity is gonna present itself *for* you to rap. Even when I get in the studio, I've already practiced what I'm gonna say and how I'm gonna say it before I get in there."

By her early teens, Megan was in rare form and ready to rap, presenting the idea of being the next of kin to her mother, though at her mother's behest, she had to wait until she was eighteen. And she did. In college in 2013, she went viral by commanding an otherwise all-male cypher. A product of the social media age, Megan took her talents to Instagram, releasing clips and garnering a fan base. That in turn led to her first mixtape, 2016's *Rich Ratchet*, which then led to her breakout EP, titled *Tina Snow,* in 2018. She rhymed from the standpoint of an already established champion, evidenced by the *Tina Snow* track "Tina Montana":

I went to pick up the torch and then lit it
They try to tell me I can't, but I did it

Megan was fierce and unrelenting. She was seasoned, even as a neophyte, due mainly to her witnessing the moves of another female rapper under her own roof. She inked a deal with music industry veteran Kevin Liles's 300 Entertainment, becoming the first female rapper signed to his label. Her debut album, *Fever,* arrived in spring of 2019 and cracked the Apple Music top five within hours of its release, solidifying Megan Thee Stallion as a hip-hop staple.

Though she arrived at a time where hip-hop's main descriptor is not in its lyrics, Megan keeps her work bars-driven. Coming off the mumble rap era (where artists would mumble their lyrics over menacing beats), Megan is introducing real lyricism back to her generation. "A lot of people who actually like hip-hop are probably appreciating it," she says of the reintroduction to lyricism, "and a lot of people who don't realize how much they like hip-hop are appreciating it. But then you have your other half that are just listening to music to feel good. It doesn't matter what the artist is saying, it's more so a feeling." She likes to strike a balance whenever she can. "I try to make sure I cover both aspects of it. I want to give my Hotties [what she calls her fans] something good to feel when they hear me spit. I want them to hear that aggression in my voice, that confidence in my tone. At the same time, when I put my words together, I want hip-hop heads to think, 'Okay, she took her time to write that down.'"

With model looks and confidence, tackling topics of bedroom behavior and rap domination, Megan Thee Stallion is the product of all female rappers' past, similar to Nicki Minaj's beginnings, though far more polished as an industry newbie. There's no character creation here; Megan is simply Megan.

I bring Rah Digga's debate of Sex Kittens vs. Nubian Goddesses to Megan and ask if people realize she has the unique position of existing in the middle. "You know what? I never even thought about it like that!" Megan exclaims. "That is so true. It's definitely true. There's a lot of guys and a lot of girls that haven't gotten into my music yet—they've probably seen a few snippets online—and they don't read; they don't do their homework. That take that clip and they run with it. 'Megan Thee Stallion, she's just so sexualized,' and it's like, you haven't even taken the time to get to know the artist. I've got layers, you know what I'm sayin'? I don't just sit and rap about fuckin' a bunch of guys, it's about me being in charge. I'm talkin' about my money, I'm talkin' about my school, I'm talkin' about what my mama taught me and my granny, all that."

Sure, she has tracks like the *Fever* single "Sex Talk," where she opens the song with "Boy, you know you need to come give me that dick," but there's also lines like "Everything I say, I do that. Bitch I'm 'bout it, but you knew that. I don't need the crowd. Pull up one deep right wherever you at" off "W.A.B." a play on Three 6 Mafia's "Weak Azz Bitch." There's more than meets the ear, here.

"It's not about the sex, it's not about the looks, it's about me not being scared to say what I want to say and do what I want to do," Megan says. "Just like how the guys are doing that and nobody's questioning it, I feel like it should be the same way for me as a woman and for other women."

So here we are, over forty years later, and that same dilemma still exists for female rappers. How do you express your individuality and creativity without being labeled as one or the other? The difference now, I suppose, is how the artist handles that situation. Megan doesn't have a male mentor advising her to pick a side. She has instinct and her mother's spirit. That kind of drive doesn't come with a road map, but she's ready for the ride either way.

"It hasn't been quick for me. I've been sittin' on this and thinkin' on this since I was like seven years old," she says. "So it feels like a long time. I feel like I've been cooking for a long time. People are finally starting to catch on." She says she might dabble in pop, but never reside there. "That's just not me," she says.

So for all intents and purposes, Megan is Thee One. I asked her, why her? "I'm just real. This is not a character pretending to be somebody else," she says. "It wasn't a gimmick. It's just a college girl from Houston, from the Southside, just being herself and I feel like people are really rockin' with that."

For the first time in female rap history, though, she's locked the top spot in the midst of many other female rappers in existence, which in essence is a new take on "the one," after all. Is this finally what we've been waiting for?

To be continued . . .

Cardi B commands the congregation like no other.

SEASONS CHANGE, MAD THINGS REARRANGE

FEBRUARY 21, 2019, 9:00 A.M.

I'm in the hallway of a New Jersey hospital, leaned up against a radiator. A few feet away in a hospital room lies my mother. My eyes are fixed on her and her breathing. Eight hours later, I'd be saying my final goodbye to her. As her only child, and the product of a single-parent home, I didn't know what I was in for once the clock struck 5:10 P.M., the time of her passing. It had always been my mommy and me. My mother was, is, and always will be my best friend. I started this book a month before she was diagnosed with cancer. I wrote this book during her chemotherapy infusions. She was there for every milestone for the first forty years of my life, including my first solo book deal. We celebrated every word I was able to type in spite of watching her fight with pain in my eyes and bravery in hers.

She was my queen. And I couldn't save her.

Anticipatory grief is strange. You know something is about to happen, but you aren't quite prepared for what the aftershocks of that earthquake will bring. In one breath you're begging for that moment to arrive, since the spoiler alert is already tattooed on your heart. In another, you know that willing that release means you're saying farewell for good. At least in the physical sense.

Two years prior, I lost my grandmother right after my first book, *Commissary Kitchen,* was released. I would lose my collaborator on the book, my good friend Prodigy of Mobb Deep, eight months after the book hit the shelves. All of this loss paired with these books. I was spiraling.

I sat on the panel of the hospital radiator with my head in my hands. All of the above thoughts swam in my head as I looked up and saw someone approaching me. It was MC Debbie D, only today she was Pastor Debora Hooper. Tucked under her arm was a Bible, and in her hand was a bottle of oil, replacing her microphone. She walked me into my mother's hospital room, we prayed, and she anointed my mom. I had met Debbie once prior to that moment, at that steakhouse to talk about her being hip-hop's matriarch, and here she was, sending off mine. I couldn't stop crying, and Debbie turned to me and said, "God has bigger plans for her." Those are the only words that still provide me with any real comfort throughout this process.

Debbie sat with me for hours. Had she not been there, I would've sat alone until the rest of my family arrived to say goodbye. It was in that moment that something really clicked for me. Yes, the subjects of my book are all women who shared a common cause, but there was one thread of significant commonality during their respective journeys. They all just happened to rap, but really they were doing what Black women do: remaining strong through the eye of every storm, holding down everyone around them, just like Debbie D was doing for me. She was holding me down—and holding me up—as I fell apart.

When I learned that Megan Thee Stallion's mother had passed away from cancer a month after my mother had, I felt Megan's pain. Even at a distance. I remembered the day I sat in my living room, eavesdropping while my friend KC interviewed Megan for her press bio. Megan was discussing how she had first presented the idea of her becoming a rapper to her mother. She spoke of her mom so fondly, laughing at the memory of freestyling for her mother over a 2 Chainz beat.

Considering her mother's past as a rapper, this was bigger than an audition for a parent. It reminded me of the day I told my mother I no longer wanted to go to law school and instead wanted to pursue hip-hop journalism full-time. Megan's mom reacted the way mine did. Skepticism, followed by intense pride for this talent we were both hiding and waiting to unfold before our best friends (our moms) when the time was right. Her mom even interjected during their interview to fact check; something my mom would totally do, too. My mom was an early childhood educator, college professor, curriculum developer, and an incredible writer. Both Megan and I have the unusual honor of carrying our mother's legacies through the talent they bestowed upon us. We get it from our mamas.

During the photo shoot for the 2019 *XXL* Freshman cover, I couldn't stop observing Megan. This cover is the last of the big deals for hip-hop media as a new artist. A spot on the *XXL* Freshman cover means you're 99.9 percent destined for greatness. J. Cole graced that cover in 2010, along with Wiz Khalifa, Big Sean, and the late Nipsey Hussle. Meek Mill, Kendrick Lamar, and the late Mac Miller in 2011. Future and French Montana in 2012. The list goes on and on. Women rarely show up on this cover, yet in 2019, Megan was the MVP. When she walked in, every other cover star was racing to get a picture with her. She recorded her corresponding video freestyle in one take. A lot of the men in the room couldn't say the same. In between takes for photos, Megan would stand and stare out the window. In a room full of people (nearly sixty, if I recall correctly), the only one she was looking for wasn't there, at least in the physical sense. Her album *Fever* was about to release, igniting what would be her moment. The moment she had been waiting for, and her mother wasn't there to celebrate it. I could relate.

But she kept going in spite of her grief: she bodied her freestyle, she posed, she smiled. It's what women do. It's what Black women do especially, and they do it especially well. *Fever* arrived a month later, and she moved forward with supreme confidence even in the face of personal adversity.

"I know that's what she would want me to do," Megan says of her mother, "and I'm pretty sure that's what your mama would want you to do."

There are common misconceptions about the strength of women in hip-hop, depending upon which era you're referencing. In the '70s, it's assuming women knew no struggles, since everyone in hip-hop back then—both men and women—were barely of high school age, and in the midst of this booming but still mysterious subculture, it was just a race to get put on. Everyone was on a level playing field, right? Wrong. Women had it harder then than in any generation that followed. Not only did they have to memorize their rhymes before even showing up to jams to perform them, but they also had to deal with the scarcity of their gender at all, and quite boldly ask for a spot to shine. Oh yeah, and they did it all for free. There was no paycheck attached to this agenda, just assisting in what would become the foundation of hip-hop culture as we now know it. Did men share similar obstacles? Sure, but let's not forget they were out there unplugging speakers and refusing to hop fences for those girls. They saw the potential for women to be competition and had the foresight to sabotage wherever possible.

Then came the '80s, where it took a teenage girl in braces named Shanté to rhyme, for hip-hop to truly flourish on radio. She looked on as she was rapidly replaced. Yeah, she was pissed, but who wouldn't be? She lost her entire childhood to become the prototype for so many to follow. That takes strength. She didn't get along with her peers, though they were the ones slowly being hypersexualized merely for existing. Male rappers were getting flashier and wanted to floss in their minks, while women like Monie Love were shaving their heads just so they wouldn't be hit on while proving their worth on a stage. By the mid-'90s they said, "Fuck it," put on that lingerie and squatted like Lil' Kim did. There was money to be made and they wanted in, to leave public housing and heal the wounds of their fathers' abuse, only to be abused by their mentors. So they rapped on their own terms about the inconsistencies of men in the bedroom and their inability to provide orgasms. They were emasculating the male competition right before our ears, yet the male audience was so blinded by their scant clothing and beauty that they didn't even realize it. Raise your hand if you're a woman and already knew men were that clueless. I see a lot of hands raised.

The 2000s were an assembly line, quite frankly. A desperation to find that lightning in a bottle that artists like Lauryn Hill and Missy Elliott had produced just a few years prior. Women had to remain persistent as their male counterparts continued to flourish. They were given barely two strikes before being out . . . on a major label shelf, contractually bound and placed there for a rainy day where no other label can grab them and offer them a chance. There's strength in even wanting to take that risk.

Then hip-hop finally struck gold (well, platinum, in fact) with Nicki Minaj, who locked her reign in tightly for nearly a decade. When Cardi B arrived, it was phrased that Nicki was being replaced, not that Cardi was widening the lane. That alone could drive a sane person crazy. *Crazy.* There's a word we've heard used to describe many women, but especially women in hip-hop.

Cardi B became the first female rapper to publicly show every angle of her flawed life. It's not like she had a choice in the age of social media, though she did so with grace and continues to do so. We saw her makeups and breakups with Offset, her pregnancy and the birth of her daughter, Kulture. We're constantly told we can't have it all, but Cardi B keeps her middle finger up, which in hip-hop sign language means "I dissent."

There's a whole new era before us now. There are so many women rapping, and it's glorious. Kash Doll, Dreezy, City Girls, Leikeli47, Rico Nasty, Asian Da Brat, Cuban Doll, Tierra Whack, Bhad Bhabie, Saweetie, and of course Megan Thee Stallion are just a few examples of women all coexisting and creating music on their terms.

I think about how cool that is. How there are so many women who have beat that sophomore-single curse (not even a whole second album) and are out here making records and thriving. I think about women who didn't get the full recognition they deserved throughout history, like Glamorous from the Juice Crew. Hailing from Freeport, New York, she was the first female MC to ever come out of Long Island and cut a record. Glamorous first came into the Juice Crew fold when Mr. Magic hired her for a *Rap Attack* promo, and she later worked at Fly Ty's Cold Chillin' Records (he also managed her). Random fact: Her cousin is Chuck Berry.

I think about the late MC Trouble, who in 1990 cut a record called "(I Wanna) Make You Mine" that had everyone in the music industry buzzing. At twenty years old, she suffered heart failure due to an extreme epileptic seizure and passed away.

I think about Sister Souljah, who has a whole political expression dedicated to her called "the Sister Souljah moment." It's derived from Sister Souljah making what was publicly perceived as extremist statements against white people, following the nationwide racial friction caused by 1992's LA riots. That same year, she dropped her first and last album, *360 Degrees of Power*. Sister Souljah was also named as a member of Public Enemy after Professor Griff left the group, and is best known for her 1999 novel *The Coldest Winter Ever*.

I could keep going all day with more and more names to add on, so many they could probably fill another whole book. Chances are, you recognize some of these names or know one of their songs. For that, they deserve recognition.

But, back to the future, where a whole slew of women are ready to take charge and continue to give hip-hop legs. Their heroes are a combination of artists over time, though they all name-check Trina. Perhaps it's because Trina was consistent, releasing music through every drought in the music industry, and as soon as a new woman hits the scene, she's there welcoming her with open arms. She knows the foundation she's laid, and she couldn't be happier.

"There's a whole other generation blossoming," Trina says to me, beaming with pride. "To see these girls and see how it is . . . it feels like 1998 all over again. There was a time when it was so many guys; now it's just so many girls. Big records and big legacies; that's the reason I'm doing this."

Yet they'll all experience the same struggles at some point, complete with the comparisons, the competition, the concerns for a work-life balance. A lot of female rappers are wives, mothers, and even grandmothers. Some stopped their career to start families; others took the show on the road. It's a testament to making it happen or making the decision to stop.

So where do we go from here? Now that desires are more frequently met and women can successfully coexist without having a bottom line immediately thrown at them. Women are in demand; women are in command. It's a beautiful thing.

"We're in control," Trina says. "All we gotta do is just do what we love and make it happen. Use the gift, the talent, the music, the artistry, everything. Make it connect and make it join forces and energies. Then everybody will get to make beautiful music, and it's amazing. It's a culture that cannot be stopped. It's growing out of control." It's time to step into the unknown.

"There is no blueprint," she says. "We are the blueprint."

If you take anything from this book, I hope it's that this road to recognition is never easy for a woman. There are loopholes, land-mines, and long hills all waiting to get in the way of who your favorite female rapper is, was, or could be. The insanity is that this has been happening for so long, and these women have shown re-markable endurance in spite of it all. So for that, here's a shout-out to every woman who ever picked up the mic. Because let's face it: every little bit, every diss track, every major single, every question-able fashion choice, and every big budget music video or grainy flip-cam freestyle has proven that when women want something, they go get it. They've pushed on through hip-hop and survived, and no matter how they did it, we salute them.

Acknowledgments

You know, some people go ahead and write books that stem from some life-altering event that they endured, where they get to thank everyone for helping them through the process. Meanwhile, I got my book deal and *then* the life-altering events piled on. Funny how that works.

But, I digress . . .

Thank you, God, for allowing me the strength, patience, and grace to weather the storms of my life that led to this rainbow of a book. My core was shaken, but my faith never was.

To my mother, Anna Acquaviva Iandoli. Mommy, we celebrated my book deal on earth, my writing process while you fought the battle of your life, and my turning in the book right before we said goodbye. Now, the celebrations are happening both here and in heaven. Thank you. You are my muse, my greatest supporter and cheerleader, my inspiration, my role model, and now my angel. I will write about you until my pen runs out of ink and continue to make you proud. I am forever #AnniesDaughter. I love you and miss you, always.

To my other angel, my grandma Josephine Acquaviva, who still comforts me from heaven. Grandma, I hope you, Mommy, Pop-Pop, and Great-Great keep sending blessings down, and that you're proud of me. Love and miss you.

To Albert "Prodigy" Johnson, my original coconspirator. P, you know I had to include you in this book. I'll continue to ride for you. Rest well, my friend.

To Debbie Harry, the real goddess of Paterson and Hawthorne. Thank you for paving the way.

To my agent, Robert Guinsler, and the team at Sterling Lord Literistic. Who knew that a frantic call to you about one female rapper would've led to a book about *every* female rapper? Thank you for being who you are and keeping my sanity and best interests in tact, especially after my whirlwind of a year. You're now stuck with me. Lucky you. Love love love you. Thank you, Neil Martinez-Belkin, for taking my call that fateful day.

To my editor, Carrie Thornton, and the team at Dey Street Books and HarperCollins. Thank you for taking a chance on another girl from Hawthorne, New Jersey. You pushed me to my creative limits, and I've left this experience a better person and writer because of it. "Bring on the next book!" she shouts, while hiding under her bed. Love you, and thank you to Tatiana Dubin for your patience.

To the amazing women who sat down with me, either in person or on the phone, to tell their stories and share their insights:

To my dear friend Debbie D . . . I finished the book, Debbie! And you were there every step of the way. Thank you for being an architect of hip-hop but also for building a friendship with me and helping me along the way. You are priceless, and I can't wait for your book.

To Monie Love, who sent the radar out when I needed to speak with people and vouched for me. Thank you, thank you, thank you.

To Rah Digga, who is simply the coolest and for years now has always helped out another Jersey girl. You're the best, Digga.

To Kid Sister . . . thanks for making our interview so difficult to transcribe because all I did was laugh. Love you, Melis, and I'm so thankful for your friendship.

To my dear friend Rapsody. Rap, no matter how busy you are, you're always there for me. I can't thank you enough for your contribution to this book but also for being my ear when I needed one and for being the brilliant artist that you are. Love you, Sis.

To Bahamadia, for your inspiration, support, and check-in texts.

To Gangsta Boo, for your friendship. Lobster mac is on me!

To Megan Thee Stallion, who came through in the eleventh hour. Our moms are smiling down. It's time to shine.

To Yo Yo (and Gabby!), Spinderella, La Chat, Snow Tha Product (and Dove), Azealia Banks, Dessa, Mia X, Sparky D, Baby D of the Mercedes Ladies, Precise, Young M.A., Ladybug Mecca (and Mary Sierra), Lady Luck, Trina, Nicki Minaj, Lil' Kim, and Remy Ma. All of our conversations and your insight (both past and present) made this book possible. Thank you.

To Kim Osorio, my sister, my friend, my mentor, and my perpetual pain in the ass (lovingly). Thank you for making calls when I needed them, for our Panera dates to write, for being a part of this book, and for always holding me down. Always.

To Vanessa Satten, for being an amazing friend, editor, and support system, and of course for taking part in this book. I can't thank you enough, V.

To Laura Stylez, my day one, who came through for this book but always comes through in my life. Love you, Sis. Thank you.

To dream hampton, for taking me under her wing ten years ago, and then letting me fly. You really didn't think I was going to allow this book to go to print without you appearing in it, did you?

To Ahmir "Questlove" Thompson. Our constant conversations over the last twenty years about you-know-who led to you-know-what (this book). Thank you for riding with me, providing your stories, and for being my friend.

To Dre (of Cool & Dre), I'm glad one of our many conversations about hip-hop could find its way into a chapter of my book.

To Thembisa Mshaka, who helped me handle my entertainment biz. You are the BEST, Sis.

To Fly Ty, Janette Beckman, Kurtis Blow, Cool V, Salaam Remi, DJ Clark Kent, Michael Gonzales, Nelson George, Lorenzo Agius, Jimmy Douglass, Styles P, and Chris "The Glove" Taylor, for your stories. It's all so appreciated.

To Marisa Mendez, who has been my right hand since day one. I legit don't know what I would do without you. I know you've grabbed the torch and are writing your own books now, but you better never leave me! Love you.

To Rachel Sonis, who jumped on board without question. Can't wait to gather again at Dos Caminos for the next one. We'll bring Robbie!

To Krista Schlueter, for the headshots; Tyrsa, for the amazing cover art; Victoria Ford and Sneakshot Photography, for the photos; and Adriana Imhof, for all your help. To Alex Boronat, Mike Sheehan, and of course Nix, who helped me recount some memories that we can all laugh about now.

To Porscha Burke, my friend, sounding board, and fellow hip-hop obsessed bibliophile. I owe this all to you. Seriously.

To Marvis Johnson, for whispering book-sales stats in my ear, which in turn inspired me to make the greatest book possible. Hahaha. You're an amazing friend, Marvis. Thank you.

To Cassandra Spangler, my friend and legal counsel. We need all of the burgers to celebrate.

To Dan Charnas, who is the greatest friend, ear, and connect. Thank you.

To KC Orcutt (my protégé and work hangs partner) and Jon Reyes (my Jonathan), who both provided love and friendship during this process but also read my pages with tears in their eyes throughout because they knew what it took to get here. I love you both SO SO SO SO MUCH.

To my best friend, Maryum, who remains by my side as my rock and puts up with me through thick and thin. Thank you for being a part of this story but also for adding to the story of my life. You are the best friend and sister in the whole world. I love you 'til infinity, Little. #bitchiloveyou

To my cousin Jenn, who has literally been a part of my entire hip-hop experience. From concerts to clubs we hated being in, you've been my partner in crime. Thank you for all of that but also for sending me a meme of Idris Elba saying "Shouldn't you be writing?" every time you knew damn well that I wasn't. I love you, Jennifah.

To my sister, Gina, who would check in to say "Are you writing your book?" at least once a day. Thith, I love you to pieces, and I welcome your constant stalking. So thankful that you (and our brother, Jimmy) exist.

To Daniel Sozomenu, for being there, reading my pages, and then getting mad at me when I didn't send more. Thank you.

To Wendy Carbajal-Ortiz (Dita), for our Thursday therapy sessions, and to Sally, for being my guide and ear whenever I need one. To Dr. Berger, for the "crack." (He's my chiropractor, calm down.)

To my godmothers, Roe and Aunt Camille, for your love and support, and thank you, Aunt Camille, for my guardian angel, Vincent.

To my father, Jimmy Iandoli, who bought me my first guitar and continues to teach me lessons in music and in life. Thank you, Daddy. I love you and Rose.

To my Acquaviva and Iandoli families, who love and support me, especially Uncle Joe; Aunt Nancy; Aunt Ann; Uncle Al; and my cousins, who all pushed me to finish this book in their own ways. I love you all. To my grandma Iandoli, who held up my over-the-shoulder high school yearbook photo and said, "Wear your hair like this on your book cover." Sorry to disappoint you, Grandma.

To the people who said "keep going" during this process:

Sowmya Krishnamurthy, my main Thotiana and Roc Girl for life. "Read it? I own it!" You're always there for a pep talk and a beat down, and you know I need both. Love you, scuzz.

Vanderslice, my brother forever and constant critic. Haha.

Janice Llamoca, hai, I love you.

Rashaun Hall, my brudder always. (Hi, Leah!)

And Nicole and Natalie of Nina Sky, my sisters for life. Thank you for always being there. Love you both so much.

Thank you to Jake Paine, Alvin "Aqua" Blanco, Chuck Creekmur, Jermaine Hall, Jerry Barrow, and Soren Baker, for all your help throughout my career and for always acknowledging me as simply a great writer, not a great *female* writer.

Shout out to some real ones: Georgette Cline (my GZA, I love you!), J57 (Shy Ronny . . . and Aerika!), Erin Magee, Jaime of WKiD Creations (my sister in art), Laura Checkoway (hi, Birdy!), Anne's Cupcakery, Esthero, Jemeni, Leah McSweeney, Your Old Droog, JoJo, Dreezy, Freeway, Vic Mensa, Russ, Mary Pryor, The Clique, Gabby Rosenthal, Tracy G, Ebro, Peter Rosenberg, Tamika Hall, Snypes, JFK, Roberta Magrini, Michelle McDevitt, Courtney Lowery, Nadeska Alexis, Danielle Cheesman, Carl Lamarre, Paul Meara, KTB, Rob Markman, Boss Lady, Mecca, Hattie Collins, Sarah Mary Cunningham, Mikey Fresh, Low Key, Kaz, Zeena Koda, Angela Burke, LaTrice Burnette, Lydia Kanuga, Clover Hope, Renata Muniz, Karlie Hustle, William Ketchum III, Matty Bernal, Angie Martinez, Miss Info, Jada Gomez, Ashley Kalmanowitz, Jason Davis, Melissa Victor, Malik Imran, Jonny Shipes, Richie Abbott, Bear Frazer, Peter Kadin, Adam Bernard, Chris Herche, Nakia Hicks, Marilyn Lopez, Jackie Reeve, Robbie Daw, Paul Cantor, Haus of Swag, Tonedeff, Datwon Thomas,

B Dot, Elliott Wilson, Nadia Ali, Adelle Platon, Dart Adams, Eric Diep, Andres Tardio, Tai Saint Louis, Ileana Diez, Dana Meyerson and the crew at Biz3, Ariela Kozin, Aliya S. King, Dan Rys, Trent Clark, Chanel McFadzean, Amir Abbassy, Jamal Jimoh, Kevin Liles, Shy Ferguson, Olu Famuyide, Chantz Brewer, Annie Chen, Nancy Byron, Jeff Clyburn, Marisa Bianco, Joe Carozza, Alex Gale, Shahendra Ohneswere, Beau Benton, Amaiya Davis, Jana Fleishman, Chaka Pilgrim, Karissa Kindy, Matt Diamond, Ariana White, Roderick Scott, Syreta Oglesby, Marjoriet Gueche, Mike Trampe, Marsha Gosho Oakes (bka Hawk), Sidney Madden, Hillary Siskind, Lauren Nostro, Victoria Hernandez, Rebstar, Jocelyn Valencia, Erica Roane, Kyle Eustice, Lisa Goins, Ashley Polynice, Rebel Child, KG Divine, Lorena (Caca), Huron (Queen Medina), Tra (Wonder Woman), Bree, Munira (Munny), Lauren (Dunny), FWMJ, D, Albania (Chica), Paulie (Boo Boo), Rabia, Ginetta, Jasmine, Priyu, Julie, Tish, Alex, Rey, Jay, Rich, Johnny, and the rest of my friends and family.

To my Riot Grrrl Book Club: Lauren, Sara, Alissa, Laina, and Kat. You already know we are stuck reading this masterpiece.

To my dogter, Indie, who barked her way through this book. Thank you for the background noise.

If I forgot anyone by name, I'm sorry, but thank you, thank you, thank you.

To all of the female rappers I wanted to write about in this book but wasn't able to: Thank you for making all of this still possible. I still bump Nonchalant's "5 O'Clock" like it's yesterday and wish I could have included something about everyone in this book. Just know you were all in my thoughts, and I hope you like this book regardless.

And last, but certainly not least . . .

To women, especially Black women. This book is a testament to strength, and it was an honor to tell this story.

Bibliography

BOOKS, IMAGES, FILM, AND VIDEO

Adler, Bill, Tom Herrell, and Janette Beckman. *The Breaks: Stylin' and Profilin' 1982–1990*. New York: Powerhouse Books, 2007.

Ahearn, Charlie, and Fab Five Freddy. *Wild Style*. DVD. Directed by Charlie Ahearn. New York: First Run Features, 1982.

Beckman, Janette. *Female Rappers, Class of '88*. 1988. Photograph. Accessed at https://www.si.edu/object/nmaahc_2015.132.65.

Bythewood, Reggie Rock, and Cheo Hodari Coker. *Notorious*. DVD. Directed by George Tillman, Jr. Los Angeles: Fox Searchlight Pictures, 2009.

"Cardi B: I Became a Stripper to Escape Domestic Violence." YouTube video, 6:26. "VladTV," January 12, 2016. https://www.youtube.com/watch?v=vzfcNl -o9bI.

"Cardi B Exposes Nicki Minaj on Instagram Rant [Full Video]." YouTube video, 8:39. "TrueExclusives," October 29, 2018. https://www.youtube.com /watch?v=cbbyxlX4ZEk.

"Cardi B Supercut (PART 1): Best Moments from *Love & Hip Hop New York* (Season 6) | VH1." YouTube video, 20:03. "VH1," January 15, 2018. https://www .youtube.com/watch?v=Hw5-zxBRQKQ.

"Eve Talks About Dr. Dre Firing Her, Rich Homie Quan's VH1 Performance and More (Video)." YouTube video, 11:11. "DJ Whoo Kid," July 20, 2016. https://www.youtube.com/watch?v=H0Lm25Ln1Ko.

"EXCLUSIVE INTERVIEW—CINDY CAMPBELL—1st Lady of Hip Hop." YouTube video, 32:32. "MC Debbie D," October 17, 2017. https://www.youtube .com/watch?v=n1B3onhCBNw.

"Full Force on Shopping Nicki Minaj, Label Suggesting Juelz Santana Ghost-write for Her." YouTube video, 15:01. "VladTV," August 21, 2017. https://www.youtube.com/watch?v=_8TShKCwbpc.

"Full Interview of Nicki Minaj and Wendy Williams." YouTube video, 7:27. "Shiyaheart11," November 18, 2010. https://www.youtube.com/watch?v=PlaO5tiQHqQ.

Furman, Leah, and Elina Furman. *Heart of Soul: The Lauryn Hill Story.* New York: Ballantine Books, 1999.

Hager, Steven, Andrew Davis, David Gilbert, Paul Golding, Harry Belafonte, and David V. Picker. *Beat Street.* DVD. Directed by Stan Lathan. Los Angeles: Orion Pictures, 1984.

"How Biggie Found Out Charli Baltimore Could Rap | I Talked to Biggie." YouTube video, 2:24. "BET," March 13, 2017. https://www.youtube.com/watch?v=bedPblgWN3I.

"How Roxanne Shante Was Sabotaged Back in 1985 Because She Was A Girl (HBO)." YouTube video, 3:33. "VICE News," February 14, 2017. https://www.youtube.com/watch?v=auM8gyH4IMo.

"Interview w/ Cindy Campbell (Kool Herc's Sister)—The First Hip Hop Party 1520 Sedgewick Ave." YouTube video, 10:48. "Davey D," March 11, 2010. https://www.youtube.com/watch?v=7SMVGLEr6nA.

"Jay-Z & Foxy Brown Interview 1996 (Rap City)." YouTube video, 4:18. "NobleChild456," February 23, 2010. https://www.youtube.com/watch?v=J32BrrmxCgc.

Jean, Wyclef, and Anthony Bozza. *Purpose: An Immigrant's Story.* New York: It Books, 2012.

"John Legend Recalls Working with Lauryn Hill in 1998." YouTube video, 0:56. "CBS This Morning," January 23, 2014. https://www.youtube.com/watch?v=wNlk-PDNLNo.

Larnell, Michael, Nina Yang Bongiovi, Mimi Valdes, Forest Whitaker, and Pharrell Williams. *Roxanne Roxanne.* Netflix. Directed by Michael Larnell. Los Gatos: Netflix, 2017.

"Lauryn Hill—The Masters Part 2." YouTube video, 8:39. "MTV," December 25, 2009. https://www.youtube.com/watch?v=d3T_ZjJtc-4.

Lazerine, Devin, and Cameron Lazerine. *Rap-Up: The Ultimate Guide to Hip-Hop and R&B.* New York: Grand Central, 2008.

"Lil Kim Keeps It Real on Nicki Minaj, Biggie Relationship, Female MC's & New Music." YouTube video, 43:12. "Hot 97," November 3, 2017. https://www.youtube.com/watch?v=kqbJCW-jxYM&t=1320s.

"Lil' Kim Reveals Private, Detailed Biggie Stories with Flex." YouTube video, 11:25. "Hot 97," March 10, 2016. https://www.youtube.com/watch?v=LjSxdy7enYY.

"Lil Kim Says Stop Comparing Her to Nicki Minaj, Women in Hip Hop, New

Music & More!" YouTube video, 8:56. "Real 92.3," August 8, 2018. https://www.youtube.com/watch?v=ubJghoqF4UM.

Martinez, Angie. *My Voice: A Memoir.* New York: Celebra, 2016.

"Missy Elliott on Behind the Scenes of 'The Rain' (1997)." YouTube video, 3:36. "ThisIsMissyExclusive," June 22, 2012. https://www.youtube.com/watch?v=QdKDEr-YZzM.

Morgan, Joan. *She Begat This: 20 Years of* The Miseducation of Lauryn Hill. New York: Atria Books, 2018.

"New Music Seminar 1985—Roxanne Shante vs Busy Bee Starski (MC Battle)." YouTube video, 7:03. "Tape Deck Wreck," June 9, 2017. https://www.youtube.com/watch?v=7wdIYJKjTzs.

"Nicki Minaj—Interview & Freestyle [The Come Up DVD]." YouTube video, 4:01. "The Come Up DVD," April 17, 2008. https://www.youtube.com/watch?v=OfqgkgMOvZs&t=171s.

"Nicki Minaj—My Time Again HD (MTV Documentary)." YouTube video, 41:09. "TaylorSwiftAccess," January 26, 2018. https://www.youtube.com/watch?v=fQloU59um5I.

"Nicki Minaj—My Time Now (MTV Documentary) (Full)." YouTube video, 41:38. "Harajuku Barbie," May 20, 2013. https://www.youtube.com/watch?v=JRPHRQyS19M.

Queen Latifah. *Ladies First: Revelations of a Strong Woman.* New York: William Morrow, 1998.

"Remy Ma Talks Lil' Kim, Nicki Minaj, and More | BOSSIP." YouTube video, 6:05. "Bossip," August 20, 2014.

"Rick Ross Speaks on Meek Mill, Female Rappers & His VH1 Show 'Signed.'" YouTube video, 29:17. "Power 105," July 24, 2017. https://www.youtube.com/watch?v=gDskuwjGtFk.

Scott, Ridley, Mimi Polk Gitlin, and Callie Khouri. *Thelma & Louise.* DVD. Directed by Ridley Scott. Beverly Hills, CA: MGM, 1991.

Sha-Rock, Iesha Brown, and Leila Jefferson. *Luminary Icon.* 2nd ed. Pearlie Gates Publishing, 2011.

Sollinger, Daniel, and Andy Robertson. *Rhyme & Reason.* DVD. Directed by Peter Spirer. Los Angeles: Miramax, 1997.

"That Time Biggie's Genius Mind Shocked Funkmaster Flex in the Studio | I Talked to Biggie." YouTube video, 1:55. "BET," March 10, 2017. https://www.youtube.com/watch?v=Z_ZX2m2Um50.

Timbaland and Veronica Chambers. *The Emperor of Sound: A Memoir.* New York: Amistad, 2016.

VIBE. *Hip-Hop Divas.* New York: Three Rivers Press, 2001.

DIGITAL AND PRINT ARTICLES

Alexis, Diamond. "Lil' Kim Speaks on Her 'Violent Relationship' with Biggie." BET.com. November 8, 2017. https://www.bet.com/music/2017/11/08/lil-kim-violent-relationship-biggie.html.

AllHipHop Staff. "Remy Martin: The Champ Is Here." AllHipHop.com. August 15, 2004. https://allhiphop.com/features/remy-martin-the-champ-is-here-QK8GIHg5jk6__dX-iT9jmA.

AllHipHop Staff. "Remy Martin vs. Lady Luck: Round by Round." AllHipHop.com. April 14, 2004. https://allhiphop.com/music/remy-martin-vs-lady-luck-round-by-round-qf9ZsrReCEq5OD1N1Adx1A.

AllHipHop Staff. "Where Are They Now? Roxanne Shanté." AllHipHop.com. March 31, 2008. https://allhiphop.com/features/where-are-they-now-roxanne-shante-iInIyts8EUKg4kf68dQh8A.

Als, Hilton. "The New Negro." NewYorker.com. October 20, 1997. https://www.newyorker.com/magazine/1997/10/20/the-new-negro.

Bass, Holly. "Rap's Raunchy Women." *Washington Post*. February 26, 1997. Accessed at LexisNexis.

Batey, Angus. "DJ Kool Herc DJs His First Block Party (His Sister's Birthday) at 1520 Sedgwick Avenue, Bronx, New York." TheGuardian.com. June 12, 2011. https://www.theguardian.com/music/2011/jun/13/dj-kool-herc-block-party.

Berr, Jonathan. "After Napster, the Music Industry Winds Up Humming." CBS News.com. February 12, 2016. https://www.cbsnews.com/news/after-napster-the-music-industry-winds-up-humming.

Browne, David. "*The Miseducation of Lauryn Hill*: EW's 1998 review." EW.com. August 17, 2018. https://ew.com/article/1998/09/04/music-review-miseducation-lauryn-hill.

Burke, Audra D. S. "La Dolce Vita." *VIBE* (May 2003). https://books.google.com/books?id=1SYEAAAAMBAJ&pg=PA129&source=gbs_toc_r&cad=2#v=onepage&q&f=false.

Burney, Lawrence. "The Age of Thee Stallion." *The FADER* (Summer 2019). https://www.thefader.com/2019/05/20/megan-thee-stallion-fever-cover-story.

Celona, Larry. "Rap Diva Has Lil' to Say on Shooting." NYPost.com. February 27, 2001. https://nypost.com/2001/02/27/rap-diva-has-lil-to-say-on-shooting.

Catucci, Nick. "Review: Lil' Kim, *La Bella Mafia*." Spin.com. July 1, 2003. https://www.spin.com/2003/07/lil-kim-la-bella-mafia-queen-beebig-entertainmentatlantic.

Chairman Mao. "Bow Down!" *VIBE* (February 1998). https://books.google.com/books?id=CywEAAAAMBAJ&printsec=frontcover&source=gbs_ge_summary_r&cad=0#v=onepage&q&f=false.

Checkoway, Laura. "Inside 'The Miseducation of Lauryn Hill.'" RollingStone
.com. August 26, 2008. https://www.rollingstone.com/music/music-news
/inside-the-miseducation-of-lauryn-hill-252219.

Checkoway, Laura. "The Heart Gently Weeps." *XXL Magazine* (September
2008). http://www.lauracheckoway.com/foxy-brown.

ClassicOne. "Eve Recalls a Rival Female Rapper Crashing Her Show." AllHip
Hop.com. November 22, 2017. https://allhiphop.com/rumors/who-s-that
-girl-eve-recalls-a-rival-female-rapper-crashing-her-show-f40m8QireUy
HtoPhd87IYQ.

Coleman, Bill. "Female Rappers Give Males Run for the Money." *Billboard*
(May 21, 1988). Accessed at LexisNexis.

Dangelo, Joe. "Lil' Kim Indicted for Lying About Hot 97 Shootout with Ca-
pone." April 14, 2004. http://www.mtv.com/news/1486360/lil-kim-indicted
-for-lying-about-hot-97-shootout-with-capone.

Dangelo, Joe. "Lil' Kim Present at Hot 97 Shootout, Police Say." MTV.com.
February 27, 2001. http://www.mtv.com/news/1441041/lil-kim-present-at
-hot-97-shootout-police-say.

Dickerson, Debra. "Lauryn Hill: Hoochie or Hero?" Salon.com. June 22, 1999.
https://www.salon.com/1999/06/22/hill.

Duncan, Andrea. "Amillion." *VIBE* (December 2000). https://books.google
.com/books?id=7icEAAAAMBAJ&pg=PA139&dq=rapper+Amil+whitehe
ad+vibe&hl=en&sa=X&ei=2CUdUsqSKKPkiwKIwoCwBw&ved=0CC0Q
6AEwAA#v=onepage&q=rapper%20Amil%20whitehead%20vibe&f=false.

Edwards, Audrey. "Independent Woman." *VIBE* (March 2001). https://books
.google.com/books?id=fiYEAAAAMBAJ&printsec=frontcover&source=
gbs_ge_summary_r&cad=0#v=onepage&q&f=false.

Ettelson, Robbie. "The New Music Seminar Battle for World Supremacy: An
Oral History." Daily.RedBullMusicAcademy.com. July 24, 2015. https://
daily.redbullmusicacademy.com/2015/07/new-music-seminar-oral-history.

ex, kris. "Eve: Natural Selection." *Complex Magazine* (September/October
2002). https://www.complex.com/music/2012/04/eve-2002-cover-story
-gallery.

ExtraLargeParty.Blogspot.com staff. "BEEF: Antoinette vs MC Lyte." Extra
LargeParty.Blogspot.com. November 11, 2010. http://extralargeparty
.blogspot.com/2010/11/beef-antoinette-vs-mc-lyte.html.

Farley, Christopher John. "Hip-Hop Nation." *Time* (February 8, 1999). http://
content.time.com/time/magazine/article/0,9171,19134,00.html.

Flick, Larry. "Single Reviews: The Lady of Rage—'Afro Puffs.'" *Billboard*
(July 23, 1994). Accessed at LexisNexis.

Forrest, Emma. "The Lil' Things in Life." *Guardian*. September 5, 1997. Accessed at LexisNexis.

Garwood, Bianca. "Lil' Kim Reacts to Eve's Story of Their Initial 'Beef': 'Why

Do You Girls Try to Make Me Out as the Bad Guy?'" Ebony.com. January 12, 2018. https://www.ebony.com/entertainment/eve-kim-the-talk.

Goldman, David. "Music's Lost Decade: Sales Cut in Half." CNN.com. February 3, 2010. https://money.cnn.com/2010/02/02/news/companies/napster_music_industry.

Good, Karen R. "Deliverance." *VIBE* (August 1998). https://books.google.com/books?id=JywEAAAAMBAJ&printsec=frontcover&source=gbs_ge_summary_r&cad=0#v=onepage&q&f=false.

Grigoriadis, Vanessa. "Cardi B and Offset: A Hip-Hop Love Story." Rolling Stone.com. June 20, 2018. https://www.rollingstone.com/music/music-features/cardi-b-and-offset-a-hip-hop-love-story-628750.

Hager, Steven. "Afrika Bambaataa's Hip Hop." *Village Voice*. September 21, 1982. https://digital.library.cornell.edu/catalog/ss:16057641.

Hall, Jake. "The Complete Beginner's Guide to Remy Ma's Rap Beefs." High Snobiety.com. March 7, 2017. https://www.highsnobiety.com/2017/03/07/remy-ma-rap-beefs.

Hall, Rashaun. "Angie Martinez Gets 'Up Close.'" *Billboard* (March 24, 2001). Accessed at LexisNexis.

Harris, Chris. "Da Brat Sentenced to Three Years in Prison for Atlanta Nightclub Fight." MTV.com. August 22, 2008. http://www.mtv.com/news/1593369/da-brat-sentenced-to-three-years-in-prison-for-atlanta-nightclub-fight.

Harvell, Jess. "Review: Lil' Kim, *The Naked Truth*." Pitchfork.com. November 21, 2005. https://pitchfork.com/reviews/albums/4995-the-naked-truth.

Hiatt, Brian. "Nicki Minaj: The New Queen of Hip-Hop." RollingStone.com. December 9, 2010. https://www.rollingstone.com/music/music-news/nicki-minaj-the-new-queen-of-hip-hop-103304.

Hislop, Rachel. "Hip-Hop Legends Unite: MC Lyte Interviews Salt of Salt-N-Pepa." GlobalGrind.com. July 17, 2012. https://globalgrind.cassiuslife.com/1863528/mc-lyte-interviews-salt-salt-n-pepa-exclusive.

Hova, Tray. "Diary of Kimberly Jones." *VIBE* (June–July 2011). https://www.vibe.com/2011/08/diary-kimberly-jones-junejuly-2011-sex-issue-feature-pg-2.

Huey, Steve. Review: Missy Elliott, *Supa Dupa Fly*. AllMusic.com. https://www.allmusic.com/album/supa-dupa-fly-mw0000594733.

Hunt, Dennis. "Female Rappers Diss and Tell: Women, Spearheaded by Queen Latifah, M.C. Lyte and Yo-Yo, Are Demanding to Join the Men's Club." LATimes.com. August 19, 199.: https://www.latimes.com/archives/la-xpm-1990-08-19-ca-3058-story.html.

Iandoli, Kathy. "10 Ways 'The Miseducation of Lauryn Hill' Changed Everything." TIDAL.com. August 25, 2018. http://read.tidal.com/article/miseducation-lauryn-hill-20-years.

Iandoli, Kathy. "Backlisting: Lauryn Hill's 'The Miseducation of Lauryn Hill'

Turns 15." Vibe.com. August 26, 2013. https://www.vibe.com/2013/08/backlisting-lauryn-hills-miseducation-lauryn-hill-turns-15.

Iandoli, Kathy. "Cardi B's 'Invasion of Privacy' Proves Her Transparency Translates into Triumph." XXLmag.com. April 11, 2018. https://www.xxlmag.com/rap-music/reviews/2018/04/cardi-b-invasion-of-privacy-album-review.

Iandoli, Kathy. "Cardi B, Girl Power and the State of Hip-Hop." Billboard.com. September 28, 2017. https://www.billboard.com/articles/columns/hip-hop/7981663/cardi-b-girl-power-hip-hop-feuds-women.

Iandoli, Kathy. "Free Remy Ma! The Bronx Rapper Is out of Prison and Talking Exclusively to I-D." i-d.vice.com. September 5, 2014. https://i-d.vice.com/en_us/article/nebwkg/remy-ma.

Iandoli, Kathy. "I Guess . . . | Lil' Kim's 'Fragility,' Nicki Minaj's 'Ego,' Blah Blah Blah." Revolt.tv. August 15, 2018. https://revolt.tv/stories/2018/08/15/guess-lil-kims-fragility-nicki-minajs-ego-blah-blah-blah-0700c87df0.

Iandoli, Kathy. "Inside Fugees' The Score, 20 Years Later, with Its Collaborators." Pitchfork.com. February 22, 2016. https://pitchfork.com/thepitch/1027-inside-fugees-the-score-20-years-later-with-its-collaborators.

Iandoli, Kathy. "Lauryn Hill Owes Us Nothing." Pitchfork.com. July 13, 2015. https://pitchfork.com/thepitch/839-lauryn-hill-owes-us-nothing.

Iandoli, Kathy. "Lil' Kim and Foxy Brown: The Thelma and Louise Tale That Never Was." XXL Magazine (Fall 2016). https://www.xxlmag.com/news/2016/11/lil-kim-foxy-brown-relationship-rivalry.

Iandoli, Kathy. "Lil' Kim Debuts New Track, 'Nasty One,' Talks Early Censorship & Everlasting Legacy." Billboard.com. July 11, 2018. https://www.billboard.com/articles/columns/hip-hop/8464926/lil-kim-debuts-new-track-nasty-one-talks-early-censorship.

Iandoli, Kathy. "Lil' Kim on Foxy Brown: 'I Literally Helped Dress Her!'" MTV.com. March 8, 2011. http://www.mtv.com/news/2495099/lil-kim-on-foxy-brown-i-literally-helped-dress-her.

Iandoli, Kathy. "Nicki Minaj: Anxious to Work on Pink Friday Follow-Up, Talks Lil Wayne, a World Tour, and Her David Guetta Collab." HipHopDX.com. March 12, 2011. https://hiphopdx.com/interviews/id.1699/title.nicki-minaj-anxious-to-work-on-pink-friday-follow-up-talks-lil-wayne-a-world-tour-and-her-david-guetta-collab.

Iandoli, Kathy. "Nicki Minaj Breaks Billboard Female Rap Album Record." MTV.com. March 3, 2011. http://www.mtv.com/news/2495252/nicki-minaj-breaks-billboard-female-rap-album-record.

Iandoli, Kathy. "Nicki Minaj's Hip Hop Awards Cypher Verse Made Me a Fan." BET.com. October 7, 2015. https://www.bet.com/news/music/2015/10/07/nicki-minaj-s-hip-hop-awards-cypher-verse-made-me-a-fan.html.

Iandoli, Kathy. "Nicki Minaj Reclaims Her Throne on 'Queen.'" Billboard .com. August 11, 2018. https://www.billboard.com/articles/columns/hip -hop/8469731/nicki-minaj-queen-album-review.

Iandoli, Kathy. "The Overlooked Genius of Missy Elliott's 'Supa Dupa Fly.'" CrackMagazine.net. 2017. https://crackmagazine.net/article/long-reads/us -rap-critic-kathy-iandoli-honours-the-overlooked-genius-of-missy-elliotts -debut-album.

Iandoli, Kathy. "We Weren't Ready for Lauryn Hill's 'Unplugged' Album . . . In More Ways Than One." Revolt.tv. May 10, 2017. https://revolt.tv/sto ries/2017/05/10/werent-ready-lauryn-hills-unplugged-albumin-ways -0700fcc471.

Iandoli, Kathy. "Why Nicki Minaj and Cardi B's Rift Is History Repeat- ing Itself." XXLMag.com. April 19, 2018. https://www.xxlmag.com/news /2018/04/nicki-minaj-cardi-b-rift-history-repeating-itself.

Jackson, John Calloway. "A Rap Session with Queen Latifah." Billboard (No- vember 27, 1993). Accessed at LexisNexis.

Jenkins, Sacha. "Ready or Not." VIBE (June–July 1996). https://books.google .com/books?id=ci4EAAAAMBAJ&printsec=frontcover&source=gbs_ge _summary_r&cad#v=onepage&q&f=false.

Jones, James T. IV. "Female Rappers Go with the Gangsta Flow." USA Today. October 5, 1993. Accessed at LexisNexis.

Judah, Hettie. "Sisters Are Saying It for Themselves." Guardian. June 8, 1999. Accessed at LexisNexis.

Kale, Sirin. "Azealia Banks: Fearless Truthteller or Relentless Troll?" TheGuard ian.com. January 24, 2019. https://www.theguardian.com/music/2019/jan /24/azealia-banks-misunderstood-talent-or-tedious-troll.

King, Aliya S. "Aliya S. King's True Hip-Hop Stories: Lady Luck Speaks." The Root.com. January 11, 2016. https://verysmartbrothas.theroot.com/aliya-s -kings-true-hip-hop-storeies-lady-luck-speaks-1822522488.

Kinnon, Joy Bennett. "Sister of Rap." Ebony (November 1999). Accessed at LexisNexis.

Krishnamurthy, Sowmya. "Lil' Kim Blasts Nicki Minaj and Foxy Brown After Summer Jam Fiasco." MTV.com. June 5, 2012. http://www.mtv.com /news/2498175/lil-kim-blasts-nicki-minaj-foxy-brown-summer-jam.

Lamont, Tom. "Napster: The Day the Music Was Set Free." TheGuardian .com. February 23, 2013. https://www.theguardian.com/music/2013/feb/24 /napster-music-free-file-sharing.

Langhorne, Cyrus. "Amil Still Loves the Jigga Man, 'I Wish I Could Talk to Jay-Z Because That Would Bring Closure.'" SOHH.com. August 19, 2011. https://www.sohh.com/amil-still-loves-the-jigga-man-i-wish-i-could-talk -to-jay-z-because-that-would-bring-closure.

Markman, Rob. "Eve on Dr. Dre: I Didn't 'Like Being Told What to Do.'" MTV

.com. November 29, 2012. http://www.mtv.com/news/1698132/eve-dr-dre-aftermath.

Markman, Rob. "Foxy Brown Makes Tearful Plea to Haters: 'Let Me Live.'" MTV.com. August 14, 2013. http://www.mtv.com/news/1712377/foxy-brown-cries-gossip-rapfix-live.

Marriott, Robert. "Blowin' Up." *VIBE* (June–July 2000). https://books.google.com/books?id=SSgEAAAAMBAJ&printsec=frontcover&source=gbs_ge_summary_r&cad=0#v=onepage&q&f=false.

Martins, Chris. "2017 No. 1s: Cardi B on Her Rise to Hot 100 History." Billboard.com. December 21, 2017. https://www.billboard.com/articles/events/year-in-music-2017/8071047/cardi-b-hot-100-history-interview-no-1s-2017.

Miss2Bees. "Rah Digga on Female Rappers: There's Only One Female That Doesn't Collab with the Others." The Source.com. December 25, 2017. http://thesource.com/2017/12/25/rah-digga-female-rappers-theres-1-female-doesnt-collab-others.

Moniuszko, Sara M. "Cardi B Injured After Fight with Nicki Minaj at New York Fashion Week Party." USAToday.com. September 8, 2018. https://www.usatoday.com/story/life/people/2018/09/08/cardi-b-and-nicki-minaj-fight-new-york-fashion-week-party/1237978002.

Morgan, Joan. "The Fire This Time." *VIBE* (November 1994). https://books.google.com/books?id=dCwEAAAAMBAJ&printsec=frontcover&source=gbs_ge_summary_r&cad=0#v=onepage&q&f=false.

Morgan, Joan. "They Call Me Ms. Hill." Essence.com. December 16, 2009. https://www.essence.com/news/they-call-me-ms-hill.

Morris, Mike. "Da Brat Jailed After Nightclub Fight." AJC.com. June 15, 2009. https://www.ajc.com/entertainment/music/brat-jailed-after-nightclub-fight/RWtZNjfGztiy93SIgoPOOJ.

Mshaka, Thembisa. "The Selling of 'The Miseducation of Lauryn Hill.'" Okayplayer.com. 2018. https://www.okayplayer.com/music/the-making-of-lauryn-hill-the-miseducation-of-lauryn-hill.html.

MTV News Staff. "Missy Elliott Discusses Her First Solo Album." MTV.com. August 1, 1997. http://www.mtv.com/news/1428558/missy-elliott-discusses-her-first-solo-album.

Murphy, Keith. "Full Clip: MC Lyte Breaks Down Her Entire Catalogue (Brandy, Janet Jackson, LL Cool J & More)." Vibe.com. January 7, 2011. https://www.vibe.com/photos/full-clip-mc-lyte-breaks-down-her-entire-catalogue-brandy-janet-jackson-ll-cool-j-more.

Murray, Sonia. "Da Brat Rapper: 'I Was Just Waiting My Turn.'" *Atlanta Journal-Constitution*. June 28, 1994. Accessed at LexisNexis.

Obst, Anthony. "Interview: Gangsta Boo." Daily.RedBullMusicAcademy.com. June 21, 2013. https://daily.redbullmusicacademy.com/2013/06/gangsta-boo-interview.

Patterson, Sylvia. "Salt 'N' Pepa." *Smash Hits*. November 15, 1988. https://
analogueboyinadigitalworld.wordpress.com/2018/07/19/magazine-archive
-smash-hits-2-11-1988.

Penrose, Nerisha. "A Timeline of Nicki Minaj & Cardi B's Complicated Relationship." Billboard.com. November 1, 2017. https://www.billboard.com
/articles/columns/hip-hop/8022232/nicki-minaj-cardi-b-timeline-motor
sport.

Platon, Adelle. "Rapsody & MC Lyte Discuss Being a Woman of Color In
Hip-Hop & Their First Encounters With Racism in America." Billboard
.com. February 1, 2016. https://www.billboard.com/articles/columns/hip
-hop/6859468/black-history-month-rapsody-mc-lyte-interview.

Preezy. "20 Veteran Female Rappers You Need to Recognize." XXLMag.com.
August 30, 2016. https://www.xxlmag.com/news/2016/08/forgotten-female
-rappers.

Ramirez, Erika. "Ladies First: 31 Female Rappers Who Changed Hip-Hop."
Billboard.com. March 31, 2014. https://www.billboard.com/articles/col
umns/the-juice/5923011/ladies-first-31-female-rappers-who-changed-hip
-hop.

Reid, Shaheem. "Foxy Brown Claims She's Misunderstood, Collaborates with
Lauryn Hill on New LP." MTV.com. February 27, 2003. http://www.mtv
.com/news/1470203/foxy-brown-claims-shes-misunderstood-collaborates
-with-lauryn-hill-on-new-lp.

Rennison, Callie Marie, Ph.D. "Rape and Sexual Assault: Reporting to Police
and Medical Attention, 1992–2000." Bjs.gov. August 2002. https://www.bjs
.gov/content/pub/pdf/rsarp00.pdf.

Rey, Michael. "Misrepresentation?" *VIBE* (February 1999). https://books.google
.com/books?id=ZCgEAAAAMBAJ&pg=PA42&lpg=PA42&dq=new+ark+
vada+nobles+vibe&source=bl&ots=dZXq3OD6UJ&sig=ACfU3U19mpbi
wMWo-Ld6ffy7swjRWWnZFg&hl=en&sa=X&ved=2ahUKEwif7fv4s_Hi
AhWjxVkKHdGUDUQQ6AEwBHoECAkQAQ#v=onepage&q=new%20
ark%20vada%20nobles%20vibe&f=false.

Ringen, Jonathan. "Missy Elliott on Her Comeback—'There Is Only One
Missy.'" *Billboard* (November 2015). https://www.billboard.com/articles
/news/cover-story/6769236/missy-elliott-comeback-wtf-new-album-graves
-disease-anxiety-super-bowl.

Robbie. "Non-Rapper Dudes: Tom Silverman Interview [Tommy Boy/NMS]."
Unkut.com. August 24, 2015. http://www.unkut.com/2015/08/non-rapper
-dudes-tom-silverman-interview-tommy-boynms.

Robertson, Darryl. "Interview: Gangsta Boo Is Still the Queen of Memphis."
Vibe.com. April 27, 2016. https://www.vibe.com/2016/04/gangsta-boo-queen
-memphis-interview-three-6-mafia.

Samuels, David. "Hip-Hop High." NewYorker.com. October 10, 1999. https://www.newyorker.com/magazine/1999/10/18/hip-hop-high.

Schwartzberg, Lauren. "Hip-Hop's First Female MCs Approve of Iggy Azalea." Vice.com. August 19, 2014. https://www.vice.com/en_us/article/nnqqx7/lisa-lee-and-sha-rock--the-first-female-mcs-ever-approve-of-iggy-azalea.

Shipley, Al. "Missy Misdemeanor Elliott's 'Supa Dupa Fly': 4 Things You Didn't Know." RollingStone.com. July 14, 2017. https://www.rollingstone.com/music/music-news/missy-misdemeanor-elliotts-supa-dupa-fly-4-things-you-didnt-know-253255.

Smith, Danyel. "Foxy Brown Is the Illest." *VIBE* (December 1998–January 1999). https://books.google.com/books?id=zywEAAAAMBAJ&printsec=frontcover&source=gbs_ge_summary_r&cad=0#v=onepage&q&f=false.

Smith, Troy L. "Pebblee Poo of Master Don and the Def Committee." November 2002. http://www.thafoundation.com/peblee.htm.

Spanos, Brittany. "Nicki Minaj vs. Remy Ma: Rap Queens' Beef History Explained." RollingStone.com. February 27, 2017. https://www.rollingstone.com/music/music-news/nicki-minaj-vs-remy-ma-rap-queens-beef-history-explained-115343.

Suskind, Alex. "15 Years After Napster: How the Music Service Changed the Industry." TheDailyBeast.com. June 6, 2014 (updated July 12, 2017). https://www.thedailybeast.com/15-years-after-napster-how-the-music-service-changed-the-industry.

Sweetingham, Lisa. "Lil' Kim Charged in Rap-Rivalry Shootout." CNN.com. April 15, 2004. http://www.cnn.com/2004/LAW/04/15/kim.

Tensley, Brandon. "How Lauryn Hill Educated the Music Industry 20 Years Ago." Time.com. August 25, 2018. https://time.com/5377938/miseducation-lauryn-hill-anniversary.

Touré. "The Mystery of Lauryn Hill." RollingStone.com. October 30, 2003. https://www.rollingstone.com/music/music-news/the-mystery-of-lauryn-hill-249020.

Tucker, Ken. "Review: TLC, *Ooooooohhh . . . On the TLC Tip*." EW.com. April 17, 1992. https://ew.com/article/1992/04/17/ooooooohhhon-tlc-tip.

VIBE staff. "Wyclef Jean Recalls Meeting Lauryn Hill, Writing Her Rhymes in New Book." Vibe.com. September 17, 2012. https://www.vibe.com/2012/09/wyclef-jean-new-book-purpose-meeting-lauryn-hill-writing-rhymes.

Virshup, Amy. "Harry's Kids." *New York* (March 12, 1984). https://books.google.com/books?id=huUCAAAAMBAJ&pg=PA30&lpg=PA30&dq=harry+belafonte+beat+street+interview&source=bl&ots=_Yrt3Z6x1I&sig=k1HVn7MVm7AeYHKPfsilCEobhrw&hl=en&sa=X&ved=2ahUKEwisjdn_yozfAhXknuAKHbPMA3g4ChDoATACegQIBxAB#v=onepage&q=harry%20belafonte%20beat%20street%20interview&f=false.

Weingarten, Christopher R. "Best of '88: MC Lyte's Machismo-Slaying Anthem 'Paper Thin.'" RollingStone.com. December 10, 2018. https://www.rolling stone.com/music/music-features/best-of-88-mc-lytes-machismo-slaying -anthem-paper-thin-762801.

Weingarten, Marc. "Freaky Tales." *VIBE* (June 2001). https://books.google .com/books?id=fSYEAAAAMBAJ&printsec=frontcover&source=gbs_ge_ summary_r&cad=0#v=onepage&q&f=false.

Winfrey, Dr. Adia. "4 Reasons Cindy Campbell Is the Mother of Hip Hop." NatMonitor.com. August 12, 2017. http://natmonitor.com/2017/08/12/4 -reasons-cindy-campbell-is-the-mother-of-hip-hop.

XXLMag.com staff. "R.I.P. MC Trouble—Trouble's in Paradise." XXLMag .com. June 4, 2010. https://www.xxlmag.com/news/2010/06/rip-mc-trouble -troubles-in-paradise.

"The Year of the Woman, 1992." History.House.gov. https://history.house .gov/Exhibitions-and-Publications/WIC/Historical-Essays/Assembling -Amplifying-Ascending/Women-Decade.

Younger, Briana. "Is Rap Finally Ready to Embrace Its Women?" NewYorker .com. December 7, 2018. https://www.newyorker.com/culture/cultural -comment/is-rap-finally-ready-to-embrace-its-women.

Zook, Kristal Brent. "The Mask of Lil' Kim." WashingtonPost.com. September 3, 2000. https://www.washingtonpost.com/archive/lifestyle/style/2000/09/03 /the-mask-of-lil-kim/b9a06fe7-adde-49fa-9259-aa1dbf71e655/?utm_term= .ed5483615bfb.

All lyrics retrieved from Genius.com.

Index